ANOTHER MOTHER

Another Mother gives voice to women who become mothers through the routes of adoption, surrogacy and egg donation, and their silent partners – the birth mothers, surrogate mothers and egg donors – who make motherhood possible for them.

Exploring experiences of motherhood beyond the biological mother raising her child, Everington draws on interviews and a range of interdisciplinary approaches to produce illuminating personal testimonies which expand our understanding of what it means to be a mother. The life writing narratives also examine the unique and hidden relationships that exist between adopters and birth mothers, egg donors and women who become mothers through egg donation, and surrogates and women who become mothers through surrogacy.

Offering a fresh approach to life writing, using hybrid form encompassing edited interview, re-imagined scenes, poetry, personal essay and quotation collage, this topical book is recommended for anyone interested in motherhood studies, gender and women's studies, life writing studies, the sociology of reproduction, creative non-fiction writing approaches, oral history and ethnography studies.

Shanta Everington is Associate Lecturer in Creative Writing at The Open University, UK, where she gained her PhD in Creative Writing. A creative and critical writer working across a range of forms, much of Shanta's writing explores recurring themes of difference, identity and belonging. Previous books include the novel *Marilyn and Me* (2007), narrated by a young woman with a learning disability who models herself on Marilyn Monroe, and young adult novel *XY* (2014), set in a dystopian world where humans are born intersex with gender assigned at birth. She is also a Royal Literary Fund Writing Fellow (2021–23) and a member of the National Association of Writers in Education (NAWE).

ANOTHER MOTHER

Curating and Creating Voices
of Adoption, Surrogacy
and Egg Donation

Shanta Everington

LONDON AND NEW YORK

Designed cover image: © Shutterstock Images

First published 2023

by Routledge
4 Park Square, Milton Park, Abingdon, Oxon OX14 4RN

and by Routledge
605 Third Avenue, New York, NY 10158

Routledge is an imprint of the Taylor & Francis Group, an informa business

© 2023 Shanta Everington

The right of Shanta Everington to be identified as author of this work has been asserted in accordance with sections 77 and 78 of the Copyright, Designs and Patents Act 1988.

All rights reserved. No part of this book may be reprinted or reproduced or utilised in any form or by any electronic, mechanical, or other means, now known or hereafter invented, including photocopying and recording, or in any information storage or retrieval system, without permission in writing from the publishers.

Trademark notice: Product or corporate names may be trademarks or registered trademarks, and are used only for identification and explanation without intent to infringe.

British Library Cataloguing-in-Publication Data
A catalogue record for this book is available from the British Library

ISBN: 978-1-032-26841-5 (hbk)
ISBN: 978-1-032-26840-8 (pbk)
ISBN: 978-1-003-29017-9 (ebk)

DOI: 10.4324/9781003290179

Typeset in Bembo
by Deanta Global Publishing Services, Chennai, India

For Etienne and Andre.
And for Andre's birth mother.

CONTENTS

Preface   *x*
Acknowledgements   *xiii*

PART I
Introduction   **1**

1 Birthing the book   3
   Shanta's story part I   *3*
   Research motivation, significance and approach   *5*
   Through the looking glass: Biographical writing as self-reflection   *6*
   Finding a form   *10*
   Collage as an evolution beyond narrative   *20*
   Reference list   *27*

2 Politics and power   29
   The personal as political   *29*
   Mother, gender and society   *31*
   Whose voice is it anyway?   *33*
   The politics of adoption, surrogacy and egg donation   *43*
   The politics of form (and the nature of truth)   *44*
   A mother writing about mothering   *47*
   Reference list   *49*

PART II
Experimental life writing — 51

3 Alison's story — 53
   The nearly son 53
   Where it all began 55
   Hers 60
   Celebrate 65
   'The sun will come out tomorrow' 69
   Reference list 71

4 Charlotte's story — 73
   The lady of the house 73
   MOT 75
   A day at the races 79
   Holes 84
   Reference list 89

5 Shanta's story part II — 90
   I like mine with a kiss 90
   Reference list 94

6 Rubi's story — 95
   Would you like something stronger? 95
   Passage to India 97
   It all started with my legs 102
   A good life 107
   Wisdom 107
   The beds in my head 108
   In her belly 108
   Everything can be fixed 109
   Reference list 110

7 Robin's story — 111
   Drama queen 111
   The farm and the full moon 112
   Yes, no, maybe 116
   Half a kiss 118
   'She's got it' 125
   Reference list 128

8 Lorraine's story　129
   Damned if we do, damned if we don't　129
   Summer of love　130
   Perfectly polite　136
   It is what it is　139
   Reference list　144

9 Shanta's story part III　145
   No babies　145
   Reference list　151

10 Margaret's story　152
   Never forget　152
   Sorry not sorry　159
   Care　159
   The wrong mother (part I)　159
   The wrong mother (part II)　160
   Elephant　160
   Blue　161
   Reference list　161

11 Contextual note　162
   Fertility treatments　162
   Egg and sperm donation　163
   Surrogacy　163
   Adoption　164
   Fostering　164
   Reference list　165

PART III
Conclusion　**167**

12 Contributing to new understandings of motherhood through expansion and analysis of life writing forms　169
   What next?　171
   Reference list　171

Index　173

PREFACE

Babies

> I see them everywhere, in the street, in cars, on buses, on trains, on planes, in supermarkets, in the park, in the dark, in vans, in prams, in slings, in the arms of a 15-year-old with tattoos and pink hair, it's not fair, with grannies and grandpas and aunties and uncles, oohing and aahing over their dimples, button nose, ten fat fingers and toes, their chuckles, their squawks, I hunt-hawk, out of the side of my eye, every time they go by, I stare at them, glare at them, it's not fair again, why her, why not me, they take root in my brain, drive me insane, fat slimy worms slither and squirm, fester in my ears, they are all I can hear, crawl out my eye sockets, they are all I can see, slide out of me monthly, flush down the drain, swim through the sewers, miniature mermaids evaporate into rain, fall down on my head again and again, they fill up the air, they are all I can breathe, they fill up my lungs, they make me scream, until I burst with emptiness, why her, why not me?

What do you think of when you imagine a 'mother-to-be'? Is it a woman in skinny jeans checking her phone every two minutes waiting to hear if her surrogate has gone into labour? Is it a woman answering a social worker's questions as she is assessed for her suitability to adopt? Or is it a pregnant woman, her baby bump protruding, her hand protectively covering it? The pregnant body is a potent image; pregnancy is the embodiment of motherhood, the ultimate symbol of womanhood. The media fully exploits this, constantly reminding us, 'This is what a mother looks like.'

But what happens if you long for a baby but find out from fertility experts that your chances of conceiving and carrying a baby to term are close to zero? Perhaps you have a medical problem. Or simply unexplained infertility. Perhaps you were waiting for the right partner to come along and it never happened. You might have the option of trying to conceive using donated eggs and bearing a child who is genetically related to another woman. Does it matter? Maybe you will adopt a child who cannot be raised by their biological mother. How might it be different? Perhaps your eggs are still ripe and able to create life but your body is unable to carry a baby. Could another woman become pregnant for you and give birth to your genetic son or daughter?

What happens if you want to help another woman become a mother by donating your eggs or becoming a surrogate? How might it feel to know there is a child out there who is part of you, who you might never get to know? How might it feel to carry a baby for nine months, give birth to her and then hand her over to another woman? What happens if you get pregnant for reasons other than to help another woman but you are not able to look after your baby and he is given to another woman to raise with or without your consent?

Facing any of the scenarios above means facing one undeniable fact: your child will have more than one mother. Maybe you will know your child's other mother(s) and maybe you won't. I became a mother for the first time through pregnancy (with my own egg) and for the second time through adoption. When my second child came into my life, I knew that his other mother and I would always be inextricably connected. Maybe one day I will meet her; maybe I won't. But she will always be part of my son's life and therefore, part of mine. I remember in adoption training, a social worker saying it is an adoptive mother's job to carry the idea of her child's birth mother until they are able to carry her for themselves. Something to do with containment. A mother within a mother. The idea makes me think of the brightly painted, wooden Russian dolls I used to play with as a child, cracking open the outer woman to reveal the woman inside and so on, until you get to the smallest, innermost doll, the baby.

This book is based on a life writing research project undertaken for a PhD with The Open University. The project focused on women who became mothers through egg donation, surrogacy and adoption and their silent partners – egg donors, surrogates and birth mothers. Of course, fathers are of equal significance – after all, women cannot become mothers without them – but this is not their book. Here I focus on the experience of women producing and/or raising children via these so-called alternative arrangements, exploring the triangular relationships between them. You'll hear mothers talk about their experiences, as they attempt to navigate the complex emotional and ethical labyrinth of motherhood via adoption, surrogacy and egg donation.

The six mothers who tell their stories here came forward after seeing information about the project circulated by a range of gatekeeping agencies. The mothers are all UK based and used services in the UK and, where stipulated, abroad. I met the women individually in locations of their choice: their own homes, a café, a hospital. All meetings were audio-recorded. Some women were interviewed only once, others up to four times, sometimes with their children present, sometimes without. A friend, a husband and an au pair accompanied them at times.

Some women skirted around their stories; others dived straight in. They offered me tea, chocolate macaroons or something stronger as they sized me up, deciding what to tell me and how to tell it. Listening to these mothers talk was a profoundly moving experience. I laughed with them. On occasions, I cried with them. Whether you are reading this as a mother, a father, a son or a daughter, you will no doubt relate these stories to your own versions of motherhood. My own children have been present in the process of writing this book, sometimes lurking in the background, sometimes shouting at me, always permeating my thoughts and feelings. To protect the privacy of those involved in the project, all names have been changed, along with other potentially identifying information. However, all the stories are real and based on recorded interviews.

Part I introduces the life writing by looking at how this book came into being, exploring the ethical, artistic, personal and political considerations involved in curating and creating voices of adoption, surrogacy and egg donation. In Part II, you will meet: Alison, who conceived her first child via an egg donor in Cyprus before going on to adopt a second child in the UK; Charlotte, an egg donor whose eggs conceived two babies for other families before she had any children of her own; Rubi, a mother who used surrogacy services in India; Robin, a surrogate mother; Lorraine, an adoptive mother who also happened to be adopted as a baby herself; and Margaret, a birth mother now in her seventies, whose baby was adopted through the Church many years ago. Part III concludes the book by summing up the ways in which this research contributes to new understandings of motherhood through the expansion and analysis of life writing forms.

Following in the footsteps of oral historians and social anthropologists (such as Tony Parker and Svetlana Alexievich), large sections of edited (italicised) interviews are included, allowing the women to tell their stories in their own words. These are interwoven with other creative forms inspired by the interviews: re-imagined scenes, poetry, collages of quotations from other published non-fiction and personal essays about my own journey as a biological and adoptive mother. In the first story, you will see Alison showing me an embroidered quilt that her mother-in-law created to tell their family story. This notion of the quilt, a tapestry, a rich woven artistic product encompassing different images, threads and stories became an interesting metaphor for the way the project unfolded, combining different voices, registers, stories and forms.

Some of the women's stories raise difficult questions to which there are no easy answers. This book gives a voice to mothers in widely different circumstances, presenting their stories, with all their complexities, stories which are open to multiple readings and interpretations.

★

To help the reader make sense of the women's stories, a contextual note is included at the end of Part II to gloss key terms and provide a basic overview of the wider context surrounding fertility, egg donation, surrogacy and adoption.

ACKNOWLEDGEMENTS

Special thanks go to the women who so generously shared their stories for this research, known here as Alison, Charlotte, Rubi, Robin, Lorraine and Margaret. I am very grateful to my PhD supervisors from The Open University, Dr Sally O'Reilly and Professor Derek Neale, for their unrelenting support and invaluable input. I would also like to thank Professor Mary Jane Kehily, for sharing the methodology of the Making Modern Mothers Project, Dr Duncan Banks, Chair of The Open University Human Research Ethics Committee, for ensuring that the research was ethically conducted, and my PhD viva examiners, Dr Siobhan Campbell and Dr Jess Moriarty, for raising a number of points that helped me strengthen my thesis. Huge thanks must go to Emily Briggs from Routledge for commissioning this book, her assistant, Lakshita Joshi, and the blind peer reviewers who helped me rework my PhD thesis into the book you have in your hands. Finally, I am indebted to my two amazing children, Etienne and Andre, for making me a mother twice over, once by pregnancy and once by adoption, inspiring me to undertake this project.

★★★

The section in Chapter 1, 'Through the looking glass: Biographical writing as self-reflection', was first published in the *Journal of Writing in Creative Practice*, volume 12, in 2019.

Some material on ethics in Chapter 2 was first published as a paper, 'Ethics and Life Writing', in the NAWE journal, *Writing in Education*, issue 83, Spring 2021.

The poems in this book were first published on the author's blog in 2022 at https://shantaeverington.wordpress.com.

PART I
Introduction

1
BIRTHING THE BOOK

Shanta's story part I

I'm already flustered when I arrive at the community centre. As I park up my new buggy, still splattered with mud from yesterday's jaunt in the park, another mother arrives.

'Hi!' I say. 'Are you going to the mother and baby group?' Stupid question.

'Yes. God, I'm a bit late. Trying to get out the house with these two, you know … The routine's all gone to pot. They're supposed to be napping now.'

It's only then that I take in the twins, peering up at me in tandem, one with a shock of poker straight, black hair, the other curly.

'Oh, I know, mine's asleep! Shall we go in together?'

I point the buggy at the double doors.

'We have to leave the buggies out here. I'm just waiting for someone to come out and help me carry one of these in.'

A smiley woman with purple lips and gold bangles jangles out of the double doors and fusses over the twins as I grapple with my baby's squirming body, outraged at being woken from his slumber. I picture a packed room full of mums chatting in cliques, like the groups I went to the first time around. This time is different though. I prepare myself for the questions. Who does he get his eyes from? The other mother introduces herself as Jyoti – it suits her. I'm a kid on my first day at school, clinging on to my new best friend. We walk through into a light, cheery room, a bombardment of primary colours. Toys are laid out on the fat, squidgy, square mats. Another member of staff sits holding a wooden drum. Noisy blonde hair.

I look around. Where are the other mums?

DOI: 10.4324/9781003290179-2

'It's a new group, ladies. We're still trying to get the word out. As it's just the two of you today, you won't need us both. I'll leave you with Sarah. Shout if you need anything, Sarah, okay?'

I exhale and settle onto a turquoise square, balancing my baby between my knees, as he grabs at a spikey, orange ball. Sarah forces us through the hello song, complete with hand actions, the type of banal activity that you never quite manage to get used to. Time for form filling. The usual questions – date of birth, health information, emergency contacts, permission to share photographs.

'Um, this question about photos...'

'We like to take photos of mum and baby doing different activities to put up on the walls and on our posters and leaflets.' Sarah smiles.

'I don't really, um, want photos of my son shared on posters and leaflets, is that okay?'

'Oh right, yeah, no problem. Just note that down on your form.'

A quizzical look.

'So where was he born?' Sarah nods her head, blonde frizz bouncing.

I answer with a carefully constructed sentence that seems to satisfy her. She turns her attention to Jyoti.

'How about the twins?'

Jyoti's eyes flick from side to side. 'Do you know what? It's really hot in here. Could we open the window?'

The cold air flows through the room. The curly twin starts to cry and Jyoti takes him in her arms, stroking his head with manicured fingertips. Then the straight-haired one joins in and Sarah pulls him onto her lap without asking.

'So are you guys still breastfeeding?' She pats his head like a puppy.

I'm starting to think coming here was a mistake.

'No.' It comes out terser than planned. I'll try to be quiet.

Jyoti smooths down her black leggings. 'It's too difficult with twins,' she says quickly, eyes darting again.

'Oh yeah, yeah. I'd love twins though.' Sarah fingers the baby's silky locks. 'When did you find out you were expecting twins? Was it at your first scan?'

The impossibly huge eyes seem to shrink. A pause.

'Look, I wasn't going to say anything but as it's just us ... the questions about breastfeeding and giving birth, well ... I had the twins by surrogacy in India. We put two embryos back, so yeah we found out after the surrogate's scan.'

The hairs on the back of my neck stand up. My son reaches up and presses his fingertips into my chin, making my mouth fall open.

'Ooh, how exciting! What was it like using a surrogate?' Sarah hops up onto her knees, still holding Jyoti's boy, kangaroo style.

Using. Jyoti's left eye twitches.

'An experience.' That's all she says at first. She glances at me. For a reaction? Because she suspects something? Oh, what the heck...

'I wasn't going to say anything either but as you've just shared your surrogacy, it feels weird to hide it. There's a bit more to our story too.'

Jyoti turns to face me, eyes huge again.

'We adopted our baby.'

A sharp intake of breath as her hand flies to her mouth.

'Oh my God, I've got goosebumps.'

Let me put the kettle on. Sarah stands up, leaving me and Jyoti together, seeing each other as if for the first time.

Research motivation, significance and approach

The short piece of auto/biographical narrative in 'Shanta's story part I', focusing on my attendance at parent–baby group, involves a classic storyline: meeting a stranger and finding a connection. This re-imagined scene sets out my experience of feeling 'other' as a mother and finding a connection with another mother who also felt outside the norm, albeit in a different way. Just as we seek connections in person, we also seek connections through literature, enabling us to 'reconfigure and create ourselves in relation to the literary text' (Campbell in Hunt and Sampson, 1998, p. 167).

Harman wrote of the 'astonishing omission' of an exploration of motherhood in women's life writing, with 'the most painful stories' being particularly rare (Harman, 2001). Contemporary explorations of motherhood in life writing can be broadly split into two categories: writing about being a mother, that is, motherhood memoir (Cusk, 2002; Enright, 2005), and writing about one's own mother, termed 'matriography' by Mansfield (2013). Both categories, it seems, have primarily focused on the biological mother raising the child she gave birth to. There is a dearth of life writing, imaginative and/or factual, by and about other types of mother: women who have become mothers through the alternative routes of adoption, surrogacy and egg donation, and their silent partners – the birth mothers, surrogate mothers and egg donors – who have made motherhood possible for them, sometimes at a personal cost.

When I was going through the process of adopting my second child, after having my first by a more conventional route, I was looking for diverse reflections and representations of mothering to help me make sense of my own journey. Jackie Kay and Jeanette Winterson have published highly moving accounts of the adoptee's experience (Kay, 2010; Winterson, 2011). Yet the voices of adoptive mothers – and indeed birth mothers whose children are adopted – are largely absent in literature. I decided to embark on a project to discover and write their stories. I was clear from the outset that I wanted to widen the net from adoption to include other routes into motherhood. Like most women who go down the adoption route, I had considered other avenues of building my family, including IVF with my own eggs and with egg donation. Finding a connection with a mother via surrogacy at the baby group opened my eyes to the world of surrogacy, not something I had personally considered.

The aim of my research was to apply and extend existing life writing methodology, to create a collection of auto/biographical portraits which extend our understanding of what it means to be a mother. This study contributes to discourse which challenges the assumptions that to be a mother a woman must be biologically related to her child/and or have given birth to her child, helping to broaden understanding of the complex nature of mothering. It also explores the unique and hidden relationships that exist between adopters and birth mothers, egg donors and women who become mothers through egg donation, and surrogates and women who become mothers through surrogacy.

The aims of life writing can be said to overlap with those of autoethnography, a method of qualitative research using writing and reflection to explore personal experience and connect it to wider cultural, political and social understandings (Ellis, 2003). This research uses life writing to explore my own personal experience of motherhood and the experience of other mothers, connecting these auto/biographical stories to wider cultural, political and social understandings.

The book curates the stories of six mothers, with three pairings spanning adoption (a birth mother and adoptive mother), surrogacy (a surrogate mother and a woman who became a mother through surrogacy) and egg donation (an egg donor and a woman who became a mother through egg donation). The rationale behind this decision was that the juxtaposition of these diverse stories and voices, alongside my own responses to the material, would allow a richer interpretation and understanding of the labyrinth of motherhood, than that afforded by a single-voiced memoir. The life writing evolved into an experimental hybrid form encompassing edited interview material, selected quotations from published works, poetry, re-imagined scenes and personal essay.

In *New and Experimental Approaches to Writing Lives*, Dr Jo Parnell speaks of the lack and need for serious scholarship into 'ways of writing lives that demonstrate an entirely new or experimental form, an unusual hybridisation … or an approach to a form that is relatively new' (2019, p. x), offering a collection of critical essays to begin to meet this need. My research contributes to knowledge in this area by developing and critically analysing an innovative hybrid form, as a way into expanding our thinking on motherhood and on life writing.

The overarching research questions were:

1) How can life writing techniques be applied and expanded to illuminate untold stories of motherhood via adoption, surrogacy and egg donation?
2) What are the methodological, ethical, artistic, personal and political considerations involved in transforming the mothers' lives into literature?
3) How can critical writing serve as a metanarrative to the mothers' stories, interrogating definitions of both motherhood and life writing?

Through the looking glass: Biographical writing as self-reflection

On a personal level, as a biological and adoptive mother, I undertook the process of researching and writing these mothers' stories as in a quest to deepen my own understanding of what it means to mother a child when your child has another mother (through adoption, surrogacy or egg donation).

After negotiating the ethics and methodologies involved in finding suitably diverse mothers to interview and conducting the recorded interviews (as discussed in the next section), I was left to focus on how to creatively transform this material into narrative. This necessitated consideration of my role – the role of the self – as a narrator and character in the text. Do I include my questions? Or do I edit myself out? How much of my own story do I include? How will I select and arrange the interview material for maximum impact? I was influenced by the work of the oral historian Tony Parker, such as *Five Women* (1965) and *In No Man's Land: Some Unmarried Mothers* (1972), testimonies of women released from prison and unmarried mothers, respectively. I found the unique, idiosyncratic voices in these published verbatim accounts utterly compelling and started to think about how I could preserve the women's voices in my stories while creatively transforming the interview material. In the preface to the reissued version of *Five Women*, editor Richard Kelly defines oral history as:

> works by a writer who conducts extensive in-depth interviews with a subject or subjects; then edits, structures and refines the verbatim transcripts so as to produce a seamless account of the subject(s) in their own words. Oral historians absent themselves from the texts they make [...]
>
> *(Kelly cited in Parker, 2013, p. I)*

This assertion that oral historians absent themselves is interesting; this is a key area in which my work differs. Alongside the production of edited verbatim material and narrated scenes arising from the interviews, I inserted myself within the text in a number of ways: as an interviewing 'life character', by writing poetry in response to the interviews and through two personal essays, recounting my own experiences of becoming a mother. It felt important to be transparent about my presence as an interviewer when deciding how to write up the stories: the interviewer is not a tape recorder or a machine but a person with values and experiences which shape the process. Lesley Forrest and Judy Giles (as cited in Polkey, 1999, p. 46) introduce the idea of interviews as a public performance. In their experience of interviewing, women 'constructed versions of themselves, drawing on a range of fictions and fantasies' for example, the 'powerful narrative that a mother's place is with her children' (Forrest and Giles, as cited in Polkey, 1999, p. 46).

> The versions of self most frequently offered to the researcher matched prevailing and normative expectations [...] each woman 'chose' a mode in which to represent herself: for example as a fighter, a stoic, as rebel, as excluded, as conformer. In doing so, the women drew upon the repertoire of myths and iconography available, choosing versions of identity

> which were both socially acceptable and *comfortable* (original emphasis) to them.
>
> *(Forrest and Giles, as cited in Polkey, 1999, pp. 46–47)*

We can argue that this idea of the interview as a public performance can apply equally to researcher and researched, as a way of constructing and presenting a self for an audience. Just as the women I was interviewing chose how to present themselves to me, I was creating a version of myself to present to them: as a writer, as a researcher, as a listener, a confidante, as a mother. Revealing that I was an adoptive mother influenced the way the women responded to me. We became more than interviewer and interviewee – we were two mothers, finding a connection. When I interviewed birth mother, Margaret, she asked me whether I had met my adopted son's birth mother, and seemed relieved to hear that my son and I shared a life story book about his origins, given to us by his social worker, so that his birth family would not be forgotten. Hearing her moving story made me reflect on the journey my son's birth mother had taken, and develop a deeper empathy for her situation. Although I would gain even more from meeting my son's actual birth mother, this was nonetheless a cathartic experience for me. Although my role was as a researcher, the fact that this was also a personal learning experience for me as an adoptive mother altered the power dynamic. I was not merely there in a professional role but also a personal one. This is discussed further in the subsection on Drafting Margaret's story in 'Finding a form'.

In *How Our Lives Become Stories: Making Selves*, Eakin discusses how we develop identity through self-narration, defining 'self' as a process rather than an entity (Eakin, 1999, p. 100). This ties in with feminist ideas on the self as a shifting, fractured, relational concept (Kenny, as cited in Polkey, 1999, p. 39). We are not one thing, we are constantly evolving and constantly recreating ourselves in the light of our experiences, our interactions with others and our interactions with text through reading and writing stories.

> A more post-modern way of perceiving the self is to see it in terms of plurality of fictions. Creativity in the construction of subjectivity signifies not so much an access to notions of authentic real selfhood as the ability to construct more than one story or narrative.
>
> *(Campbell in Hunt and Sampson, 1998, p. 166)*

In her memoir, *Why Be Happy When You Could Be Normal?* Jeanette Winterson states, 'It took me a long time to realise that there are two kinds of writing; the one you write and the one that writes you' (Winterson, 2011, p. 54). Winterson discusses how the act of writing about life with her adoptive parents, and her reunion with her birth mother, was an act of discovery: 'When I began writing this book I had no idea how it would turn out. I was writing in real time. I was writing the past and discovering the future' (Winterson, 2011, p. 226). Fellow adoptee Jackie Kay's poetry collection, *The Adoption Papers*, presenting the voices of three speakers who are distinguished typographically: the daughter, the adoptive mother and the birth mother, seeks to present multiple versions of events (Kay, 1991). In *The Autobiography of My Mother*, Jamaica Kincaid writes about her mother who died in childbirth (Kincaid, 1996). The title itself could be seen as an oxymoron – how can we write the autobiography of another? Surely, writing on another person's life is a biography? Kincaid writes a story of her 'unknown' mother in an attempt to story herself, as explored in Alison Donnell's essay, 'When Writing the Other Is Being True to the Self: Jamaica Kincaid's *The Autobiography of My Mother*':

> The explosion of criticism surrounding autobiography, and particularly women's autobiography, over the last twenty years, has demonstrated that as a genre autobiography can be likened to an unmade bed; a site on which discursive, intellectual and political practices can be remade, a ruffled surface on which the traces of previous occupants can be uncovered and/or smoothed over … Many of the most influential women writers of the twentieth century have chosen to make this bed and some to lie in it too. Virginia Wolf, Zora Neale Hurston, Gertrude Stein, and their more contemporary bedfellows Sylvia Plath, Maxine Hong Kingston and Meera Syal have produced inventive and insightful works between its covers.
>
> *(Donnell, 1999, p. 124)*

Liz Stanley offers a definition of auto/biography as a collision and conflation of the two sub-genres:

> The notion of auto/biography involves the insistence that accounts of other lives influence how we see and understand our own and that our understandings of our own lives will impact upon how we interpret other lives.
>
> *(Stanley, 1992, p. i)*

Hearing Margaret's story influenced my understanding of what a birth mother goes through when her child is adopted, in turn influencing how I saw part of the role as an adopter to carry the idea of her child's birth mother until they are able to carry her for themselves. Conversely, writing about the lives of mothers through the lens of my own experience and world view, the 'biographical' narratives of other mothers are coloured and shaped by my unique perspective. This cyclical process can therefore be seen as an 'auto/biographical' act. The dynamic of writing another's story is summed up by bell hooks as 'I want to know your story. And then I will tell it back to you in a new way. Tell it back to you in such a way that it has become my own. Re-writing you, I write myself anew' (1989, p. 22). A positive interpretation of this statement is that biographical writing can serve as a process of re-storying our own lives within the context of other. However, this raises questions of authorship and ownership of stories – who do they belong to, the biographical subject or the biographer? (The ethical issues of speaking for and representing others will be discussed in Chapter 2, 'Politics and power'.)

In response to Carlyle's suggestion that writing about a life should be an act of sympathy, biographer Sally Cline regards the process as an act of empathy, stating that she 'tried to understand my subjects better, get inside their heads, their world', a process Cline says is easier if you admire aspects of someone's character (Cline, cited in Cline and Angier, 2010, pp. 22–24). Empathy, unlike sympathy, is not about feeling sorry for someone but attempting to put yourselves in someone else's shoes, to feel an affinity with them. Within my research, as an adoptive mother, it was easy for me to empathise with fellow adopters Lorraine and Alison, as we had a shared experience. However, it was also powerful to imagine myself on the other side of that experience, by interviewing birth mother Margaret. Despite having no personal experience of egg donation or surrogacy, I felt for Rubi as she spoke about the pain of infertility and her quest to become a mother, and deeply admired Charlotte and Wren for their altruistic acts, as an egg donor and surrogate mother, respectively.

Writing about mothers involved in adoption, surrogacy and egg donation, in widely different circumstances, led me to deepen my understanding of rich, multifaceted experiences of motherhood, as both lived experience and as social construct. Journeying through this project, interviewing mothers in an attempt to capture their stories, has led me to position myself in relation to their selves.

Finding a form

One of the biggest challenges of the project was deciding how to creatively transform the raw material into a compelling read illuminating the mothers' lives. On starting the project, I had early ideas about how I might shape the material, mainly in terms of a prose narrative. However, on interviewing the women and attempting to match content and form, these ideas evolved. As I began to assemble the work, I saw patterns emerging that I wanted to replicate, so insights gained during the process of writing informed its direction. It was only after completing a full draft of the life writing that I fully understood the rationale behind the form that I was creating. On reflection, I understood that the choice of form has not only ethical and artistic connotations but also political ones, explored further in Chapter 2, 'Politics and power'.

After transcribing the first interviewee's recorded interviews, I found Alison's voice so riveting that I wanted to preserve it rather than transform it. I turned to the work of social anthropologist Tony Parker (*In No Man's Land: Some Unmarried Mothers*) and journalist Svetlana Alexievich (*Voices from Chernobyl*), as examples of finely edited interviews and set about editing Alison's transcripts.

> Constructing narrative is more than a matter of transcribing interviews and erasing the questions. It involves communicating character and content in

a form that remains true to the subject while commanding the reader's attention. These are properly the skills of the writer. John Banville, the novelist, makes the point in his review of Parker's (1991) *Life After Life*: 'Tony Parker's material is tape-recorded speech but he is a very cunning writer. By means of arrangement and pattern, rhythm and tone … he makes out of these tape-recorded testimonies a kind of art that is all the more affecting because it springs from fact.'

(Barton, 2018, p. 251)

Five years into my research, a book was published by Jo Parnell called *New and Experimental Approaches to Writing Lives* (2019). In the introduction, Hugh Craig explains how Parnell's concept of the 'literary docu-memoir' has its roots in Tony Parker's work, and further explains Parnell's invented form:

> Colour and texture is given by the documentary effect of incidental factual materials and photographs. Literary docu-memoir also creates a three-dimensional experience for the reader, by rendering in detail the context of the interviews and the experience of the interviewer. The interviewer puts on a 'fictional cloak' as a writer, striving, paradoxically, to create truth by acknowledging the context of imagination and feeling for both subject and interviewer.
>
> Parnell takes from Parker the belief that ordinary people in their interaction with a sympathetic interviewer can touch on 'deeper realities', philosophical and poetical insights which might otherwise have not emerged over the course of their normal reflective and interpersonal life.
>
> *(Craig in Parnell, 2019, p. 3)*

My invented life writing form builds on these ideas, in providing colour and texture through a tapestry of creative and factual components. Angier talks about life writers more generally having 'a sort of immigrant status in literature; admired for their "investigative skills", but only rarely noticed for the quality of their writing', but goes on to say, 'The truth is that stories are only ever noticed because of the quality of their writing; good research alone is just statistics … every act of giving meaning is creative' (Angier cited in Cline and Angier, 2010, p.6). Eventually, the stories evolved into a complex hybrid form, combining edited interviews, re-imagined prose scenes, poetry, personal essays and quotation collages.

> The Russian critic and literary theorist Bakhtin coined a useful (if overused) term for this variety. Heteroglossia is the translation of his Russian word raznorecie – literally, "manylanguagedness" … Bakhtin privileged heteroglossia: works that make present the clashes and incongruities of different voices are preferred to those that create a "unified" narrative surface…
>
> *(Mullan, 2005)*

As stated in the beginning of this chapter, my rationale for using heteroglossia was that the juxtaposition of diverse voices and forms, this manylanguagedness, would allow a richer interpretation and understanding of motherhood, than that afforded by a single voiced or unified account. Creative decisions were made for each woman's story in turn, and then reviewed and reworked once all the stories had been drafted.

Drafting Alison's story

The first mother to come forward to be interviewed was Alison, a mother by egg donation and adoption. After transcribing her interview, I was left with the task of experimenting and shaping the material. Initially, I opted for the format of an edited interview, narrated in first person, interspersed with descriptions of childhood photographs (both from Alison's childhood and of her children). I attempted to replicate the approaches taken by oral historians, Parker (1972) and Alexievich (1997), who convey the uniqueness of each subject's voice by including the idiosyncrasies of each interviewee, such as conversational tics and repeated phrases, e.g. 'in a way', 'like' etc. The key challenge here was to decide how far to go in editing the original transcript, recognising that although some grammatical 'errors' add to the idiosyncrasy of the voice, there is a fine balance between capturing an authentic voice and confusing or irritating the reader. The decision to use descriptions of photographs was also influenced by Janice Galloway's approach in her memoir, *This Is Not About Me* (2010), which makes the reader feel as though they are flicking through family albums with her.

I chose to write up the interviews in first-person present tense narration as I wanted to position myself as a character in the text, to be overt about my role rather than pretend to write 'objective' biography. This is explored further in Chapter 2, 'Politics and power'. Initially, in 'The nearly son', covering my first meeting with Alison, the first-person narration dominates before I retreat into the background, allowing Alison's voice – and images – to tell the story. Rather than restrict the writing to an edited interview format, I opted for a different treatment of Alison's account of meeting her son's birth mother, 'Hers', writing it as a re-imagined memory – re-entered and creatively transformed in third-person present tense. This method allowed me to play around with the material, providing more freedom and elasticity. I 'invented' some of the dialogue – although it is heavily based on what Alison told me about her interactions with others, I do not have their exact words in the same way that I have hers from the transcripts. To distinguish between presentation of actual dialogue and 'invented' dialogue, I italicised the verbatim dialogue and used quotation marks for the invented dialogue. The mode of re-imagined memory felt more like fiction, so it felt natural to follow the convention of quotation marks. I was also influenced by other memoirists' use of italicised dialogue (e.g. Kay, 2010; Myerson, 2009).

The re-imagined memory allowed me to creatively combine material. Alison's meetings with William's birth mother, Tracey, are juxtaposed with the birth of

Alison's daughter, Emily. I was struck by Alison telling me that when her daughter was born, she felt like a fraud, because she had conceived using another woman's egg. She said she felt guilty somehow, a feeling that also resonated with her emotional state on meeting Tracey. Alison's feeling, that she was 'not entitled' to her baby, interested me, linking to the idea of 'ownership' which is found in other stories of adoption by both adoptees (Kay, 2010; Winterson, 2011) and adopters (Donovan, 2013). I also found Alison's words, 'I could only look at her out of the corner of my eye', particularly powerful and wanted to weave this in the narrative somehow. I wanted to portray Alison's unease rather than have this explicitly told in the reported speech sections. I spent a long time thinking about how to portray this before settling on the method used, interjecting dreamlike sequences into the main contact narrative, initially referring to her daughter impassively as 'the baby' rather than 'her baby' and withholding Alison's name to create some ambiguity as to whether it was referring to Alison or Tracey. I wanted to juxtapose the idea of Alison feeling inadequate at not being able to comfort her new baby, with the scene where she is called to return to comfort William, assumed to be competent and in control, to be able, even, to stem a nosebleed. The result is a rather fragmented, disorienting narrative, mirroring the bewilderment of new motherhood. The re-imagined third-person scene is 'sandwiched' between the narrated interviews, a significant structural decision as the re-imagined section feels like the core of the piece, to be exposed once the layers are peeled away.

Writing Alison's section felt very organic and fluid. After creating the form of combining edited interview with re-imagined scenes, I initially aimed to replicate it and use it for the other stories to create a sense of rhythm and shape. However, it didn't quite work out this way as the form further evolved.

Drafting Charlotte's story

The second mother to be interviewed was Charlotte, who donated her eggs for other couples to conceive. The link with Alison's story interested me as Charlotte is far removed from Alison's fantasy of her egg donor being someone coerced or trafficked into donating eggs; juxtaposing their stories therefore seemed appropriate. I tried to mirror the make-up of Alison's narrative in the way I interwove images with edited interviews, and included a central section consisting of key re-imagined scenes, 'A day at the races'. Similar to the way I contrasted Alison's experience as a new mother with donor-conceived Emily and as a foster carer with William, I contrasted Charlotte's experiences at the time of the birth of the babies conceived via her eggs (Macey and Jake) with her first birth experience with her 'own child', Tahlia. As with Alison's narrative, I edited material to make sense thematically rather than chronologically, somewhat manipulating the text to fit. For example, Charlotte's comments about her mother's background in care have been edited to appear directly above the comment about egg donation, 'serving to fill a whopping hole', when actually the two sections of dialogue came at very different points in the interviews.

There are stylistic differences between my treatment of Alison and Charlotte's stories. The sections interweaving photos differ, as in Alison's case, we were looking at and discussing photo albums together, whereas Charlotte sent me a Facebook link to images after the interview. This new way of sharing mothering online was discussed at Dr Heather Elliott's seminar, 'Storying Mothering Online', as an emerging form of publication of stories and voices (Elliott, 2016). Therefore, the interweaving is more artificial; the text does not directly relate. My aim is for the form to work with the content to suggest a disconnect. Some of the themes identified in Alison's narrative reoccur here, e.g. competitiveness and absences. Charlotte's story also explores new thematic areas of fate and superstition, which echo in some of the other women's stories. I was struck by the way Charlotte uses the idea of destiny as a comfort, a way of reassuring herself that everything is as it should be. In this regard, there are two layers to the narrative: what is directly said and what can be inferred (as with Alison's narrative). For example, Charlotte says she has no regrets but there is clearly a lot of repressed anger towards Stephen and Anthony. I found the body language in some of the photographs, particularly with Anthony and Stephen, very revealing (e.g. the new fathers on all fours, surrounding Macey, in a protective stance) and attempted to convey this through visual descriptions of the photographs woven into the text.

Drafting Rubi's story

Rubi was the third mother to come forward for interview: an Anglo-Indian woman who travelled to India to use surrogacy services and now had two children by two different surrogates and two egg donors. I interviewed Rubi on two separate occasions in her own home. Deciding how to present Rubi's material was challenging. Unlike Alison and Charlotte, Rubi opted to have her husband present during the interviews – the complication here is that 'Rubi and Sunni' very much came as a pair. Although the interview was with Rubi, she kept calling out to her husband and asking him to verify information and he drifted in and out of the room, making comments. In some ways, he is more present in the story than her – he gave up his job and stayed in India, continuing to provide sperm to multiple surrogates until one got pregnant, while Rubi went back to the UK; he falsified a pregnancy scan to be sent to his dying mother to pretend they were having a baby before there was any pregnancy; essentially, he pursued parenthood on their behalf after she had given up. Her absence from parts of the story fascinated me and was something I wanted to explore. During the first interview, Rubi did not reveal very much at all, yet during subsequent conversations, once trust and rapport were established, she opened up much more. However, there were still a lot of gaps to fill in. Rubi's selective storytelling links to the idea of 'interview as a public performance' (as discussed previously).

One of the key difficulties I experienced with arranging and editing the material was that Rubi contradicted herself often, e.g. at the first interview, she told me that when they started with the first surrogate, Dawn, they used IUI at the clinic, where Sunni's sperm was injected into her eggs. During the second interview, she told me they started with artificial insemination, where sperm is inserted directly into the surrogate's vagina. To avoid confusing the reader, the edited version refers to artificial insemination from the outset – although in some ways, the editing loses the way Rubi conceals and possibly 'sanitises' parts of her experience. During editing, I have had to strike a balance between rearranging (often repetitive) material to group content thematically or chronologically, with editing to preserve the tension by allowing 'plot hooks' to be planted and information revealed later.

On reviewing Rubi's transcripts, I identified a number of narrative arcs including Rubi's childhood and how that provides context for her self-image, relationships and her infertility; and tension with Rubi's sister-in-law (and the reveal as to the reason). After I had written up the first draft, I had a look at Sunni's e-book, which is published online in instalments on his website. As there were a number of images in there, I used visual descriptions of some of these, as I did the visual images from photo albums in Alison's story and Facebook in Charlotte's story. Initially, I attempted to replicate the form used in Alison and Charlotte's stories by including a 'fictionalised' or re-imagined constructed memory scene, juxtaposing Rubi meeting the first surrogate for the first time with her teenage experiences with her older sister. This decision was influenced partly by Rubi revealing that the surrogate called her 'sister' combined with how she felt inadequate next to her actual sister, highlighting themes of competition (also present in Alison and Charlotte's stories). My intention was to foreshadow the revelation of Rubi's eating disorder, low self-esteem and body image, revealed in the final section.

However, following supervisory feedback I decided to remove the reconstructed chapter, which wasn't working for a number of reasons. There was unnecessary repetition of information between the edited interviews and re-imagined scenes; the section was much more heavily 'fictionalised' than Alison or Charlotte's re-imagined scenes, which I would define as prose life writing rather than fiction; and perhaps most importantly, the fictionalised scene included some fairly salacious, unsubstantiated content, inferred from the gaps in the interview, which detracted from Rubi's account. I decided that I needed to hand the story back to her and decided to completely cut the scene. At this midpoint in gathering the six women's stories, I was starting to feel somewhat restricted by my own imposed form in attempting to repeat the approach used in presenting Alison's story, sandwiching a reconstructed scene between edited interviews. After removing the scene from Rubi's story, I knew something was missing. It was only when I finished transcribing all the stories that I realised what I needed to add.

Drafting Robin's story

The fourth participant was Robin, who acted as a surrogate mother in the UK. Her story worked well alongside Rubi's, to provide a voice for the absent surrogate character. In the process of writing Robin's narrative, I didn't want to be unnecessarily bound by the structural decisions I made at the beginning with Alison's story, as I felt it was important to be open to reworking the form. However, to an extent, I did retain the structure: the opening section, 'Drama queen', introduces Robin to the reader through our meeting scene; there follows Robin's edited verbatim voice dispersed with descriptions of what is happening in the room, with the analogy of the green chair taking the place of descriptions of photographs; a middle reconstructed scene, 'Yes, no, maybe', focuses on Robin taking her daughter to a surrogacy conference where she met the couple she went on to be a surrogate for. Initially, this was written in third person limited omniscience from Robin's point of view but later rewritten in her daughter's perspective.

A key area of supervisory discussion on this story was the extent to which my role as a narrator and character within the text was working. It was felt that my interjections were somewhat tagged on and superficial in the story, and I needed to consider whether to remove myself as a character or enhance my role. I believed it was important that I remained present as a character in the stories for reasons of transparency (after all, I was there), and to reflect my influence and role within the process. Eventually, after writing up all the interviews, I decided to enhance my role as a character by including two personal essays about my own experiences (one essay on pregnancy loss and one on adoption) to be discussed in the next section on 'Collage as an evolution beyond narrative'. Supervisory feedback also addressed the reconstructed scene. Robin was a very self-assured storyteller, not revealing any vulnerabilities in the way that Rubi and Charlotte did. I could not 'get between the cracks' of her story very easily. Robin's story is very much intended mother Sara's story – the motif of the other mother as a haunting absence does not occur here. These factors resulted in her reconstructed chapter being more 'straightforward' and less fragmented, and as a result, less compelling. After supervisory feedback, I decided to interrogate the gaps in her story by rewriting the scene from her daughter's point of view, in an attempt to get inside the mind of a child tasked with deciding whether or not her mother should act as a surrogate. The final section explains exactly what happened in Robin's words, mixed with descriptions of photographs. Quite a bit of 'technical' information about surrogacy is delivered in this section. (I asked her a lot of probing questions on exactly what happened to try to get this clear.) However, after supervisory feedback it was agreed that to avoid confusing readers who may be unclear about fertility processes, additional factual content would be presented via a contextual note to be included at the end of the stories.

Although I retained the form of sandwiching a reconstructed scene within the narrated interviews, I was left with a nagging feeling that something was missing here.

Drafting Lorraine's story

Lorraine was the next woman to volunteer for interview. She was an adoptive parent of two siblings, who had herself been adopted as a baby. Lorraine opted to be interviewed twice, both in public places. At this stage of interviewing, I had a vague idea that I might include some separate autobiographical writing about my own experience of adopting, and connect it with Lorraine's story. As a result of this thinking, I experimented with keeping myself fairly absent from the text in Lorraine's story, resulting in minimal authorial intervention, in contrast with the previous narratives.

After trying out a different point of view in Robin's reconstructed scene, I decided to use a dual perspective to create a re-imagined scene, 'Perfectly polite', for the meeting between Lorraine's birth mother and adoptive parents. The meeting is recounted in the alternating perspectives of Lorraine's birth mother and her adoptive mother, contrasting their experiences. The re-imagined scene is more heavily 'fictionalised' in the sense that I have not interviewed these women but imagined the scene from Lorraine's detailed descriptions of how both her mothers acted.

During our first interview, Lorraine told me:

> 'I gave a talk to the Natural Parents Network, it was a group of women in their fifties and sixties, birth parents who would have been mothers around the time I was born. I was there in a dual role as an adoptee and adopter so I was liked and disliked in equal measures. I saw how painful it was for these women.'
>
> *(Quote included in Lorraine's story from Part II)*

This stayed with me afterwards as I prepared to meet the final participant, a birth mother in her seventies whose child was adopted, she felt by coercion.

Drafting Margaret's story

Birth mother, Margaret, was recruited through the Natural Parents Network that Lorraine referred to. I am aware that I delayed seeking out a birth mother to interview until the end of the project, reflecting my anxiety about this meeting. How would she view me, a woman who adopted another woman's child? How would I feel on meeting her, a woman who was unable to raise her baby and felt she had no other choice but to allow a woman like me to adopt her child? As anticipated, Margaret's interview was the one I found the most personally challenging. Coming face to face with a birth mother whose child had been raised by another mother, hearing her pain and witnessing the impact of the loss of her child triggered complex emotions in me as I imagined the experience of my adopted son's birth mother. Maybe one day I will meet her, if my son decides to trace her and is successful, and if he wants me to be part of that journey, and if she wants me to. There are a lot of 'ifs'. Maybe interviewing Margaret is the closest I will come.

Unlike the other narratives, Margaret's story, 'Never forget', is one continuous section without a re-imagined scene, and is significantly shorter, partly due to her reticence and the fact that we only had one meeting together. After becoming increasingly frustrated by the limitations of my own self-imposed format, and following my own emotional response to Margaret's interview material, I decided here to experiment with a different response to the material: as an alternative to the re-imagined scene, I produced a set of six poems. These poems are not exclusively related to Margaret's story – some fuse ideas from various stories and other influences. In discussing the creation of the submitted poems, I would like to draw on the work of Sarah Hesketh and Dave Swann, who both created poetry arising out of interviews (in Hesketh's case with elderly people with dementia, and in Swann's case with prisoners), while also discussing the influence of poets Jackie Kay, Carrie Etter and Selima Hill. On her blog, 'Where the Heart Is', poet Sarah Hesketh (2014) discusses her project with Age Concern Central Lancashire, working with the staff and service users in four dementia care settings: 'The established model for writers working with people with dementia is to record the words of the person with dementia and for the writer to then perform the role of editor, shaping those words into poem-like texts' (Hesketh, 2014). This is the approach I have taken in my first poem, 'Sorry not sorry', which takes verbatim words from different sections of Margaret's interview and rearranges them. There was an interesting link here with memory, as the slogan of Natural Parents Network is 'We never forget', yet Margaret had repeatedly forgotten key details. I was interested in juxtaposing Margaret's anger and need for an apology from the government with her anger and need for an apology with her (now late) mother, which seem very intertwined. The lines in italics (*My mother kept telling me/ It would kill my father if he knew/ She just did what she wanted*) relate to her discussing her mother and the non-italicised lines (having looked at all the evidence/I don't want to hear about what happened to you/ it's not worthy of an inquiry/adoption is completely different now) relate to the government response. However, by juxtaposing them, a new meaning is created – what I 'heard' reading between the lines of the interview – that her mother didn't want to hear about what happened, and that it would have been Margaret's maltreatment rather than the adoption that would have killed her 'kind' father. I was also influenced here by Jackie Kay's use of typography/alternating fonts in her poetry collection, *The Adoption Papers*, to reveal the alternating 'voices' of birth mother, adoptive mother and adoptee.

In Swann's poems, rather than use the interviewee's own words, he variously presents his own voice or a fusion of partly 'fictionalised' voices. Swann talks about the influence of Tony Parker's work and how it reminded him 'to concentrate not only on the words, but on the patterns hidden within cadences and syntax, and to watch for elliptical, fragmentary, and evasive turns-of-phrase' (Swann, 2017). In his poem 'Denial' he fuses the confessions of two 'evasive prisoners':

> The fusion of the two inmates seemed to be demanded by the poem, which hankered after the physicality granted by trees and cameras. Otherwise,

the poem would have lacked a material grounding, and the voice would have floated away. To that extent, I was learning not only about the fictionalisation made possible by poetry, but about the need to balance verbal utterances with concrete detail, so that the work operated through a wider range of senses.

(Swann, 2017)

My poem, 'Care', is similarly a fusion of real-life stories: Margaret's suggestion that everyone wanted blonde blue-eyed babies and the idea that the adopters were told they could return the baby if it didn't work out; an adopter friend who adopted a 14-month-old baby who was eventually diagnosed with Foetal Alcohol Syndrome (FAS) aged ten, after she spent years trying to get help for him due to his disturbing behaviour (e.g. holding a knife behind her back) but was told it was down to her parenting and sent on parenting courses instead; stories on Adoption UK forums (torturing pets is apparently quite a common behaviour among children adopted from care due to abuse and neglect as is engaging in sex work); a training session I recently attended on Child Sexual Exploitation about how disused properties are used by groomers. I wrote 'Care' as a prose poem, setting it out as prose rather than verse, while utilising some poetic devices such as fragmentation, compression, repetition (When you, you might not, you might, you will) and sound patterns such as full rhyme (wetting/getting) assonance/part rhyme (fantasising/hanging/candy, room/soon) and alliteration (picturing play dates and packed lunches), metaphor (pass the parcel) and juxtaposition of childhood innocence suggested by words such as 'Christmas and candy' with the sexualized words 'fantasizing, stockings, strangers' which foreshadows the flash-forward scene aiming to create a stark and poignant effect.

The prose poem form here was influenced by the form used in *Imagined Sons* by Carrie Etter, which consists of a series of first-person prose poems narrated by a birth mother imagining her son in all different guises, from a businessman to a prisoner. Etter's 'imagined sons' are interspersed with Birth Mother's Catechisms, which repeat questions to reveal different answers, forming the basis of 'The wrong mother (part I)', where the answers twist to reveal the narrator's inner turmoil. I also decided to write an autobiographical counter poem in the voice of an adoptive mother, 'The wrong mother (part II)', using a first-person voice to describe how I felt when I saw the photo of my son's birth mother – a very bizarre, almost violent reaction. I was told by the social worker that this was positive as it was about me feeling he was mine and having protective instincts. The line 'I couldn't bear your face' also refers to me being unable to 'child bear' the baby who looks like her.

'Elephant' explores Margaret's attempted 'abortion', using the serpent-like imagery of the douche tube fused with the elephant's trunk and phantom umbilical cord (the elephant being the symbol of The Natural Parents Network). This is as close as I got to incorporating mythology: the mythological symbol of the serpent (variously representing fertility/phallus, and Satan/evil) and the reference to Lot's wife (opening with 'pillar' and ending in 'Don't look back', i.e. the opposite of never forgetting). In addition to symbolic imagery, I've used sound patterning and enjambment. This poem was also partly influenced by Selima Hill's work, often anchored in 'domestic domains' using juxtapositions and surrealism to illuminate emotional truths, particularly the poems in *Portrait of My Lover as a Horse* (2002), such as 'Portrait of My Lover as a Swan' and 'Portrait of My Lover as an Elephant'.

My final poem, 'Blue', is a 'simpler' poem using imagery, metaphor and rhyme, written in a first-person voice to narrate an experience of loss that happened in the past but is very present for the narrator ('so long ago/that it's now'). It was inspired by the idea of birth mother Margaret 'never forgetting' but also echoes the post-traumatic stress of pregnancy loss discussed in Robin's story. In the first stanza, imagery centres on water evoking waves as contractions, waters breaking, and the moon, a key symbol of the menstrual cycle. The second stanza explores a partner unsure how to console her, grief depicted by the blanket as a shroud and the infantilising action of patting on the head. After experimenting with writing poetry as an alternative to the re-imagined scenes, I was creatively energised to experiment with other forms. Now that I had gathered the material from all the women's interviews in its entirety, it was time to look again. This is when the hybrid format started to take off.

Collage as an evolution beyond narrative

After drafting the women's stories, I took a break from writing, returning to the manuscript a few months later, offering the opportunity to look at the work with fresh eyes and consider different ways to experiment with form. Before the break, the writing had taken the form of edited interviews, re-imagined third-person scenes and emerging poetry. I began by re-reading Alison's story and two aspects stood out for me: firstly the embroidered quilt that her mother-in-law created to tell the family story and secondly, the silver locket Alison bought to give to her son's birth mother, which has echoes of the film, *Annie* (1982). The notion of the quilt, a tapestry, a rich woven artistic product encompassing different images, threads and stories seemed an interesting metaphor for the way the project was unfolding, combining different voices, registers, stories and forms.

During the period in between writing up the interviews and looking at them afresh, I was influenced by some of the creative non-fiction materials I had been teaching as a visiting lecturer at the University of East London, focusing on a wide range of forms within creative non-fiction. I was interested in Roland Barthes' work, *A Lover's Discourse*, which includes a note on 'How this book is constructed', which essentially serves as a note on how to read it. This is a book which requires the reader to do some work, not least in working out how to approach the reading:

> What is proposed, then, is a portrait – but not a psychological portrait; instead, a structural one which offers the reader a discursive site; the site of

> someone speaking within himself, amorously, confronting the other (the loved object), who does not speak.
>
> *(Barthes, 1984, p. 3)*

Inspired by the hybrid-layered forms encountered on the syllabus I was teaching, I began to apply similar thinking to *Another Mother*, which requires the reader to work, providing a 'structural portrait' of motherhood via adoption, surrogacy and egg donation, a 'discursive site' from which to explore voices and stories and themes. In this case, each interviewee speaks in a way that confronts 'the other' in terms of the other mother(s) to their child, who does not get to speak here. For example, Alison confronts the idea of birth mother Tracey, not to speak to her but about her. Inspired by the idea of Alison's embroidered quilt as a method of storytelling led me onto consideration of a collage approach as used by David Shields in *Reality Hunger* (Shields, 2011) and I decided to experiment with building/assembling/stealing/creating a response to Alison's story via collage. According to Robert Root's 'Collage, Montage, Mosaic, Vignette, Episode, Segment', a collage is 'the technique … of assembling disparate images into an integrated whole which expresses a specific theme … through the interrelationships of the parts' (Root and Steinberg, 2005). Shields' book is itself a collage of numbered quotations, with intentional ambiguity surrounding which quotes are Shields' own words and which (the majority) are from other sources. Shield's opening chapter consists entirely of quotations about collage.

> Conventional fiction teaches the reader that life is a coherent, fathomable whole that concludes in a neatly wrapped-up revelation. Life, though – standing on a street corner, channel surfing, trying to navigate the web or a declining relationship, hearing that a close friend died last night – flies at us in bright splinters.
>
> *Quote 319 (Lance Olsen, 10:01) in Shields (2011)*

'I'm interested in collage as (to be honest) an evolution beyond narrative' Quote 328 (Shields, 2011). 'Momentum, in literary mosaic, derives not from narrative but from the subtle, progressive buildup of thematic resonances' Quote 334 (Shields, 2011). These quotes resonated with me as they fit with my experience of working on *Another Mother*. It isn't one neatly wrapped up story; it's a myriad of stories, some narrated, some existing in the gaps between lines. Interviewing the mothers, reading and researching other sources was an overwhelming experience of bombardment, of material flying 'in bright splinters'. The 'subtle, progressive buildup of thematic resonances' has emerged with through-lines of 'ownership', 'competition', 'otherness', 'absence' etc. Reflecting on Barthes and Shields made me feel strongly that *Another Mother* needs to be presented in hybrid form, that marrying content and form in this way is the only approach that could work for such a project, where a linear narrative, or series of mono-voiced edited interviews, would fail to provide the necessary 'discursive site' or 'literary mosaic'.

This gave me confidence to further experiment in my response to Alison's story, presenting a collection of quotations from other published non-fiction linked to the material.

I couldn't get the image of the silver locket Alison gave to Tracey out of my head, and this became the central symbol for a clustering exercise, starting with the film *Annie* (1982), which inspired the title quotation, 'The sun will come out tomorrow'. The locket from *Annie* led to me researching foundling tokens in orphanages, which led to the idea of a transaction, and so on. I wanted the quotes to lead on to one another almost in a story spine, as well as providing contrasts between quotations, and oblique connections (such as Bible quotes to highlight the hypocrisy of religion). Ultimately, I wanted the collage to act as a kind of kaleidoscope, presenting different views and perspectives, not demonising any parties but illuminating common humanity.

The quotation collage consists entirely of published quotations from other non-fiction texts. Unlike Shields, I have not included my own words within the quotes. I believe my response can be felt by the way the material is shaped, shown rather than narrated. Elsewhere in the wider project, I do include my own words, e.g. as poetry, re-imagined scenes and personal essay. Having created poetry in response to Margaret's story and curated a quotation collection in response to Alison's, I went back over the other women's stories to consider how other forms best fit my response to the material. I wrote the personal essay, 'I Like Mine with a Kiss', after re-reading Charlotte's story of being an egg donor. I knew I wanted to write something linked to eggs, ovulation and pregnancy, in other words, the quest for biological motherhood, but I wasn't quite sure what, so I started to freewrite to generate raw material. I hadn't planned to write something quite so personally revealing but this was the response that emerged, recalling the start of my personal journey towards adoption. Writing a personal essay served as an act of discovery rather than a premeditated form.

> Yet few other genres commit the writer's "I" so relentlessly and few other genres are able to force the writer to confront himself so absolutely. The personal essay allows writers to discover their own complexity – and that includes their hatreds, as well as the rawness and sustainability of their wounds. Among the legacies of the personal essay is that it has been used to describe so many different kinds of pain and self-discovery.
>
> *(Kriegel, 2008)*

The process of writing the personal essay encouraged me to examine the 'rawness and sustainability' of my 'wounds', to 'confront' myself and my pain. The essay title comes from a line in the song 'D'Ya Like Your Eggs in the Morning' (Brodszky and Cahn, 1951).

Trying to conceive can end up feeling like a cold, clinical experience; the line, 'I Like Mine with a Kiss', sums up the desire for love and affection to be part of the process.

Much of what characterizes true essayists is the ability to draw out a point through example, list, simile, small variation, hyperbolic exaggeration, whatever. The great essayists have all had this gusto in fleshing out an idea, which becomes not a chore but an opportunity.

(Lopate, 1995, p. xxxix)

Structurally, my essay begins with a specific memory scene and recounts a series of linked vignettes about the experience of trying to conceive a second child. I decided to splice these with quotations from the NHS website about the stages of pregnancy. This serves the dual purpose of juxtaposing increasingly emotional content with 'clinical/factual' content, and also of informing the reader how an embryo develops to the stage it would have been when I experienced an ectopic pregnancy. We then reach the 'reveal' of the ectopic pregnancy, which sets up the 'turn' for wanting to adopt, although this is not fully reconciled. I left the essay on a 'cliff hanger' about what happens next (which was continued in the second personal essay, 'No Babies', about my experience of applying to adopt). I attempted to use metaphor in the piece, e.g. the opening 'faded black knickers' which are now 'worn, patchy material, barely held together by nearly snapped elastic' is a metaphor for my psychological state at this stage of trying to conceive. Mimicking the splicing, I also juxtapose imagery – the clinical 'antibacterial soap' and 'thermometers' with sexually suggestive phrasing 'stick it in my mouth and suck hard'. I have also used hyperbolic exaggeration, e.g. 'I am drowning', as well as imagery and lyrical language in the final scene. In mentioning other mammals (dolphins, skunks and cats), I attempt to relate the human experience with the wider animal experience, reinforcing the idea of reproduction as a 'natural' occurrence.

After deciding to use the personal essay in response to Charlotte's story, I saw the following pattern emerge:

Collage of quotations; personal essay; poems; collage of quotations; personal essay; poems

This led me to write a quotation collage in response to Robin's story, a personal essay in response to Lorraine's and a poetry sequence in response to Rubi's. As the first quotation collage focused on adoption, I decided that the second one, following Robin's account as a surrogate, would curate quotations focusing on the female body as a vessel/biological motherhood/pregnancy and birth. I took the title quotation, 'She's got it', from the pop song *Venus* (Shocking Blue, 1969), as a reference to the Roman goddess, a symbol of desire, fertility, prosperity and victory, choosing a song from popular culture as a nod to celebrity. As the first personal essay focused on pregnancy loss, I decided that the second (placed after Lorraine's stories on adoption) would recount my own experience of preparing to adopt; here I replicate the form of the first essay by interweaving interview personal testimony with published quotations, in this case, highlighting powerful statistical information on adoption. As the first poetry sequence written (in response to Margaret's story) focused on adoption, I decided that the second one to be written (placed first in the final order) would be on infertility and surrogacy following Rubi's story. The heteroglossia of voices and forms began to build.

Part II, the experimental life writing, was not written in chronological order. It was only after writing poetry in response to Margaret's story that I decided to go back and write poetry in response to Rubi's story, aiming to explore the themes raised using a range of poetic forms. Although not originally written in the order presented, I was conscious of how they worked against one another and decided to re-order them as a sequence with their own narrative arc – opening with the longing and jealousy in 'Babies' (which was eventually separated from Rubi's story and placed at the beginning of the manuscript), we move on to the judgement and desperation in 'A Good Life', through the sadness leading to hope in 'Wisdom', the unravelling and trauma fall-out of 'The Beds in My Head', the anxiety leading to joy in 'In Her Belly' and the tender ending of 'Everything Can Be Fixed'.

The continuous breathless text of 'Babies' with its lack of line breaks makes it read almost as a prose-poem. However, it does make use of poetic devices, most importantly sound patterning, including full rhyme (e.g. 'on trains, on planes', 'in the park, in the dark', 'I stare at them, glare at them') and slant rhyme/assonance (e.g. 'in vans, in prams'). The poem has a sing-song quality, mimicking a children's story book, inspired by Dr Seuss's style of lyrical prose. About halfway through the poem, the theme of longing turns to something darker, 'they take root in my brain, drive me insane'. The poem then uses imagery and metaphor, representing the babies as 'fat slimy worms … crawl out of my eye sockets', moving onto the experience of periods signifying the lack of pregnancy, 'slide out of me monthly, flush down the drain, swim through the sewers, miniature mermaids' building to the crescendo of suffocation and emptiness.

'A Good Life' is a 'found poem' created entirely of words from the interview text. Distilled into seven lines, alternating lines representing words spoken by Rubi with lines representing reported words spoken to her (by her husband, wider relatives and a potential surrogate), I aimed to convey both Rubi's desperation and the impact of the external messages she receives. Images from the verbatim text take on new metaphorical meaning with the juxtaposition of lines, e.g. 'curtains' works with the idea of being gossiped about in the previous line, the idea of 'curtain twitching', of being watched, scrutinised.

In 'Wisdom', the opening lines in each stanza are 'This womb/This body/This woman/This marriage/This family' widening the focus of Rubi's 'faulty' reproductive organs to the family she eventually creates in her own way, with the enjambment before 'together' marking the turn. The poem also uses full and slant rhyme to hold it together.

I use refrains in the next three poems to create different effects. 'The Beds in My Head' repeats 'I line up the beds in my head' to create a nightmarish, almost obsessive account of Rubi's journey to motherhood. I played with a more traditional form of end rhyme with 'In Her Belly', consisting of quatrains with an AABA rhyme scheme, written in a lullaby style as words spoken to a child birthed via a surrogate. The poem uses the refrain 'When you were in her belly' to move from the narrator's anxiety while her baby was inside the surrogate to her amazement on bringing her baby home. I have attempted to play with cliché with the ending to capture the surreal nature of obtaining a baby without going through pregnancy but perhaps this needs further transformation. 'Everything Can be Fixed' uses a refrain, 'It's okay, it's okay' but in a much more fluid and unstructured way. This is a narrative poem, telling a mini-story of a broken teapot as a metaphor for the series of ruptures and fixes of the mother–child bond.

The final hybrid form was assembled as follows:

Alison's story (*mother by adoption and egg donation*)
The nearly son (*edited interview*)
Where it all began (*edited interview*)
Hers (*re-imagined scene*)
Celebrate (*edited interview*)

'The sun will come out tomorrow' (*collage of quotations – mainly focusing on adoption*)

Charlotte's story (*egg donor*)
The lady of the house (*edited interview*)
MOT (*edited interview*)
A day at the races (*re-imagined scene*)
Holes (*edited interview*)

Shanta's story (*biological and adoptive mother*)
I like mine with a kiss (*personal essay – focusing on my experience of secondary infertility/pregnancy loss – the turn considering adoption*)

Rubi's story (*mother by surrogacy*)
Would you like something stronger (*edited interview*)
Passage to India (*edited interview*)
It all started with my legs (*edited interview*)

(*Poetry sequence*):
A good life
Wisdom
In her belly
The beds in my head
Everything can be fixed

Robin's story (*surrogate mother*)
Drama queen (*edited interview*)
The farm and the full moon (*edited interview*)
Yes, no, maybe (*re-imagined scene*)
Half a kiss (*edited interview*)

'She's got it' (*collage of quotations – focusing on the female body as a vessel/biological motherhood/pregnancy and birth*)

Lorraine's story (*adopter/adoptee*)
Damned if we do, damned if we don't (*edited interview*)
Summer of love (*edited interview*)
Perfectly polite (*re-imagined scene*)
It is what it is (*edited interview*)

Shanta's story
No babies (*personal essay – picks up where the other left off, focusing on adoption training/assessment ending on meeting son*)

Margaret's story (*birth mother*)
Never forget (*edited interview*)

(*Poetry sequence*):
Sorry not sorry
Care
The wrong mother (part I)
The wrong mother (part II)
Elephant
Blue

In this way, I began to view the entire form as a sort of collage – a collection of pieces slotting together to form a whole. The final form also includes a preface, conclusion and contextual note. Incorporated edited interviews and weaving in personal essay, quotation collage and poetry in response, completed the hybrid form, the rich tapestry curating and creating voices of adoption, surrogacy and egg donation.

Boyd Tomkin comments on the move away from linear form:

> If this new biographical – or even post-biographical – literature tends to rob both writers and readers of faith in the solid, full-dress portrait, it yields many compensations in return. It feels closer in its sidelights, speculations and digressions to how we understand people we know … And if it often shatters the subject of biography into multiple fragments, pieces of a jigsaw that might never wholly fit, then it can also show us how the smallest life can illuminate not just its times but our shared condition.
> (*Tomkin cited in Cline and Angier, 2010, pp. 149–151*)

This idea of 'the smallest life' illuminating 'its times' and 'our shared condition' will be discussed further in Chapter 2, 'Politics and power'.

Reference list

Alexievich, S. (1997) *Voices from Chernobyl*, New York, Picador.
Annie (1982) Directed by John Huston [Film]. Columbia Pictures.
Barthes, R. (1984) *A Lover's Discourse*, New York, Hill & Wang.
Barton, L. (2018) *Disability and Society: Emerging Issues and Insights*, Abingdon, Routledge.
Brodszky, N. and Cahn, S. (1951) *How D'Ya Like Your Eggs in the Morning*, Beverly Hills, CA, Sony/ATV Music Publishing LLC, The Bicycle Music Company.
Cline, S. and Angier, C. (2010) *The Arvon Book of Life Writing*, London, Menthuen Drama.
Cusk, R. (2002) *A Life's Work: On Becoming a Mother*, London, Fourth Estate.
Donnell, A. (1999) 'When Writing the Other is Being True to the Self: Jamaica Kincaid's *The Autobiography of My Mother*', in Polkey, P. (ed.) *Women's Lives into Print: The Theory, Practice and Writing of Feminist Auto/Biography*, London, Macmillan Press, pp. 123–136.
Donovan, S. (2013) *No Matter What: An Adoptive Family's Story of Hope, Love and Healing*, London, Jessica Kingsley Publishers.
Eakin, P. (1999) *How Our Lives Become Stories: Making Selves*, New York, Cornell University Press, pp. 142–146.
Elliott, H. (2016) *Storying Mothering Online* [Postgraduate Seminar at Thomas Coram Research Unit, UCL Institute of Education, University College London], 3 May 2016.
Ellis, C. (2003) *The Ethnographic I: A Methodological Novel about Autoethnography*, Walnut Creek, AltaMira Press.
Enright, A. (2005) *Making Babies: Stumbling into Motherhood*, London, Vintage.
Etter, C. (2014), *Imagined Sons*, Bridgend, Seren Books.
Galloway, J. (2010) *This Is Not About Me*, London, Granta Books.
Harman, K. (2001) 'Motherhood and Life Writing', in Jolly, M. (ed.) *Encyclopedia of Life Writing: Autobiographical and Biographical Forms* [Online]. Available at: http://libezproxyopen.ac.uk/login?qurl=http%3A%2Fsearch.credoreference.com.libezproxy.opn.ac.uk%2Fcontent%2Fentry%2Froutlifewrite%2Fmotherhood_and_life_writing%2FO (Accessed 16 October 2014).
Hesketh, S. (2014) 'Poems for Dementia Awareness Week 2014', *Where the Heart Is* (n.d.) [Blog]. Available at: http://wheretheheartispreston.tumblr.com/ (Accessed 28 December 2017).
Hill, S. (2002) *Portrait of My Lover as a Horse*, London, Bloodaxe Books.
hooks, b. (1989) 'Choosing the Margin as a Space of Radical Openness', in *Framework: The Journal of Cinema and Media*, No. 36, 15–23.
Hunt, C. and Sampson, F. (eds.) (1998) *The Self on the Page: Theory and Practice of Creative Writing in Personal Development*, London, Jessica Kingsley Publishers.
Kay, J. (1991) *The Adoption Papers*, Glasgow, Bloodaxe Books.
Kay, J. (2010) *Red Dust Road*, London, Picador.
Kincaid, J. (1996) *The Autobiography of My Mother*, London: Vintage.
Kriegel, L. (2008) 'The Observer Observing', in Lazar, D. et al. (eds.) *Truth in Nonfiction: Essays*, Iowa City, University of Iowa Press, pp. 93–99.
Lopate, P. (ed.) (1995) *The Art of the Personal Essay*, New York, Anchor Books, p. xxxix.
Mansfield, S. (2013) 'Fashioning Fathers: An Interview with G. Thomas Couser by Stephen Mansfield', *Life Writing*, vol. 11, no. 1, pp. 5–19.
Mullan, J. (2005) 'Colliding Voices: John Mullan Analyses Personality by Andrew O'Hagan' [Online]. Available at: https://www.theguardian.com/books/2005/feb/05/featuresreviews.guardianreview23 (Accessed 2 February 2018).
Myerson, J. (2009) *The Lost Child*, London, Bloomsbury.
Parker, T. (1972) *In No Man's Land: Some Unmarried Mothers*, London, Faber and Faber.

Parker, T. (2013 [1965]) *Five Women (Faber Finds)*, London, Faber and Faber.
Parnell, J. (ed.) (2019) *New and Experimental Approaches to Writing Lives*, London, Red Globe Press.
Polkey, P. (ed.) (1999) *Women's Lives into Print: The Theory, Practice and Writing of Feminist Auto/biography*, London, Macmillan Press.
Root, R. and Steinberg, M. (2005) *The Fourth Genre: Contemporary Writers of/on Creative Nonfiction*. New York, Longman.
Shields, D. (2011) *Reality Hunger: A Manifesto*, London, Penguin Books.
Shocking Blue (1969) *Venus*, Blaricum, Pink Elephant Label.
Stanley, L. (1992) *The Auto/Biographical I: The Theory and Practice of Feminist Auto/Biography*, Manchester, Manchester University Press.
Swann, D. (2017) 'Life after Life': The Influence of Tony Parker, unpublished PhD chapter, Chichester, University of Chichester.
Winterson, J. (2011) *Why Be Happy When You Could Be Normal?* London, Vintage.

2
POLITICS AND POWER

The personal as political

'The personal as political' is a mantra of second-wave feminism that still carries significance in contemporary life writing today. Recording the personal stories of mothers can be seen as a political act in itself, highlighting the importance of women's experiences of motherhood, essentially saying, this is worth hearing, it's worth recording.

> I think that without the women's movement … none of the women we now celebrate would have had the support required to be so visible … It took a revolutionary change in thinking about who can speak and who can be heard to make this possible.
> *(Morreau in Sumner, 2011, p. 155)*

In the late 1960s to the 1970s, Anne Oakley carried out two research projects – one about housework and one about transitioning to motherhood:

> Both projects employed in-depth interviewing as a way of generating personal narratives about experiences which, at the time, were viewed within mainstream social science (and society more generally) as unimportant, because they are private, domestic and belong to women's lives.
> *(Oakley, 2005, p. 246)*

In 1977, Adrienne Rich published *Of Woman Born: Motherhood as Institution and Experience*. She says she wrote it as resistance to the idea that 'the abstract' is a 'more developed or "civilized" mode than the concrete and particular' and to 'the ascription of a higher intrinsic human value to men than to women'

DOI: 10.4324/9781003290179-3

(Rich, 1976, p. ix). She wanted to examine motherhood – her own included – in a social context, as embedded in a political institution: in feminist terms.

Although things have undoubtedly changed for women since the 1970s, asking whether women's voices – indeed mothers' voice – are being heard remains a valid question. Since the beginning of the twenty-first century, there have been a spate of published memoirs focussing on motherhood, such as Rachel Cusk's *A Life's Work: On Becoming a Mother* (2002) and Anne Enright's *Making Babies: Stumbling into Motherhood* (2005), which sought to capture the complexity of individual lived experience. *Making Babies* opens with a chapter titled 'Apologies', in which Enright says that when an essay from her book, discussing pregnancy, was featured in *The Guardian* magazine, 'there was a ferocious response on the letters page. Who does she think she is?' (Enright, 2005, p. 1). 'MARRIED WOMAN HAS CHILDREN IN THE SUBURBS – it's not exactly a call to arms, and I genuinely apologise for being so ordinary' (Enright, 2005, p. 2). 'My only excuse is that I think it is important. I wanted to say what it was like' (Enright, 2005, p. 4).

> Motherhood is a subject touched upon, but very rarely explored, in both autobiographical and biographical accounts of women's lives. If female experience has been sidelined by "male" conceptions of selfhood and self-importance, maternal experience has been doubly silenced and ignored.
>
> (Harman, 2001)

Harman's article, 'Motherhood and Life Writing', published in the *Encyclopedia of Life Writing: Autobiographical and Biographical Forms*, charts the development of motherhood in life writing, looking at the way women's life writing reflected the social context of the times. Prior to the seventeenth century, women's autobiography focused mainly on spiritual experience, and although women diarists in the seventeenth and eighteenth centuries began to touch on motherhood, in the nineteenth century, women's writing moved away from motherhood to focus on 'their contributions to public life, their literary and artistic achievements, and their political struggles', reflecting the new role of women in public life. Harman concludes that by the twentieth century, women had begun to write autobiographically about motherhood within certain confines: 'Although many of motherhood's experiences are being explored in writing, some of the most painful stories – e.g. of termination, miscarriage, infertility, or the death of a child, – seem rarer than ever' (Harman, 2001). The six stories produced for *Another Mother* deal with many of these experiences: Alison, Rubi and Loraine's infertility, Margaret's attempted termination and loss of her child through adoption and Charlotte's pain from both the estrangement of her own mother, and her strained relationship with the parents of the child she 'gifted' them through egg donation.

Added to the fact that women, like Enright, still apologise for publishing accounts of motherhood is the fact that contemporary explorations of motherhood in life writing have, with a few notable exceptions, primarily focused on the biological mother raising the child she gave birth to. Yet the landscape of motherhood is changing. As many women delay entering motherhood to focus on their careers, and women become mothers in same-sex couples or as single mothers, many are building families by the so-called 'alternative routes' of adoption, surrogacy and egg donation.

As highlighted in Chapter 1, this research uses experimental life writing to explore my own personal experience of motherhood and the experience of other mothers, connecting these autobiographical and biographical stories to wider cultural, political and social understandings. It borrows from an autoethnographical approach in that it embraces and foregrounds the researcher's subjectivity rather than trying to limit it; autoethnographers reject the idea of social research as objective and neutral knowledge (Ellington and Ellis, 2008). Brochner and Ellis (2016) set out two forms of autoethnography: analytic and evocative, the former developing theoretical explanations of phenomena and the latter offering a narrative presentation that opens up conversations and evokes emotion. This research can, therefore, be said to offer an evocative autoethnographical exploration of motherhood via adoption, surrogacy and egg donation through the method of experimental life writing.

Sally Cline speaks of biography as serving as a window on the times, that her writing on Zelda Fitzgerald's life 'became not merely a window into a destructive marriage but also a window into an unjust time in history for women who wished to achieve' (2010, p. 25). Similarly, I wanted my biographical portraits on motherhood to illuminate the diverse and changing landscape of motherhood. In this way, writing the lives of others causes the life writer to reflect on the wider context of the subjects' lives, leading to a deeper understanding, not just of one particular life, but of the wider social and cultural factors impacting on that life.

Mother, gender and society

A definition in the *Oxford English Dictionaries* of 'mother' is the 'female parent of a human being'. In the thought-provoking article 'Is Motherhood Gendered?' Clarissa Sebag-Montefiore explores how issues of gender, identity and self-identification further expand the definition of motherhood:

> Reproductive medicine has seen definitions of motherhood expand to embrace egg-donor mothers and adoptive mothers, in addition to the gestational, or birth, mother. Today there is a fourth category: the transgender mother. This can mean, among a variety of possibilities, a man with a uterus who has transitioned from a woman, and who stops taking hormone-replacement therapy to conceive; or a woman who has transitioned from a man using frozen sperm with a surrogate.
>
> *(Sebag-Montefiore, 2015)*

While the six mothers interviewed in this book are cisgender women (where 'cisgender' is a term used to describe a person whose gender identity corresponds to their sex assigned at birth), the term 'mother' can be expanded. Philosopher Sara Ruddick supports this expanded view, arguing that 'mothering' is a practice, promoting the use of the verb 'mothering' as gender-neutral (1989). Although traditionally, mothering has been primarily associated with 'femaleness', the practice of mothering, of raising children, can be undertaken by any gender. In addition to transgender parents (who have a different gender from the sex they were assigned at birth), the definition and practice of 'mothering' can also apply to non-binary or other non-cisgender individuals (gender diverse, non-conforming and genderqueer), who may have a fluid conceptualisation of gender and 'a questioning or performative stance' (Tasker and Gato, 2020). Gender identity and parenthood is an emerging area of study (more information can be found via the references at the end of this chapter).

As with the concept of gender, the concept of mother can be seen as socially as well as biologically constructed:

> That 'motherhood' is a cultural entity, shaped by time and place, is clear from the vastly disparate concepts of what mothers are and how they should behave. In many aboriginal nations – in Australia, for example – children are raised not just by the biological mother but by multiple 'aunts' in tight-knit communities. In the Victorian era, the aristocracy's offspring were routinely given over to wet nurses, nannies and governesses. In contrast, the 'super-mom' of 1950s and early '60s America marked a historic milestone … This apron-clad mother (a product of cookie-cutter suburbia) stayed at home and dedicated her life solely to her husband and children.
>
> *(Sebag-Montefiore, 2015)*

Despite advances in fertility treatments and babies being conceived in 'test tubes', we have not yet reached a stage where foetuses can be grown to term outside a human uterus, a process called 'ectogenesis' (Overall, 2013). Many questions remain surrounding the future of motherhood, e.g. In the future, will ectogenesis be possible? Will human bodies continue to be needed to procreate? Will society need mothers or simply male and female gametes, i.e. eggs and sperm? Could there be a future where child rearing is no longer seen as an individual responsibility but a communal or societal one, replacing the role of mother with something more collective?

Of course, not all women want to bear or rear children; not all women enjoy motherhood. In her controversial book, *Freeing Ourselves from the Mad Myths of Parenthood* (2000), psychotherapist Susan Jeffers explores the downsides of becoming a parent, voicing the taboo 'bad thoughts' that parents may have but feel unable to share. She 'confesses' that after becoming a parent, she did not feel like raising a child was a good fit with her personality or life, and explains how on divorce she agreed to her son going to live with his father. In the book, she draws on conversations with a range of other parents, and their answers to the question of whether they would still have chosen to have children, if they knew then what parenting would be like. Although the stories in *Another Mother* speak of the longing for motherhood, the thesis is not intended to imply that *all* women long for motherhood. Women who are child-free by choice may proudly assert that decision; others may have made peace with the realisation that they will not become mothers (Pine, 2019).

Few mothers confess regret at having had their children. The birth mothers' stories researched for my PhD speak of yearning for the children they gave up. It is rare to find an autobiographical account of regret at having – and keeping – a child, although fiction explores this terrain, e.g. Joan Barfoot's novel, *Gaining Ground* (1980), presents the story of a mother who walks out on her family when her two children are young, portraying the sensitivities of a woman deemed 'abnormal'. Rosie Jackson's *Mothers who Leave* states that 'In Britain, an estimated 100,000 women live without their children; in the United States at least half a million. Yet mothers who've left are still thought of as unnatural, deviant, even immoral' (1994). Of course, fathers who walk out on their families receive a different societal reaction and judgement from mothers who do the same. It strikes me that researching the experiences of mothers who walk away from their children, opting not to participate in raising them, would be a fascinating area for further life writing study.

Whose voice is it anyway?

When we think about creative writing, what it is and what it means, we often think of fictional stories invented from the imagination. We admire a writer's skill in 'making things up', conjuring ideas and words like a magician. How does the genre of life writing fit into this? Life writers are not making things up, but writing about real lives. My research involved interviewing, recording and transcribing six women talking about their experiences, then editing and creatively transforming the material, raising questions of authorship and ownership of stories. If the words and ideas are not entirely the writer's own, who owns them? Life writing, like all writing, is a literary construction. Life writers impose narrative strategies on the material to influence the reader's experience of that material. This raises questions around the ethical issues of speaking for and representing others in life writing.

Procedural ethics

Ethical considerations were involved at all stages of my research. The first step before I could embark on recruiting and interviewing women for the project was to obtain approval from the university's Human Research Ethics Committee (HREC). The first few months of the project in 2014 were spent preparing to submit my plans to the HREC. This enabled me to consider good practice issues in recruiting and interviewing biographical subjects (referred to as 'research participants' by the HREC), as well as to network across disciplines with other researchers using related methodologies. The Open University Faculty of Health and Social Care research on The Making of Modern Motherhoods Project, *Making Modern Mothers* (Thomson, Kehily, Hadfield and Sharpe, 2011), used ethnography and biographical methods to explore the experience of pregnancy and new motherhood for biological mothers. A meeting with Professor Kehily, who worked on the project, helped me to identify some pertinent ethical and methodological issues relating to recruiting and interviewing mothers. For example, bearing in mind that participants may be at home with children, a suitable methodology would be to offer to travel to their home for the interviews or another place which suited the participant, such as a local café, should they not feel comfortable being interviewed at home. It was important to stipulate that any children present during interviews must be fully supervised by their parent at all times, and that I, as the researcher, would not be able to be left alone with the children. We discussed that stories should be anonymised using pseudonyms (for the participants and all other people featured in the story) even if the participants were happy to be named, due to the invasion of privacy for others involved, and that if there were other potentially identifying details, e.g. a specific location, these should be omitted or altered to avoid possible identification.

Following Professor Kehily's advice, I drew up an 'Information Sheet for Participants' and 'Consent Form' and submitted these, along with other relevant documentation, to the HREC, for project approval. Two versions of the documents were produced: a full-length detailed version and a shorter plain English version for accessibility reasons (e.g. if being accessed by a potential participant with literacy issues or learning disability). The Information Sheet set out the following:

- What am I studying?
- Who do I want to talk to?
- What will participation involve?
- What will happen to the material from the meetings?
- How can I find out further information?

The Information Sheet invited volunteers to email me as the researcher to have an initial informal, confidential telephone conversation, to discuss the project without any obligation. Further to an initial conversation, if the woman wished to participate in the face-to-face interviews, a Consent Form was provided for signature. This was an official agreement to participate in the project, setting out key boundaries including confidentiality. The Consent Form set out the agreement to take part in interviews and to the conversations being audio-recorded, on the understanding that the audio-recordings would not be used as broadcast material but transcriptions of part of them may be used in the life writing narrative and related publications. Participants were also given information about their rights to withdraw from the project. Signing the consent form assigned the copyright for the transcriptions of interviews/meetings to me, the researcher for use in my PhD thesis, and other publications, on the understanding that this would not affect participant's right to publish their own autobiographical account in the future. Participants were given contact details of the project supervisor and Head of Department.

A number of stipulations were made by the committee before I could commence, including that the participants could only be recruited via 'gatekeeping agencies' (such as charitable organisations offering information, advice and support services related to adoption, surrogacy and egg donation) and not via any existing contacts (to prevent the possibility of personal persuasion, bias or coercion) and that a suitably qualified counsellor must be involved to offer optional debriefing to participants in case the interviews triggered painful memories. Particular concern was expressed over interviewing a birth mother whose child had been adopted. There was discussion about the participants' rights to withdraw their interview material and the level of input they should be given in the writing up and presentation of the material. It was advised not to allow participants the option to review and amend their stories as this could cause unnecessary delays and create complications of co-authorship. The committee also advised against an open-ended right to withdraw, as this could potentially leave a PhD researcher in dire straits if participants withdrew just before thesis submission. We settled on allowing participants thirty days from their last interview to withdraw consent. This was considered reasonable by all parties and was discussed and agreed upfront with all participants, when presenting them with the Information Sheet to read and Consent Form to sign. I was reminded that the committee's role was to oversee procedural ethics 'to ensure procedures adequately deal with informed consent, confidentiality, rights to privacy, deception, and protecting human subjects from harm' (Ellis, 2007). The committee serves a legal function to protect the organisation (e.g. from law suits) as well as research participants.

Once my reworked proposal was approved, I set about contacting relevant organisations to act as gatekeepers for recruitment. Membership organisation, Donor Conception Network (DCN), expressed interest and circulated a call-out for participants, resulting in enquiries from several women, who were sent the Information Sheet. The first woman to come forward, Alison, was very enthusiastic and had a wealth of interesting experience. As she has a child via donor conception and an adopted child, proceeding with Alison did threaten to jeopardise the six-woman approach, but I decided to go ahead and allow the project to evolve organically. Indeed, subsequent participant, Lorraine, recruited as an adoptive mother, also happened to be adopted herself, so again presented a dual perspective and experience at interview. The second participant, Charlotte, a woman who donated her eggs to five different recipients, was recruited via the National Gametes Donation Trust (now the SEED Trust). The other women were recruited via Surrogacy UK, Adoption UK and the Natural Parents Network (a user-led organisation for birth parents whose children have been adopted). My approach to the research was to interview and write up one woman's story at a time before moving on to recruiting the next to allow me time to digest and reflect on each woman's story, and also to not keep women waiting once they had expressed an interest in being interviewed. There was no shortage of volunteers wishing to be interviewed and the six women fell naturally into place.

My initial plan for the interviews was formed after meeting with Professor Kehily and learning about some of the interview methods used in the Making of Modern Motherhoods Project. I undertook four interviews with Alison, over a period of several weeks, with the following focuses: (1) childhood photographs – looking at photos from the participant's childhood and photos of her children; (2) a day in the life – shadowing the participant in her everyday life; (3) objects – looking at an object that is significant to the participant as a mother, in Alison's case an embroidered quilt that her mother-in-law made to tell the family story (discussed as an analogy to the quilting method of storytelling in 'Finding a form' in Chapter 1) and (4) important dates – discussing birthdays, Mothers' Day and other celebrations. Formats varied from participant to participant, depending on their wishes. For example, there were several meetings in the participants' homes for Alison, Charlotte and Rubi; Lorraine preferred to be interviewed in a café (two meetings) and Robin and Margaret both opted to one longer home meeting each. The women were in control of the way the meetings were set up.

Social sciences researcher, Ann Oakley, has written extensively on her experience of in-depth interviews of women in the late 1960s–1970s for research on 'housework' and 'transitioning to motherhood', In her article 'Interviewing Women: A Contradiction in Terms?' (Oakley, 2005, pp. 217–232), Oakley talks about how academic researchers tend not to describe the research process beyond the basic facts such as how many interviews were carried out, duration, frequency, whether a standardised question format was used etc. and do not generally comment on the social, personal or emotional aspects of the interviewer–interviewee relationship. She says that sociology methodology textbooks on interviewing mainly operate a 'masculine paradigm' of legitimate and illegitimate interviewing behaviour, establishing a rapport as a means to an end to get interviewees to answer set questions, which offers a reductionist view of interviewers and positions interviewees in a passive role, exploring this as at odds with women's models and not being a good fit for feminist interviewers interviewing women. Oakley talks about the significance of the interviewee's and interviewer's feelings, interviewees asking the interviewer personal questions (e.g. do you have children?), hospitality (being offered tea etc.), transitioning to friendship, and views the 'textbook code' (e.g. do not get involved) as adopting an exploitative attitude to interviewees as purely instruments of data rather than human beings. While Oakley's observations differentiating masculine and feminine ways of approaching the interview relationship were important at the time her social sciences research on housework and motherhood in the 1960s and 1970s, in the current climate, the interview dynamic may be viewed as a more personal and nuanced relationship, depending on the individuals involved. The traditional, more transactional approach might involve trust and hospitality. Equally, there is perhaps a transactional element in human interactions, regardless of gender. Oakley argues that in practice it is difficult to establish rapport without answering interviewees' questions (which in sociology research would traditionally be batted away by commenting that it is the interviewer's job to gather opinions rather than offer them), claiming there is 'no intimacy without reciprocity' (p. 226).

Certainly, the women I interviewed wanted to know about my own experiences of motherhood, and they were particularly interested in asking me questions about my experience of adoption (e.g. egg donor Charlotte asked how old my son was when I adopted him, birth mother Margaret asked if he has any contact with his own birth mother). Sometimes, women told me information 'off the record'. It seemed the moment the Dictaphone was turned off and my coat put on was often the moment a participant would open up and say, 'Don't write anything about this but … ' This was extremely frustrating to me as a researcher as interesting material often emerged during these moments. Understanding that women had the right to control what information was recorded (and thirty days after the last interview to withdraw consent), I, of course, never used any of the unauthorised material. However, at times, I wished they hadn't disclosed it when I couldn't use it if it was to be of no use to me. However, to varying degrees, the women opened up to me as more than a researcher. This leads onto the issue of relational ethics.

Relational ethics

Of course, ethical dilemmas did not cease to exist after the research had been passed by the committee. Questions abounded: Was it ethical to expect my subjects to reveal their innermost secrets for possible publication when I was wary about revealing my own experience, particularly around the adoption of my youngest child? How should I walk the tightrope between researcher and friend? And what about the children, who did not consent to having their lives exposed for public consumption?

In 'Telling Secrets, Revealing Lives – Relational Ethics in Research with Intimate Others', Ellis (2007) deals with ethics from an ethnographer's point of view, defining a type of ethics differing from procedural ethics, which she coins 'relational ethics'. Ellis's article discusses dilemmas arising in three separate ethnographical works that she undertook, in situations where she either had a relationship with the biographical subject or developed a relationship (or became 'friendly') with the subjects over the period of research. Many of her ideas could be applied to creative life writing, as the same dilemmas ensue. Ellis discusses writing about her mother, without her mother's knowledge or consent, in 'Maternal Connections', and the feedback from her college students on reading this writing that it made them uncomfortable reading intimate details of her mother's experience in hospital, knowing that her mother was not aware of this information being shared. She also discussed writing about her experience of bereavement after the death of a romantic partner, and the issues arising in sharing personal information about the deceased. The third project, less personal perhaps, concerns one of her earliest ethnographical studies, with a small fishing community, who she lived alongside for the duration of the research, and became friendly with, discussing the limitations of pseudonyms, detailing how anonymised subjects recognised themselves in the text of one of her books, exploring the fall-out:

> In my mind, the dissertation and book that followed were separate from my relationship with the Fisher Folk. Thus, I failed to consider sufficiently how my blunt disclosures in print might affect the lives of the people about whom I wrote. Instead I cared about how committee members reacted to my dissertation and whether my manuscript would be published as a book. Although I didn't appear often in the text as a character, I considered the story I wrote to be my realist, sociological story about them, not their story … Wasn't this what getting a PhD was all about?
>
> *(Ellis, 2007, p. 10)*

As a mother interviewing other mothers, I felt a connection with my participants and a responsibility as a researcher, leading me to deliberate over potentially unflattering character portraits, ruminating on the inherent moral ambiguities. I asked myself how I would like my own complex experiences of motherhood presented. My own motives were something I had to carefully consider at each stage: I was researching motherhood through adoption, surrogacy and egg donation to help illuminate women's experiences and increase understanding but, of course, there was also the matter of personal gain in terms of the academic award of my PhD.

Couser's *Vulnerable Subjects: Ethics and Life Writing* (2004) discusses the issue of informed consent and who is capable of giving it, exploring the inherent problems of parental memoirs, straddling an authorised and unauthorised biography, whereby parents assume rather than request rights: 'What are intended by parents as beneficent acts may be perceived by their children, once grown, as violations of their autonomy, acts of appropriation or even betrayal' (Couser, 2004, p. 57). When, as adults, we write about, or agree to have published, accounts of our parenting, laying bare accounts of our children's lives, how can we possibly know what they will think of these publications when they are older? If we ask our children whether they give permission to have their lives exposed, how can we be certain that they understand the full implications of what they are agreeing to? At what age are children able to give informed consent? Is there always an element of coercion in the power dynamic of parent–child? Are some children more vulnerable than others?

To highlight these ethical dilemmas, I draw on Julie Myerson's publication of *The Lost Child* in 2009. Myerson was commissioned to write a biography of Regency painter, Mary Yelloly, a girl who died of tuberculosis in the 1820s, leaving behind a collection of watercolours. However, during the process of writing the book, Myerson became distracted by her teenage son, Jake, developing what she described as a drug addiction to skunk (a potent form of cannabis), leading her to decide to rework the book-in-progress as a dual narrative of two lost children: Mary Yelloly and her son, Jake Myerson. The book reveals very intimate information about Jake's drug use and personal life at the time, including his parents' decision to ask him to leave (and lock him out of) the family home aged 17 years, and his mother's offer to pay for a termination of pregnancy for a teenage girl he got pregnant. It makes for uncomfortable, voyeuristic reading in places.

In an interview with *The Independent* at the time of publication, Jake, then 20 years old, insisted he told his mother he didn't want the book to be published, despite her claims in the press that he had given permission:

> My mother seems to have suggested that I somehow agreed to this book which isn't really correct. The book contains some poetry that I wrote when I was about 15 or 16 and I remember getting a call from my mother saying she'd pay me £1,000 if she could use it. I was scrabbling around for money at the time so of course I took it but that doesn't mean I wanted it to be published.
>
> *(Myerson cited in Taylor, 2009)*

Five years later after detox, in an interview with *The Daily Mail*, Jake takes responsibility for his drug use and agrees with some of his mother's actions in terms of 'tough love'. However, he still does not agree that she did the right thing in publishing his story. He reveals that since the publication of his private life: 'He's attempted to kill himself more than once. He's been admitted to psychiatric wards twice. He's shoplifted tens of thousands of pounds worth of goods, been arrested, and self-harmed' (Foster, 2014). Clearly, then, it would seem fair to say he is a vulnerable person, by anyone's definition. Five years after the account of his troubled teenage years were published by his mother, he says:

> Obviously, I still don't agree that my mother should have written *The Lost Child*. I was put into a position totally out of my power and felt very vulnerable. She should have held onto it and published it 20 years down the line — no one would've batted an eyelid. But she did what she did and she's tried to apologise.
>
> *(Myerson cited in Foster, 2014)*

Mindful of the impact of autobiographical writing on my own children, I had to make an ethical decision over how much of my own story as a biological and adoptive mother to include in the creative writing for my project, and how this could potentially violate my children's privacy. My decision to include two personal essays was discussed in 'Finding a form' in Chapter 1. The essays explore my experience of loss and trauma with an ectopic pregnancy, and also my experience of training and preparation to adopt, ending on seeing a video of the baby who went onto become my son. I took a decision not to include any other discussion of either of my children in the creative writing, nor reveal other aspects of their personal stories, which I see as belonging to them. Likewise, although I adopted as part of a couple, I decided to present only my own parenting journey; my children's father has his own story.

Myerson claimed in her book that she wrote it to help other families dealing with teenage drug addiction (Myerson, 2009). The claim that publication may serve the 'greater good', possibly at the expense of individuals portrayed, raises wider ethical dilemmas. If more people may be helped by publication than those harmed, is the damage balanced out? In 'The Unseemly Profession: Privacy, Inviolate Personality and the Ethics of Life Writing', Paul Eakin unpicks the concept of 'the individual' and the concept of 'privacy', which he says can be said to be peculiar to Western culture. In some other cultures, the rights of an individual may be seen as less important than the rights of the community. Indeed, a person may be seen to exist in terms of their role within a group rather than as a separate individual (1999, pp. 165–166). Eakin critiques the publication of the controversial memoir, *The Kiss*, by Kathryn Harrison (1997) which explores an incestuous relationship with her father, which began in her twenties. Although some commentators lauded her as being courageous for sharing her story, other critics condemned her for ignoring the consequences of publication for her two young children, calling the book an 'exhibitionist display' and 'narcissistic act' and accusing her of 'merchandising pain' (Eakin, 1999, pp. 153–155).

Another key consideration for life writers, according to Eakin, is whether the life writer has objectified the person whose life is being documented, transforming him or her into a 'thing' (p. 166). This links with Couser's critique of adoptive father Michael Dorris's memoir of raising an adopted son, *The Broken Cord*, which Couser says reduces his son to a 'case study' (Couser, 2004, pp. 56–73). Couser explores how after diagnosis of foetal alcohol syndrome, literary treatment of Dorris's son, Adam, changes from 'a fully individualized character' to becoming 'a type and his story a case history' (Couser, 2004, pp. 60–61). This made me question whether my initial decision to select six women to interview by category (adoptive mother/birth mother/egg donor/mother via egg donation/surrogate mother/mother via surrogacy) was reductionist, reducing the women to 'types' rather than individuals. In reality, the women who came forward did not fit easily into one category – the first, Alison, being a mother through adoption and egg donation, the second, Charlotte, being an egg donor, biological mother and stepmother. All aspects of these women's lives that were discussed were fascinating, not just the ring-fenced aspects associated with their 'categories'.

Appropriation and authentication

Linking these discussions on appropriation and Oakley's assertion of the 'masculine paradigm' of social sciences interviewing, likewise a biographer has been traditionally reviewed as an 'expert/authority' narrating the life of their 'subject'. The biographer has traditionally remained absent in the text and/or presented as being objective, their processes invisible to the reader. Literary editor, Boyd Tomkin (as cited in Cline and Angier, 2010, pp. 149–151), talks about 'a new wave of biographical literature' over the past two decades, highlighting the example of Philip Hoare 'once a conventional biographer' whose 2009 non-fiction book, *Leviathan, or The Whale*, 'puts the storyteller centre-stage, and makes a drama out of his quest for the subject' (p. 150). The idea of having the biographer centre stage may be viewed as an innovative way of working but the inclusion of a metanarrative, writing about the process of life writing, doesn't eliminate the risk of appropriation. Indeed, Julie Myerson's narration of her son, Jake, very much put her own character centre stage. Placing oneself centre stage as a biographer also presents the risk of narcissism; by staying on the sidelines, it might be argued that the author at least avoids gratuitous self-dramatisation. If the biographer is no longer an absent voice but acknowledged as a person with their own role in the journey of narrating another's life, how does this shift the paradigm?

This idea of the storyteller as a pivotal character can be seen in Alexander Masters's biography, *Stuart: A Life Backwards* (2006), which relays the author's meetings with a homeless man named Stuart over a period of two years. However, despite the apparent progressive approach of Masters including himself as a character in Stuart's story, as a middle-class author writing the biography of a vulnerable homeless person, Masters can be said to be 'articulating the other'. This can be problematic in terms of the unbalanced power dynamic, with its inherent potential for appropriation or even exploitation. A number of ethical issues are involved, including Stuart's vulnerability and ability to give informed consent; relational ethics (as Masters interviewed Stuart over a period of two years, developing a relationship with him; and how Stuart is represented, the notion of exoticising 'the other', which can be inferred via the language used in the book jacket blurb:

> the story of an extraordinary friendship between a reclusive writer and illustrator ('a middle class scum ponce, if you want to be honest about it, Alexander') and a chaotic, knife-wielding beggar whom he gets to know during a campaign to release two charity workers from prison.

Masters examined homelessness from the 'outside in'. My project differs in that I am exploring motherhood via adoption, surrogacy and egg donation from the vantage point of a biological and adoptive mother, one could say 'from the inside'. Although I cannot claim to know what it feels like to be anyone other than myself, and have not experienced what my interviewees have, the overlaps and shared experiences with the mothers interviewed alter the dynamic between researcher and researched. Can I be defined as articulating the other, if I am the other? Clearly, there are still delicate issues to be negotiated. I was not a vulnerable birth mother who felt she was coerced into adoption; I was a writer-researcher seeking to gain an academic qualification from the interviews. I was a White British interviewer interviewing women from cross-cultural backgrounds. There is a fine line between 'appreciation', seeking to deepen understanding of another's experience, and 'appropriation', using an aspect of another experience/culture/identity that is not your own for your own personal interest.

Issues of appropriation and authentication needed to be negotiated with all aspects of using the women's interview material; however, there were particular questions around cultural appropriation when interviewing women cross-culturally. Rubi referred to attitudes of her Indian family with language such as, 'You know, it's a typical Asian thing.' I did not want to present her experience in a culturally stereotyped way; I wanted to capture and convey the reality of her experience, including her family's response to her infertility and surrogacy, in a way that was authentic. Rubi and her husband, Sunni, both had English sounding names, although deviating slightly from traditional spellings by changing 'y' to 'i'. When I presented her story to my supervisors using the names Ruby and Sunny, my supervisors queried whether I had changed their names from Indian names. Dr Sally O'Reilly, who writes historical fiction, highlighted that sometimes real historical details appear so implausible to the reader that they have to be falsely edited to offer an illusion of authenticity, which I found fascinating. However, I was uncomfortable with the idea of using traditional Indian pseudonyms for this couple, as I did not feel this reflected their identity. In the end, we settled on changing my suggested pseudonyms of Ruby and Sunny to Rubi and Sunni to reflect the nature of their actual names.

In *Art and Ventriloquism*, David Goldblatt uses the metaphor of ventriloquism to examine 'how the vocal vacillation between ventriloquist and dummy works within the roles of artist, artwork and audience as a conveyance to the audience of the performer's intentions, emotions and beliefs through a created performative persona' (2005, book blurb). This relates to novelists using fictional characters as dummies to direct their own voice through and project ideas, themes and emotions. Thinking about biography, we can also see that the biographical subject can serve as a kind of 'dummy' too, with the biographer acting as a ventriloquist, controlling the words allowed to escape through the subject's mouth in terms of how material is edited and presented, as explored in 'Finding a form' in Chapter 1. 'If the ventriloquist is to be understood as a controlling or at least intentional figure, the dummy is the medium for another voice, one different from the ventriloquist's yet a voice of the ventriloquist' (Goldblatt, 2005, p. 76).

There are no easy answers to ethical conundrums, no set rules that apply to every situation. Rather there are principles that can be applied, other writers and researchers' experiences – good practice and mistakes – to draw on.

We do not act on principles that hold for all times. We act as best we can at a particular time, guided by certain stories that speak to that time, and other people's dialogical affirmation that we have chosen the right stories .... The best any of us can do is to tell one another our stories of how we have made choices and set priorities. By remaining open to other people's responses to our moral maturity and emotional honesty … we engage in the unfinalized dialogue of seeking the good.

(Frank, 2004, pp. 191–192)

This chapter attempts to reflect on the ethical decisions made throughout researching and writing up *Another Mother*, knowing it remains an area of open dialogue.

The politics of adoption, surrogacy and egg donation

Half a Million Women (1997), written by a group of social workers, provides insight into the experience of an estimated half a million women who, at the time of the book's publication, had given children up for adoption in the UK, outlining the social context of adoption. Before embarking on my research, I held, perhaps naïvely, the belief that adoption in the past and present were two radically different realities: in the past, adoption was a result of young, unmarried women being pressured or forced to give babies up for adoption, whereas in recent times, adopted children were more likely to have been removed from their birth families by social workers on the grounds of abuse or neglect. However, authors Howe et al. (1997) present this in a slightly different way – that society's views on what constitutes a fit or unfit mother shifts over time. At the time of the Adoption of Children Act, 1926, unmarried mothers who wanted to keep their babies were deemed 'mentally unstable' and social workers therefore operated under the moral standards and psychological perspectives of the time, just as they do now (Howe et al., 1997, pp. 12–18).

As highlighted in the preface, a recent research study by the Nuffield Foundation on Inequalities in Child Welfare Intervention Rates (2014) found that women living in the UK's poorest neighbourhoods were ten times more likely to have their children taken into care than those in more affluent areas. There are also socioeconomic inequalities involved in egg donation and surrogacy. As shown in Rubi's story, women from poorer nations may become egg donors or surrogates for financial reasons (it is illegal to offer financial reward for surrogacy or egg donation in the UK), often to provide a better life for their own children (Wilkinson, 2003, pp. 168–197; Deveaux, 2016, pp. 1–48). There are additional ethical issues involved in adoption, surrogacy and egg donation, including 'the nationality of the baby, the role that religion and race should or should not play, the adoptive parents' age and sex/gender … that are different or at least thought to be different from the issues about having one's own biologically related child' (Overall, 2012, p. 12).

Some of the interviewed women's stories raise difficult ethical and political questions to which there are no easy answers. My research attempts to give a voice to mothers in widely different circumstances, to present their stories, with all their complexities, stories which are open to multiple readings and interpretations. Mainstream media, on the other hand, often appears to have an agenda in how mothers' stories are interpreted. *The Mommy Myth: The Idealization of Motherhood and How it Has Undermined All Women* (2005), written by Susan Douglas and Meredith Michaels, details research into the way motherhood has been represented in the media over a 30-year period. Chapter 5, 'Threats from Within: Maternal Delinquents' (2005, pp. 140–172) explores how both surrogate mothers and 'abusive' mothers are portrayed in the media. Analysis of the media portrayal of the 1986 custody battle between surrogate mother, Mary Beth Whitehead, and the 'legal mother', Dr Stern, discusses how both women were caricaturised. It looks at the ways in which mothers are cast in various roles as 'unfit', 'antimother' and 'she-devils'. Discussion of media imagery of 'crack babies' explores how the media characterises mothers via an 'us/them account of decent folk versus abusers', failing to show complexities, such as 'a crack mother who cared about her kids'. The explicit intention of my creative output for this research is to avoid all forms of stereotyping and caricature, and to present the women featured (both those directly interviewed and those who appear as absent characters) as complex, fully individualised characters.

The politics of form (and the nature of truth)

Feminist scholars, Adrienne Rich and Ann Oakley, both write in the first person, reclaiming the 'I', deviating from the traditional patriarchal mode of the 'grand narrative', Rich says that *Of Woman Born* 'was both praised and attacked for what was sometimes seen as its odd-fangled approach: personal testimony mingled with research, and theory which derived from both' (p. x). Rich justifies her approach, discussing her distrust of the absent author who 'lays down speculations, theories, facts, and fantasises without any personal grounding' (p. x). Using a hybrid form for *Another Mother* allowed me to include my own reflections on motherhood in the form of poetry and personal essay and in the selection and arrangement of quotations from a range of sources. In this way, my response to the interview material adds a seventh voice to the project.

In *Writing a Woman's Life*, Heilbrun says, 'there still exists little organised sense of what a woman's biography or autobiography should look like', discussing how some of the narratological issues of constructing a biography are deeply entwined with the way we see women in society (1988, p. 27).

> There is no objective or universal tone in language for however long we have been told that there is. There is only the white, middle class, male tone. But the question is not only one of narrative and tone, it is also one

of language. How can women create stories of women's lives if they only have male language with which to do it?

(Heilbrun, 1988, p. 40)

This is not only a feminist issue but relates to wider historical and political context. Jerome de Groot's *The Historical Novel* (2010) explores postmodernism and the historical novel, rejecting ideas of authenticity, absolute truth and 'grand narratives' (p. 110). History itself is seen as an imaginative narrative, using metaphor and narrative style, 'to interpret a version of something that is innately other and unknown' (p. 113); this can also be applied to life writing, which reinterprets personal histories, re-imagining lived experience. De Groot talks about metafiction 'as a way of turning away from traditional methods that correspond to ordered reality', e.g. chronology, linearity, the omniscient narrator etc., 'demonstrating the play of the linguistic and representational system and loss of assurance in articulation' (p. 117); a similar metanarrative can be applied to life writing. Choosing to be transparent about my role as a (subjective, biased, human) researcher and mother, I have inserted myself within the text of the life writing, making my research processes, such as the interviewing context, explicit, thereby providing a metanarrative to the life writing. De Groot's concept of 'turning away from traditional methods that correspond to ordered reality' in historical fiction can also be seen in the approaches of many life writers:

> Of course that is not the whole story, but that is the way with stories; we make them what we will. It's a way of explaining the universe while leaving the universe unexplained, it's a way of keeping it all alive, not boxing it into time. Everyone who tells a story tells it differently, just to remind us that everybody sees it differently. Some people say there are true things to be found, some people say all kinds of things can be proved. I don't believe them. The only thing for certain is how complicated it all is, like string full of knots … Claw it, chew it, rearrange it and at bedtime it's still a ball of string full of knots. Nobody should mind.
>
> *(Winterson, 2011)*

Vesna Goldsworthy's memoir, *Chernobyl Strawberries: A Memoir* (2005), written for her son after being diagnosed with breast cancer is presented in a fragmented way, reminiscent of Winterson's approach. The chapters focus on themes, rather than presenting a chronological account. For example, Chapter 1, 'The Beginnings, All of Them', offers a range of starting points. The Afterword (almost a critical commentary) dated London, 27 July 2004, includes some interesting reflection on memory and writing process, where she talks about autobiography as a 'doubly edited life': 'Memory edits the first run, the writer edits the second, as she imposes provisional boundaries on her recollection' (2005, pp. 186–187):

> [Memory] connects people and places and things which may superficially seem unconnected, and imposes its own patterns across time. To have written a linear narrative of my life – from birth to the present – would have been to force my story to acquire a shape which it doesn't have in the way I remember it, and to jettison those very patterns and leitmotifs which seem to me the most interesting.
>
> *(Goldsworthy, 2005, p. 186)*

To have constructed linear narratives from the mothers' interviews would have felt similarly forced; discovering the emerging patterns, themes and symbols was the most interesting aspect of curating and creating the text. Fiona Sampson, when writer-in-residence at Age Concern Swindon, says of her experience of creating poetry out of verbatim material: 'When I type up the poem for an exhibition, I am like a photo-journalist framing and cropping the image' (Sampson in Hunt and Sampson, 1998, p. 131). This aspect of Sampson's creative writing gives a voice to marginalised people: when one of the residents saw her own words, she did not attribute them to herself; she found it difficult 'to believe that what she said had a literary shape or even a textual one' (p. 130). This raises the idea of writing as reification: 'Reified as text, literary and imaginative writing … has a higher status than whatever they might say in conversation' (p. 139), a concept which resonated with me as I considered both Rubi's and Margaret's voices being reified through the poetry written from their interviews, as well as the edited interview text itself (which is also a construction of voice and story). In some ways, all the creative forms in the project, including those not created from verbatim words, can be said to reify the women's voices and experiences as a collection of artistic representations. The project transforms the raw material of reported experience into a carefully constructed and sculpted artefact.

In *Interpreting Interviews*, a text on social sciences research, Mats Alvesson states that 'some people would argue … all knowledge is metaphorical in that it emerges from or is "constructed" from some point of view.' He goes on to talk about our experiences and ways of thinking and seeing as being organised by metaphors. 'Metaphors can be seen as *crucial elements in how people relate to reality*' (Alvesson, 2010, p. 63). 'The ability of metaphors to explore and express experiences … indicates shared ground between poets and researchers' (p. 65). Of course, in creative writing research, we do not differentiate between 'poets' and 'researchers'; they are one and the same thing, but identifying common ground between social science researchers and creative writing researchers is particularly relevant here. The 'fictionalised' or 'poeticised' sections in *Another Mother* are no less 'true' than the verbatim sections. As a researcher using creative writing to explore and express women's experiences of motherhood via adoption, surrogacy and egg donation, I believe that the use of metaphor and imagery is a powerful tool in the creation of voice and story, and ultimately in ways of seeing and understanding experiences of motherhood.

A mother writing about mothering

> It's hard not to feel guilty that you are not doing the research and writing projects you planned to do; that you *are* doing the research and writing projects you planned to do; that you can no longer spend the entire weekend prepping and grading; that you do sometimes spend the entire weekend prepping and grading; that you are no longer as available for school [university] events; that you are not available enough for family events; that you are happy in the maternal sphere; that you are happy in the career world...
>
> *(Chun et al. in Evans and Grant, 2008, pp. 244–245)*

It would seem remiss to reflect on the process of researching mothers' lives without addressing my own role as, and the inherent challenges of being, a mother of two children, aged two and nine years at the beginning of my PhD and nine and fifteen at the end. I undertook my PhD part-time over seven years (with two study breaks) at the same time as teaching creative writing both within The Open University and outside of it. Harman writes that 'the mother who would write is so often gagged – by forces that range from the mundane (lack of time) to the highly theoretical (a Lacanian view of language that would forever separate a mother from the words in which she might describe her experience)' (Harman, 2001).

There have been several significant anthologies of personal essays by mothers who are creative practitioners in various disciplines, which have spoken to my practice. In *The Fruits of Labour: Creativity, Self-Expression and Motherhood*, artist Jacqueline Morreau writes: 'The first need of an artist is solitude. How can she find it within a ten-to-twelve-hour working day, such as I had when I was a single, working mother and a mature student' (Morreau in Sumner, 2011, p. 154). Being a single, working mother and a mature student has presented me with many practical challenges; finding the time that Harman speaks of and the solitude that Morreau raises were constant struggles throughout my research. Of course, it was my choice to undertake this research when my children were young (although I was not a single parent at the beginning of my PhD, but part of a partnership which broke down during the PhD). The obsessive passion for the project came about shortly after adopting my youngest son; if I hadn't had this experience, I wouldn't have been motivated to undertake the research. Hence, motherhood has been an intrinsic part of my research process, acting as both a driver and at times, a barrier. My research has been carried out almost exclusively when my children have been at school, at afterschool clubs or in someone else's care. The COVID-19 pandemic complicated this arrangement, especially during the nationwide schools closure, which necessitated another six months study break.

Academia is not always conducive to supporting mothers, especially single mothers, and institutional barriers still exist. *Mama, PhD: Women Write about Motherhood and Academic Life*, edited by Elena Evans and Caroline Grant (2008), explores the continued inequality of the sexes in higher education:

> The sociologist Arlie Hochschild observes that the feminist revolution stalls as soon as one has a baby. Academy's no ivory-tower exception. Even this far into the second wave, nothing's been done to fix the fact that our prime childbearing years coincide with the years in which we are supposed to move all around the country for postdocs and visiting positions, brave the job market, prepare new courses, publish our dissertations, and get tenure.
>
> *(Sanders in Evans and Grant, 2008, p. 247)*

'Prime childbearing years' may not be so relevant to those of us who become mothers through adoption, surrogacy or egg donation, yet as a mature PhD student, I was essentially in a similar space. For example, when asked to present on my research at a recent OU online departmental research meeting, although I was grateful for the opportunity, it presented me with practical challenges as a single mother. At this time, my children were back at school and I was able to work uninterrupted during the school day. However, afterschool childcare options were still highly restricted due to the continuing COVID-19 pandemic, and the meeting was being run from 4.00 pm to 6.00 pm, when my children would be home (and in need of their tea). Thankfully, at this time, support bubbles and childcare bubbles had been legalised, allowing my mother to travel to my house, look after my children and prepare their tea downstairs while I balanced my laptop on my bed. However, the options were severely limited and it was only by luck that I was able to present. Running research meetings after school at key parenting times disproportionately effects women who still tend to be the primary carers of young children. This remains a political issue.

As an antidote perhaps, *Mamaphonic: Balancing Motherhood and Other Creative Arts*, edited by Bee Lavender and Maia Rossini (2004), is an anthology of practical role models:

> We collect other mothers in our heads – mothers who have published books, mothers who have opened show, mothers who sell their art, mothers who act in movies, mothers who sell millions of records, mothers who go on the road.
>
> We repeat their names like prayer: Toni Morrison, Louise Erdrich, Exene Cervenka, Kim Gordon, Sinead O'Connor, Diane di Prima, George Sand, Kristen Hersh, Erma Bombeck, Mary Wollstonecraft, Patti Smith, Tillie Olsen, Grace Paley, Ursula le Guin, Muriel Rukesyer, Diane Arbus, Lorrie Moore, Louise Nevelson, Sally Mann, Maya Angelou, Loretta Lynn.
>
> ...
>
> Somehow they did it, we think. So we can do it too.
>
> *(Lavender and Rossini, 2004, pp. 2–3)*

Reference list

Adoption UK (2022) 'About Adoption UK' [Online]. Available at: https://www.adoptionuk.org/Pages/Category/about-adoption-uk (Accessed 10 November 2022).

Alvesson, M. (2010) *Interpreting Interviews*, London, Sage Publications.

Barfoot, J. (1980) *Gaining Ground*, London, The Women's Press.

Brochner, A. and Ellis, C. (2016) *Evocative Autoethnography: Writing Lives and Telling Stories*, New York, Routledge.

Cline, S. and Angier, C. (2010) *The Arvon Book of Life Writing*, London, Methuen Drama.

Couser, G. T. (2004) *Vulnerable Subjects: Ethics and Life Writing*, New York, Cornell University Press.

Cusk, R. (2002) *A Life's Work: On Becoming a Mother*, London, Fourth Estate.

De Groot, J. (2010) *The Historical Novel*, Abingdon, Routledge.

Deveaux, M. (2016) 'Exploitation, Structural Injustice, and the Cross-Border Trade in Human Ova', *Journal of Global Ethics*, vol. 12, pp. 1–48.

Donor Conception Network (2022) 'Who Are We' [Online]. Available at: https://www.dcnetwork.org/who-are-we (Accessed 10 November 2022).

Douglas, S. and Michaels, M. (2005) *The Mommy Myth: The Idealization of Motherhood and How it Has Undermined All Women*, New York, Simon & Schuster Ltd., Free Press.

Eakin, P. (1999) 'The Unseemly Profession: Privacy, Inviolate Personality and the Ethics of Life Writing', in *How our lives become stories: Making selves*, New York, Cornell University Press, pp. 142–146.

Ellington, L. and Ellis, C. (2008) 'Autoethnography as a Constructionist Project', in Holstein, J. and Gubrium, J. (eds.) *Handbook of Constructionist Research*, New York, Guilford, pp. 445–465.

Ellis, C. (2007) 'Telling Secrets, Revealing Lives – Relational Ethics in Research With Intimate Others', *Qualitative Inquiry*, vol. 13, no. 1, pp. 3–29.

Enright, A. (2005) *Making Babies: Stumbling into Motherhood*, London, Vintage.

Evans, E. and Grant, C. (eds.) (2008) *Mama, PhD: Women Write about Motherhood and Academic Life*, New Jersey, Rutgers University Press.

Foster, J. (2014) 'Repentance of a Drug Rebel', *The Daily Mail* [Online]. Available at: https://www.dailymail.co.uk/femail/article-2887951/Repentance-drug-rebel-novelist-Julie-Myerson-outed-son-cannabis-user-split-thier-family-polarised-opinion-Six-years-fighting-heroin-addiction-finally-admits-RIGHT-tough.html (Accessed 5 March 2021).

Frank, A. (2004) 'Moral Non-Fiction: Life Writing and Children's Disability', in Eakin, P. (ed.) *The Ethics of Life Writing*, New York, Cornell University Press, pp. 174–194.

Goldblatt, D. (2005) *Art and Ventriloquism* [Online]. Available at: http://ebookcentral.proquest.com/lib/open/detail.action?docID=1619363 (Accessed 19 February 2021).

Goldsworthy, V. (2005) *Chernobyl Strawberries: A Memoir*, London, Atlantic Books.

Harman, K. (2001) 'Motherhood and Life Writing', in Jolly, M. (ed.) *Encyclopedia of Life Writing: Autobiographical and Biographical Forms* [Online]. Available at: http://libezproxyopen.ac.uk/login?qurl=http%3A%2Fsearch.credoreference.com.libezproxy.opn.ac.uk%2Fcontent%2Fentry%2Froutlifewrite%2Fmotherhood_and_life_writing%2FO (Accessed 16 October 2014).

Harrison, K. (1997) *The Kiss*, New York, Random.

Heilbrun, C. G. (1988) *Writing a Woman's Life*, New York, W. W. Norton.

Hunt, C. and Sampson, F. (eds.) (1998) *The Self on the Page: Theory and Practice of Creative Writing in Personal Development*, London, Jessica Kingsley Publishers.

Howe, D. et al (1997) *Half a Million Women: Mothers Who Lose Their Children by Adoption*, London, Penguin.
Jackson, R. (1994) *Mothers who Leave*, London, Pandora.
Jeffers, S. (2000) *Freeing Ourselves from the Mad Myths of Parenthood*, London, Hodder Paperbacks.
Lavender, B. and Rossini, M. (eds.) (2004) *Mamaphonic: Balancing Motherhood and Other Creative Arts*, New York, Soft Skull Press.
Nuffield Foundation (2017) *Inequalities in Child Welfare Intervention Rates* [Online]. Available at: https://www.nuffieldfoundation.org/project/inequalities-in-child-welfare-intervention-rates (Accessed 15 January 2020).
Oakley, A. (2005) *The Ann Oakley Reader: Gender, Women and Social Science*, Bristol, Policy Press.
Overall, C. (2012) *Why Have Children? The Ethical Debate*, London, MIT Press.
Oxford Dictionaries (n.d.) *Definition of 'Mother'* [Online]. Available at: www.oed.com (Accessed 29 September 2022).
Masters, A. (2006) *Stuart: A Life Backwards*, London, Fourth Estate.
Myerson, J. (2009) *The Lost Child*, London, Bloomsbury.
Natural Parents Network (2022) 'About' [Online]. Available at: https://www.facebook.com/NPNNaturalParentsNetwork/about (Accessed 10 November 2022).
Pine, E. (2019) *Notes to Self*, London, Penguin Books.
Rich, A. (1986 [1977]) *Of Woman Born*, New York, W. W. Norton.
Ruddick, S. (1989) *Maternal Thinking: Toward a Politics of Peace*, Boston, Beacon Press.
Sebag-Montefiore, C. (2015) 'Is Motherhood Gendered?' *Aeon* [Online]. Available at: https://aeon.co/essays/when-trans-people-become-parents-who-gets-called-mother (Accessed 29 September 2022).
SEED Trust (2022) 'About Us' [Online]. Available at: https://seedtrust.org.uk/about-seed/ (Accessed 10 November 2022).
Sumner, P. (ed.) *The Fruits of Labour: Creativity, Self-Expression and Motherhood*, London, The Women's Press.
Surrogacy UK (n.d.) 'About Us' [Online]. Available at: https://surrogacyuk.org/aboutus/ (Accessed 3 November 2022).
Tasker, F. and Gato, J. (2020) 'Gender Identity and Future Thinking about Parenthood: A Qualitative Analysis of Focus Group Data with Transgender and Non-Binary People in the United Kingdom', *Frontiers in Psychology*, vol. 11, no. 865.
Taylor, J. (2009) 'Now For My Side of the Story: Myerson's Son Hits Back', *Independent* [Online]. Available at: https://www.independent.co.uk/arts-entertainment/books/news/now-for-my-side-of-the-story-myerson-s-son-hits-back-1636845.html (Accessed 5 March 2021).
Thomson, R., Kehily, M. J., Hadfield, L. and Sharpe, S. (2011) *Making Modern Mothers*, Bristol, Policy Press.
Wilkinson, S. (2003) 'The Exploitation Argument against Commercial Surrogacy', *Bioethics*, vol. 17, pp. 169–187.
Winterson, J. (2011) *Why Be Happy When You Could Be Normal?* London, Vintage.

PART II
Experimental life writing

3
ALISON'S STORY

The nearly son

Alison is waiting for me at the train station outside WHSmith: a woman with a grey-streaked bob, in jeans and trainers squatting down on the floor, talking to two young children with mousy hair. The girl holds a teddy and the boy a biro and rail leaflet. Alison's face lights up when she sees me looking at her. *Shanta?* She offers a hand but I have already gone in for an air kiss. The children talk at me in stereo in words I cannot fathom. Alison leads me outside to her car where we spend a few moments deciding who will sit where. *The children want you to sit with them in the back but it's a tight squeeze and a bit of a mess. I think you should go in the front.* After a spot of musical car seats, I end up in the front, talking to Alison but turning round every few seconds to engage with the children. They look just how children should look, ruddy cheeked and dishevelled and full of curiosity. William wears a navy tee-shirt, khaki shorts, navy wellies with matching pen scribbles on his legs. Emily wears a floral raincoat with star-spangled wellies topped with long navy socks. Frantic questions are fired, random comments uttered. *We're all a bit overexcited!*

 We park up outside a terraced house. Black door, metal door number, outside light, a few weeds on the pavement. And now we are inside a surprisingly spacious house with a huge, airy, sparkly kitchen that looks as though it belongs in a television advert. Crates of wooden toys sit under the kitchen island; fabric craft creations are scattered on its surface. In a room off to the side, there is a wooden table and a piano. The perfect family. *Who plays the piano?* I ask. *None of us really. I used to but ...* William is climbing up to get biscuits and Emily shows me her self-portrait; she wears a tiara and holds a bunny rabbit. *That's lovely*, I say, thinking that I should really get Alison to sign the consent form before we start the session. But we have already started, haven't we? We started the moment

DOI: 10.4324/9781003290179-5

we greeted one another at the station, the moment they welcomed me into their home. *Would you like some tea? Normal or herbal?* We sit around the wooden table and Emily spreads out a game of matching pairs, which I am useless at, much to Emily's amusement. Soon William's bored and starts to knock the cards onto the floor shouting.

Let's go to the park, suggests Alison brightly and we set about putting our coats and shoes back on before I remember the consent form and fish it out of my bag for signing just as William starts to get agitated. Once out in the fresh air on their scooters, the children settle down. *We try to get out every day. We all feel better when we get out.* We chat about holidays, theirs, mine. William speaks with an impressive vocabulary for a not yet three-year-old. *We saw dinosaurs. I thought they were real but they were models. Dinosaurs are very, very old so they are dead but some are alive.* As we walk through the park, the trees swaying overhead, the sun half in, half out, rain threatening, I think about the information gleaned from Alison prior to meeting.

It's a familiar story – failed IVF attempts leading to fertility treatment and adoption. *We got a long way down the process; we were approved for adoption and matched for another little boy. I'd seen his photo, watched him on a video, I knew his name. We'd even accidentally seen him in person when we were out choosing beds and popped into a railway station and there he was in his buggy and I heard someone call his name. But it didn't work out. It left me angry and sour. We went back to fertility treatment, first in London and then found an anonymous egg donor in Cyprus. After a while, I was pregnant with Emily. It was wonderful.* I consider the three of them strolling along, their movements in tune with one another, their speech patterns mirroring one another, and think about this other boy. Questions for another time. *One wasn't enough. I wanted a sibling for Emily. We went back to adoption with another agency. William was placed with us when he was a very young baby under a scheme called concurrent planning; legally we were his foster carers and we didn't know whether we would get to keep him. I took him for regular supervised contact sessions with his birth mum. She and I have a lot in common – we are the only two people who could look at photos of William all day. I liked and respected her. She was vulnerable; as she grew up, the system didn't provide the basic level of care for her. The adoption order was granted a year later. Once the adoption was approved, contact stopped.*

There is a sandpit in the middle of the playground; plastic sand toys sit in a pile to one side. *Can you both play with me in the sand?* asks Emily, selecting three rakes in yellow, blue and green. Alison is side-tracked by a woman with two young daughters. I smile while busying myself with the children, leaving Alison to decide whether and how to introduce me. *Generally, I'm quite private*, she told me over the phone. *Though everyone knows about William as I suddenly turned up at a birthday party one day with a new baby in tow. Emily knows how our family was made. She came out of school one day shouting at the top of her voice that William was adopted and she was donor conceived. I don't mind her telling people but I wasn't really in the mood that day at the school gates, you know.* Alison has stepped aside to chat with this woman. I'm sensing from her body language that she doesn't want to introduce me as someone who is researching her family life story. I pretend to eat a sand ice-cream that William has made me, while Emily runs off to play with one of the school friends she has spotted. He piles more sand into my hands instructing me to eat. *More ice-cream! More!* Alison returns, apologising for her absence, explaining that the friend is going through a hard time. We walk around the playground chatting, watching the children, welcoming their interruptions. Later, Alison walks me back to the station and tells me about the career she had before children. *Time goes so quickly,* she says. *I think it's good for them to have me at home.* We walk through the car park and William chatters about the motorbikes. *But I'm not always sure I'm doing the best for me.*

Where it all began

I am back at Alison's table with a steaming mug of tea, surrounded by photo albums. We are alone, children occupied at school and nursery.

I don't know where to start. She fidgets and pushes the albums around.

All I can think about is the nearly son. I imagine Alison being passed his photograph for the first time, a sharp intake of breath, then a sigh of relief through a smile. Nervous laughter.

Start wherever seems natural to you, I say.

I see him wrapped in a blue fleece blanket, ensconced in a dark grey buggy. His hair is dark and wispy. Alison hasn't seen him yet. She is looking at the information boards, reading the train times off the screen, clutching her receipt from the bed shop. I hear trains thundering past. *Caleb!* someone calls and Alison's head turns in slow motion, her eyes locked into his eyes. Then he is gone.

She flicks open an album, seemingly at random. *Ooh, ooh, that's really funny maybe we should start there.* I lean over the page to see four photos – the first shows a postcard view from a balcony, looking out to the azure sea; the second, two empty sun loungers side by side; the third, a smiling man I presume is her husband, and the last, an artistic shot of Alison's naked back. They look unreal, somehow.

I was thinking about that today. I haven't thought about this in ages. So this is Cyprus. And what happened was we went to a hotel the week before Christmas. And it was empty. Was it Cyprus? Yes it was Cyprus. And there was this bay. Isn't it beautiful? And it's Christmas and everybody in London is like getting pissed and having a terrible time and then you are doing that thing where you go for drinks after work and you don't want to and we arrived and they say we've upgraded you. We looked out over the bay and there was a gay couple in like some really posh room down here. I spent the first two days of the holiday reading on one of these [points to sun loungers] *and then we went and had treatment and it worked so that was Emily.* Pause for breath. *I've never forgotten how wonderful it was to lie on that sunlounger in a bath robe and just read a book and feel under no pressure to do anything, which is weird, oh I am feeling conscious about that* (points to the naked photo and laughs) *because you do feel during the whole of treatment under pressure but I didn't. Wasn't that lovely? The clinic was grim, it was really grim but once we'd done that* we were just on holiday. I don't think we stayed for Christmas; we mustn't have stayed for Christmas. Where did we have Christmas? Did my mum come over? I can't even remember. I remember driving around the island. I remember my boobs being a bit prickly – I remember thinking ooh, you mustn't be excited. Then it all went a bit grim with the pregnancy in part but um, yeah so that's where she started off.

Should I show you a bit about William's start? I've only got pictures on my phone though. Just talking about beginnings now. I just found this before you came.

On Alison's phone, there is a picture of her sitting on a dark-coloured sofa holding a baby. The baby is dressed all in white – white romper suit, white booties and little white scratch mittens. It looks as though he's wearing a gold tinsel Christmas hat – a Christmas angel – but on closer inspection, I can see that the gold is an embroidered throw on the sofa. Alison looks barely recognisable. She is smiling with her eyes closed, her hands wrapped around the baby's body. He stares at something off screen. He looks startled.

So poor William, you see. I feel so sorry for him. There was a massive widescreen television and he was strapped in a bouncy chair but they put the bouncy chair to the side so he just sat the whole time and had a flat head on one side when he came, just being kept in a chair. So I think this picture is the first time I met William. It all happened really quickly. The social worker who introduced us to William said to meet him at the station. I wondered if he was an alcoholic but didn't think he was. He was from Glasgow so he had a really thick accent, he was often unshaven, and I heard subsequently that he might have had thyroid problems. It was just hard to tell what he was saying. But when I first met William he was really late so I came at the top of the station and waited at the ledge, partly sheltered but partly in the wind. It was really windy; the wind was just racing. Anyway he came and you know those flats where you have those green and white boards and he said he'd had to find flats here so many times, I know how to do it, so he kind of found the address of the flat. I'll show you the foster carer, who I've got really mixed feelings about. You can hold the phone if you want. He was nine weeks old. So she had this … I've never been in a flat like it and I um, she brought him in and I remember just looking at him thinking what a runt. And I don't mean that in the nasty way but I think you are allowed to say it. She had her agency supervisor there and she was this young American woman and I thought God, love, you haven't got a clue. And our social worker was there and they took a few photos and I was just freaking out. I look like I was laughing but I was terrified. It was complete mania. I just thought, oh take him away. I didn't mean that literally take him away but I just thought I'd got to get this over with. Just get me out. Two days later she brought him up to ours, look.

In the second photo, William is looking directly at the photographer. He is sitting on the lap of a woman dressed in a black crewneck jumper, her hair tied up in a top-knot, a shock of jet black to finish the look. In this picture, William is dressed in a coloured patterned baby suit, and wearing a red-rimmed bib. His hands are clasped together in a clap or a prayer. The foster carer looks at him side on, smiling.

He was so hungry, poor thing. I don't think she fed him. To be fair to her, she ran a mother and baby unit. Her point of view was that I help mums look after their babies, I don't look after babies. So she was cross, knackered, she was cross with her agency. She kept ringing her agency and saying I don't want this baby, get rid of it. And when she walked in, she said your house looks like one of those off the telly programmes, off the property programmes and that made me laugh. But she was cool, you know, and I feel bad because I haven't kept in touch with her and I should, you know. The next day we went to her house to get him. That was just the most stressful day of my life.

In the next photo, a man is sitting on a leather armchair with two children on his lap. Light reflects off mirrors on the wall. His right hand holds a bottle of milk in William's mouth. His left hand obscures Emily's face; he appears to have his little finger in her mouth like some kind of pseudo-dummy. His face looks tired, the muscles in his cheek tense. *Oh that was Waterstones! We were sitting in the cafe in Waterstones. I think there's another one here when I was trying on jeans. Let me see. I don't know why I was trying on jeans five minutes after William arrived. But I remember always being so grateful to Joe because look I'm trying on jeans which is a bit of normality and he's just like coping with both of them. He's feeding this really hungry baby and handling this ruffled child who was used to being cherished and the total focus of our attention and I remember thinking thank you Joe, you're so cool. It's really weird talking to you because it brings back so many memories.*

We sip tea in silence for a few moments. Alison looks into her mug, fiddling with the handle.

I think deep down perhaps most adopted children would want to stay with their birth family and that is a loss they will have to carry with them. It's not that I feel second best but I acknowledge there is loss in William's life. But I think if you can respect your mother, maybe I can't respect my own, but maybe he can respect his. As I've become a parent I grappled with my relationship with my mum. I genuinely feel William's birth mother is a woman he can respect and that right at the beginning she genuinely wanted a child for really good reasons and I think that's really important for William. For William it's quite straightforward in a way. We know who his birth mother is and we can explore contact but for Emily who's donor conceived it's very different. She has an anonymous egg donor and the day before we flew to Cyprus, talk about messing with your head, I listened to a Radio Four programme, and I'm pretty sure it was Jenni Murray so it must have been Woman's Hour and they were talking about human trafficking and they talked about Eastern European women being trafficked to Cyprus for sex work and all that sort of stuff and then I immediately think who's our donor, where did she come from, is she genuinely altruistic or is she being coerced? We've got very limited information about the donor so I remember the minute we touched down in Cyprus it was like I had antennae. Anyone who was not from Cyprus, I was kind of thinking are you our donor, are you being coerced?

So for William, his story is quite complete and though it's very sad and complex, I've got it worked out. For Emily not only is there a hole compared to William, because his birth mum is such a well-drawn picture we know her so well, but the donor is anonymous and I had this anxiety that she was in some kind of, you know, someone's trafficking her and she was made to give her eggs. I imagine they traffic people to go and work in clubs as sex workers and dancers and it strikes me that it's a really short step, you know the club's there, the clinic's around the corner. In this country you get £750 expenses as an egg donor. It's not payment for your eggs, it's for your expenses. How are we doing for time? I have to pick

William up from nursery soon. It's a payment of your trouble. I don't know but if you're a pimp, just say to a woman here, you know, stimulate your ovaries, go and have your eggs harvested. So I rang the clinic after Emily was born, partly because I wanted to try again and I wanted them to pass on my thanks, and at every conversation my ulterior motive was to try to glean information, to kind of comfort myself, to fill in some gaps. And that's me, you know. And it's not even my story.

When we came out from the embryo planting, I think they call it, the clinic is really basic, so you could hear through the walls and I heard the nurse say how are you, Mrs Smith? Please anonymise this name. So I don't know this person, I never saw them and I heard the woman's voice say I'm really sorry, I just got upset. So she had just had some kind of procedure and the woman had got upset, had a go at somebody and calmed down. They were kind of making up. There was all this stuff that I constructed in my mind that is probably all crap. It's a complete head fuck. It's funny you coming because all of that stuff I could hardly remember and that's why opening that page this morning was so interesting because the hotel came back to me. Holidays aren't like that anymore, are they? You don't get to sit on a sun lounger, not for two days half naked in a four-star hotel with a loaded gay couple down the end. You know, we wouldn't even be admitted to that hotel now. They don't take children under 12.

I feel I ought to show you this now. I'm on a roll of beginnings. You said to bring some photos of me, of my childhood, but I don't really have many. I feel a bit sad.

Alison opens a new photo album to reveal her childhood photos. There is a picture of a woman holding two children on her lap. The baby is crying, wrapped in a huge swaddling blanket, an elder sibling sits beside her with his hand on the baby. The woman looks down at the baby, her face difficult to read. She wears a navy blue blouse with large white buttons, her dark hair is cropped short, held back off her face with a pale blue Alice band. In the background, I can see an old-fashioned pram, the spokes of the wheels glistening in the sun.

So that's my older brother and that's my mother, my poor mother, looking a bit harangued. The story about me is that my mum always said I cried for the first 18 months and she said the only time I didn't cry was when I ate so I was massively fat.

Next, they pose on a settee. The baby is smiling, the boy has what looks like a choc-ice in his mouth and the woman again stares down at the baby's head. At the bottom of that page is a picture of mother and daughter on the beach. Both wear frilly white hats resembling lampshades. The brother doesn't feature, the baby a toddler now, leaning against her mother's red and white striped shoulder, her mother's eyes trained directly onto the child. Her mother never looks at the camera; she has eyes only for the baby.

We used to go on holiday. I don't know, it might be Majorca. Or it could be Blackpool because my mum grew up in Blackpool. That's Grannie and Grandpa. There's a myth in the family that all men are bastards. Grannie's mum was in a wheelchair and died quite young and her dad remarried and my grannie got so upset. Her mother's jewellery went to the stepmother and everything. When my dad left, my mum says he's like those bastard men. But Joe is liked, he's okay.

A sepia picture of two elderly people sitting cross-legged in a field. She wears a polka dot dress and clutches her knees. He wears a light-coloured formal jacket and black trousers. Huge sunglasses hide their expressions.

She flicks through pages. *I don't think there's much else after that. Oh, that's me in a ballet class; we must have been doing teddy bears' picnic. And that's a boyfriend; he's probably running a bank now. That was a friend; that friendship didn't survive infertility. It's a bit sad. She was a good egg. Then it all gets very boring. That was me at university. That was an exchange at university. I went to America for a year and this is me in America. I might have a photo of my dad. Oh I can see him now. He left the Christmas I was nine and it was a massive bust up. My mum saw her best friend and him exchange a glance. I think it was on Christmas Eve or Boxing Day at a drinks party; they went home and had a big row, he packed his bags and left. It transpired he was having an affair with her best friend. It was all horribly acrimonious because we lived in quite a small village and lots of people got divorced after that but they were the first. The whole village cut down the middle; some went with him and some stayed with my mum. The first six months I did see him. So I can picture him, I can picture him at home where we grew up but after I was ten, I didn't see him. The next time I saw him, this is a bit weird, was at his funeral. I was 25 when he died. I went to see a counsellor but I didn't really lose him then.*

I am, in a way, being passive aggressive against my mother and grandmother for creating an environment at home where a child who wasn't really in a position to make an objective decision probably chose not to see her dad because it made life easier. But it's not as simple as that. Perhaps deep down I just thought that parent's gone, this parent's freaking out and I just need to calm everything down here. So I'm a vulnerable child; I don't know what's going on. I remember the first time we were going to see him, my brother and I, after he was gone. We were driving down a bumpy road. I might have said something a bit like, you know, maybe we'll get more presents and go out and do something nice and I remember my mother just freaked. And I have some sympathy, because I know that when my daughter is tired she can say horrible things and I can feel really stung. But I think what I'm saying is it wasn't really my decision. Am I making any sense?

Maybe me thinking about the possibility of having contact with William's birth mother is me, I think intellectually, having a relationship, having the facts is better for you even if he might feel it's something he's scared of. I can see myself on the phone to my dad, those old phones and brown carpet. At the time, my dad was too bad to burn but now I feel kind of sorry for him in a way. His dad went off to war and didn't come back, chose not to come back. His mum drove a library van all around Europe while she had a son in the UK, sent him to boarding school and he was just palmed off so he had no relationship with his parents so really difficult for him actually, probably. It's kind of funny how these things play themselves down in generations and yet in the intensity of everyday life nobody could, well nobody in that generation was going to forgive infidelity, but they couldn't unpick it.

I found parenting the biggest challenge I've ever done. It's taken me a really long time and once my wealth of goodwill and patience has dried up, you know seven years in, then I start playing out these default parenting strategies and I don't like them at all and I feel this kind of crusade to parent differently. But when I'm in the middle of it and about to shout, how do I stop myself and think of a different strategy? I'm over the fish fingers shouting. Why am I saying it like that? As I'm criticising Emily's maths, she must feel shit. Stop it!

So those poor two women, William's birth mother and that woman who was trafficked for her ovaries.

Hers

Alison recounts a series of meetings at a contact centre with William's birth mother, Tracey. During their final meeting together, the last time Tracey would ever get to see her birth son as a child, the social workers presented her with a scrapbook and a DVD of William to remember him by. Alison wanted to give her something too, so she bought her a silver necklace engraved with William's fingerprint. I picture Tracey, a small, pale, hunched woman, walking away from the contact centre, fingering the chain around her neck, twisting it, worrying it. A final reminder of the son she lost, the son who was nearly hers.

★

Alison walks into the building, pushing the pram, and is immediately stopped by two women.

'Ooh, isn't he sweet?' says the taller one, peering into the pram at William who stares blankly up at her.

'He's gorgeous,' says the other, making a face at the baby. 'Aren't you gorgeous?'

Alison basks in their attention for a few moments, before her eyes are drawn to the commotion at the other end of the corridor. Her heart thumps.

'They'll be ready for you soon.' The tall woman smiles reassuringly at Alison. 'They're just reconfiguring the room.' Her hands are still on the pram, making it impossible for Alison to move closer to her destination.

She sees people, lots of people, milling about. Which one is *she*?

'I think I need the loo. Is that alright?' says Alison, half-smiling, half-grimacing. 'It's small in there, isn't it? Can you watch him for a moment?'

She pushes open the door, letting her face fall slack, beginning to exhale.

'Sorry,' says a small, pale, hunched woman scurrying out of the bathroom, head down.

Alison stands there stunned, staring after the woman. Could it be? Her throat constricts at the thought of William outside in his buggy. She pees as quickly as she can, washes her hands, stares at her face in the mirror, noticing the lines, the fear in her eyes. Outside, the social worker is standing with William in her arms. Alison swallows.

'Oh my God, I think I've just bumped into her.' She hops from side to side.

'It's okay, pet. Take a deep breath. You can take William through now.'

Alison watches as the social worker places him back in the buggy, nodding at her. They both turn to look through the open door to the meeting room. The last time Alison was in that tiny room was for the planning meeting. There were lots of people crammed in, sitting round in a circle, squashed into small chairs, like adults in a primary school classroom. William's first foster carer, Alison's social worker, William's social worker, Tracey's social worker, Tracey's advocate, the contact supervisor, the social work manager and Alison. Not Tracey; she was not invited to the planning meeting. But Alison remembers the social work manager well. Liv, that's her name. A fixed expression, set shoulders, eyes that don't smile. Hard-bitten.

This time, Tracey is invited. Everyone is standing or shifting from foot to foot. Nobody sits except the hunched woman. Liv thrusts a hand in Alison's direction for a brisk shake.

'So, we've just had the preliminary meeting with Tracey where we've explained how contact will work. Just to recap for your benefit then, Alison, you will hand over to Tracey, tell her how William's been getting on since you last met and then leave for two hours. Zainab, the contact supervisor, will stay in the room with Tracey and William. You will return at the end of contact and Tracey will hand over to you. Is everyone agreed?'

'Yes, yes.' Alison's eyes dart around the room before meeting Tracey's. Tracey's forehead is creased, her hair scraped back. Alison tries to smile.

'OK. We'll leave you to it.' Liv saunters out, followed by her entourage, leaving Alison, Zainab, Tracey and William.

Alison looks to Zainab to facilitate, seeming to remember something about the contact supervisor modelling parenting for the birth mother. Zainab stares at her clipboard, scribbling notes in biro. Tracey's eyes flick between Alison and the buggy.

'He's been great since we've had him, really good,' says Alison, wondering what the hell to say.

'Oh! Oh, yeah.' Tracey smiles tightly, clasping her hands together, as if in prayer.

'Let's get him out, shall we?' Alison leans in to William and pulls him out of the buggy. She spent ages getting him ready for today, wanting to make the right impression. She takes in his JoJo Maman Bebe outfit now, wondering what it says, feeling suddenly embarrassed. He's cared for, looked after. We have money that you don't have.

Tracey breathes loudly, her body swaying as she looks at her son.

'Let's put him down here, shall we?' says Alison slowly and calmly, placing William on his tummy on a play mat scattered with toys. He kicks his legs and reaches out for a rattle. Alison looks at him for a moment; looks at the clock.

'Okay, so I think I'm supposed to leave now. Is that right? Let you have your time together?'

Tracey's eyes are wide. She peers down at William on the floor but does not make any move towards him.

'Yes, you can go now.' Zainab clicks her pen.

Alison stands as if to leave, then turns, watching Zainab chew her painted nails. Still, Tracey is motionless.

'Do you want to hold him?' Alison edges forwards, then backwards. 'Do you want me to…'

'You can go now,' says Zainab. 'Come back in two hours.'

Alison's eyes connect with William's. He starts to frown. Her stomach lurches.

'Okay.' She is rooted to the spot. Both William's mothers, paralysed.

'I'll take it from here.' Zainab stands and ushers Alison to the door.

Outside, Alison leans against the brick wall, the cold air rushing to her head. Tears well up and fall quickly, messily. She walks without thinking where she is going, wandering into a coffee shop. She doesn't notice the woman holding the door open for her. She doesn't notice the men chatting at the next table. She sits holding a cappuccino, which she does not drink, checking her watch again and again. They have been together for two weeks, apart for 15 minutes. She wants to, she needs to, look into William's eyes again. Needs to hold him. Right now.

★

She is in theatre, lots of people rush about, the baby is whisked to the side to be checked over. She feels as though she is fading, the room disappearing, she feels herself drifting away, a voice saying, 'Something's wrong', a stab in her arm. Then she is awake in a side room. The baby is presented to her all swaddled up. She shifts in the bed and holds the baby for the first time, feels the weight of this new little person, outside of her body now. She can't look at the baby's face. Not yet. She looks at the blanket wrapped around the baby, white and soft. She looks at the shape of the baby. Surprisingly long. Solid. Real. She looks at the tuft of hair peeping out from the top of the blanket, thinks maybe it looks a bit like Joe's hair. She wonders what she looked like when she was born, before she got massively fat, knows she would not have looked like this little person. Finally, she allows herself a glance, out of the corner of her eye. A dark pink little face, all scrunched up.

'It's a girl.'

She jumps. Forgot there was anyone standing there. A girl. Joe thought it was going to be a boy, but Alison knew. A daughter. They'll call her Emily.

She remembers being wheeled along in a bed and the nurse saying, 'Here comes the Queen.' That night, Emily cried. Alison held her but she wouldn't stop. She cried and cried and cried. The nurse came and took her and swaddled her and she stopped.

★

The ring of her mobile startles her and she knocks her coffee, spilling it onto the table. The display flashes with the contact centre's phone number and she snatches at the phone, thudding it against her ear.

'Hi Alison. Can you come back? He won't stop crying.'

Alison darts out of the coffee shop and sprints back to the contact centre wondering what has happened to make her baby cry so much. Back in the tiny, suffocating room, Zainab holds William while Tracey paces up and down, her face crumpled.

'Is everything okay?' Alison looks from woman to woman. She is all too aware that William is not hers, that she is only fostering him for now. But a tiny voice in her head says, 'He soon will be.'

The next time she sits holding her coffee, she doesn't take her eyes off her phone display. It takes 20 minutes.

'He's got a nose bleed. We don't know how to stop it. Can you come back?'

★

She puts Emily on her breast, tries to get her to latch on. The mouth clamps shut. A shot of pain. It's not working. Why isn't it working? All around, her women breast feed their babies with ease, bond with their babies with ease. She looks at the daughter who does not share her genes, the baby who will not latch on.

★

Alison waits for the call, quietly confident.
'No one could calm him except you.'

★

She sits in the car on the ride home, wearing a pair of pyjamas and a fleece, feeling sweaty. Emily sleeps in the car seat in the back. Joe drives slowly all the way home.

★

'You may as well stay in the building. We'll come and get you if we need you.'
Ten minutes later, Alison is in the room with Tracey and William.
'Shall we sing some nursery rhymes to him together? He likes this one. Row, row, row the boat...'

★

She transfers Emily out of the car seat and into a Moses basket, carefully carrying her upstairs. The laundry basket is overflowing. Her body aches all over but she'll have to put a load on before she can go to bed. When she finally gets to bed, she lies with her eyes open, watching, waiting.

★

Tracey puts William in the buggy and pushes him to the door, followed by Alison, who holds the door open for her. She pushes the buggy out onto the ramp. Alison itches to take hold of the handles. There is a frisson in the air. Alison's chest is tight. Tracey doesn't let go of the buggy; she's supposed to let go now.

'I wanted to ask you something,' she says, now Zainab is out of earshot. 'Why do you think he cries with me and not you?'

'I, I …' Alison searches for the right words.

'And another thing I wanted to ask … I'm worried William might have something wrong with him, you know, like I've got. D'you think he's got something wrong with him?'

★

Visitors queue up to visit Emily, bearing gifts and cuddles. Alison wants to sleep.

★

Alison gets off the train and starts to make her way out to the contact centre. William smiles up at her, blissfully unaware she is about to hand him over again.

'Yes, my darling.' She reaches into the buggy and strokes his hair, feeling her phone vibrate in her pocket. 'Hello?'

Tracey hasn't turned up for contact. Alison can go home.

★

'She looks just like her daddy.'

Alison feels slightly light-headed as Joe's family coo over a sleeping Emily. She never wonders what her own genetic child would have looked like. She never thinks about it. Never at all. All she thinks about is when Emily is due to wake from her nap. She wishes the visitors would all leave so she could slide under the duvet.

★

Alison loiters at the station for a few minutes, checking her phone, wondering whether Tracey will turn up. There are no messages. The meeting has not been cancelled. As she makes her way into the room, she sees the bruises on the side of Tracey's face, then the woman sitting next to her, holding her arm, bolstering her.

'Hello, I'm Tracey's advocate. Pleased to meet you.' She holds out a hand to Alison.

Alison stares at the purple and yellow marks. The voice in her head asks, 'How will you keep the baby safe if you can't keep yourself safe? The court will never find in your favour.'

Celebrate

It's January. A New Year. I am sitting in my local library looking out to the frozen sea, earphones in place, playing back the recording of our last interview. At first, all I can hear is Alison crunching on her toast. There are muffled noises and clicking, conversation stopping and starting. We spoke about Christmas just before I turned the Dictaphone on.

Talking about celebrations, did I show you this photo? It's weird because that's where it all started; that was the night I met Joe. So that's me in the good old days.

There are three photographs arranged on one page, each displaying a rake-thin Alison wearing a skintight, red PVC jumpsuit, completely encasing her body from the neck down, featuring a black zip down to her belly button. I wonder how on earth one gets into such a thing; for some reason, baby powder springs to mind. The outfit is finished off with matching pillar box lipstick and black high-heeled boots. In the top image, Alison stands at the bottom of a grand staircase, with her arms round another, plumper, young woman, who wears a long, grey gown, grey wig and a black mask. Both women stare at the camera. The grey woman's expression is hidden behind her mask but Alison's exudes enough excitement for two. It's as though she can sense that something incredible is about to happen.

That's Jane. I went to school with her; she was quite frightening at school. She's a year older than me and we ended up at university together. So this was her house in Kensington so you can imagine they lived a different lifestyle to us. Then we went to uni together and we were kind of in different cliques but we were quite close, quite tight. We hung out a lot, we went sailing together. She got me into sailing actually. And then um, she went to work for this ad agency and met Joe. The company had this fancy dress party in their basement, so she invited me to this party. Parties. Do you remember that life? Anyway, so I went to this fancy dress shop and came out in this outfit and the guy there said, 'Wow.' Whatever! The outfit's outrageous really.

In the next image, the pair are joined by a man, who poses in front of them, wearing a green, yellow-and-red-checked kilt, and a wide grin. In the third, Alison sits alone at a white Formica table, wearing a self-satisfied smile, holding a spoon to her mouth, heaped with an unidentifiable morsel of food. A white mug and empty white plate sit in front of her. The morning after the night before? Her red lipstick is intact.

Joe went as Jon Paul Gautier and he went with his friend who was dressed as Zorro. I gave my number to Joe because I had some concert tickets to Bjorn Again, an Abba tribute band, so we went to the concert together a week later and I wore that outfit again and it was really funny because somebody else was wearing it too but she was fatter than me. Oh, look that's us all singing Abba songs in my flat. When you look at that, to the wedding photos, to these of me and I think, Oh God, I've aged.

For some reason I wanted to show you a picture of the adoption celebration day.

The children sit at a wooden desk in front of rows of black ring binders. They are dressed smartly – William in a blue-checked shirt and Emily in a grey buttoned jacket. William looks down, totally engrossed in stamping ink on paper. Emily looks up at someone off camera, adoringly.

There was this really sweet photo with the judge. I don't know if I can find it. Let me see. So only the four of us went because I was so anxious. It was just the family thing, you know, it's nothing more than a celebration, so the four of us went and the clerk came out to get us and there we were in our best gear and we all stood up and the clerk said something quite formal and we couldn't keep William still and Emily was up and down so he said, Oh forget it! Do you want to come and sit on my chair? And Emily literally climbed over all the seats to go and sit on his chair and he was really such a nice guy. So William started stamping on the paper and Emily's just not – her first babysitter said she's the only little girl she knows who's not eager to please an adult. That picture of her, I've never ever seen her look at someone with such admiration. She's like, oh my God, you're a hero. So I adore that picture. I wish I could find the one with the judge but I can't find it. We had our photo taken and the official one with us all standing with the judge and the clerk said, you all look so nervous and I said, I am really nervous! It was really nice of the judge that he would let William just get on with it and sit at the desk. And I thought what a nice bloke.

So afterwards we went on to a playground so here's me and William in the playground. There's Emily in the playground. Then we had a really small lunch in a really nice café with a few friends, so this was us, and the lady round the corner did us a cake and there was a photo of us and Emily was grabbing the cake. I really liked that one. I might have put the one of the judge away actually, not in the family album. It's not something you really want to broadcast, you know. It's not your average situation, is it?

Alison pulls out a picture of herself, an elderly woman and Emily walking hand in hand. Shot from the back. Three generations of backs. I think of her naked Cyprus shot. I wonder what it is with Alison and backs.

That's a really current one of Grannie Pat. That was Emily's seventh birthday at Lego Land. The relationship between my mum and the children is quite good. This Christmas she just said, oh I'm tired and she's not used to the house being so noisy and kids all over her so I think she was just a bit shell shocked by it all. But I think she is completely adoring and to be honest, I think she's been brilliant about it all because I was quite tentative about it, thinking, oh what would she think. So, for example, um, Joe's stepdad, Paul, he's a real, you know, traditional, I want to say 1950s. So I just get the picture that there's a bit of undercurrent. But Grannie Pat has been really accepting, totally not batted an eyelid. And my brother, you know I've got an older brother, and I'd arranged to meet him for lunch and I was really anxious. I had spent ages thinking how I was going to tell him that Emily was donor conceived and what this means that she's your niece but you are not genetically related but he was like, Alison, she's still my niece. He didn't give a shit. Joe's mum has been hugely accepting that our family has not traditionally come about. I think it's so interesting that notion of family.

That's quite a cool photo actually. That's Joe's lot.

A large family gathering – your typical wedding photograph – rows of women in pastels and men in grey suits, a few children dotted between them, all smiling at the camera in a forced fashion.

Joe's mum and her family are big Quakers. There's Joe's stepfather, grumpy Paul. The reason I think it's interesting, so this uncle got divorced and that's his first wife and that's his second wife. My parents had a really acrimonious divorce, but in this family they just all get along, and the first wife always rocks up at these events and everybody comes and is included and it's okay. Nothing kicks off and there's no tension so I interpret it as a theme of everyone is included and they are accepting. So I'm really proud of how accepting my family have been and I'm not surprised at how accepting this family have been. Except Joe's stepdad Paul.

A picture of Emily, wearing a school uniform with white socks and a bright green mock graduation hat, standing on what appears to be a wooden table in a garden, shaking hands with a middle-aged woman who is handing her a scroll. The woman has greying blonde hair, in an easy wash 'n go style, and wears a black and white patterned top and black skirt.

Just thinking about celebrations and there's a picture of Emily's school graduation and her teacher, Mrs Fanshaw, was the first person to see William. So that's her, look, she's quite a character locally, she's got ten children and she set up this nursery. She's got this huge house that just got bigger and bigger to accommodate them all. She's got grandchildren now and two of her children work in the nursery. It's a really successful business, her husband just does the admin. The day William arrived was so, so stressful going to pick him up and get back in time to collect Emily from nursery but we were late and I think it was one of the most stressful times of my life. Have I told you about this? Yeah, he was wearing the yellow knitted thing from the foster carer and when Mrs Fanshaw came out I was really embarrassed because everyone round here wears JoJo Maman Bebe. And she looked into the car and said to Emily, 'He really loves you.' Then when we got home there was this card and big bouquet of flowers from her. We hadn't really told many people that we were adopting, so we couldn't expect any big 'wow wee' because nobody really knew until we rocked up a few weeks later at this party with this new party. But she sent the cards and flowers and it was so lovely and accepting and that was her whole thesis as a devout Catholic. You know the first day I was really tense, thinking is he okay, how am I going to get him to sleep, when will contact start. And there were these flowers and I really appreciated it, I thought it was so kind.

Alison gets up from the table and goes over to the worktop, taking something out of a bag. A mound of colourful fabric heaps out towards me. I want to touch it. She lays it out on the floor, so I can see it properly.

I wanted to show you this. Joe's mum's a really 'can do' person. She's retired now but she made this quilt for William; she's made one for all her grandchildren. I'm sure she's largely self-taught. So she wanted to incorporate the story for William in a way that nobody would know but William would know. So each of these pictures tells a story and each of these outlines could be any people but is supposed to be key people, like this one is supposed to be the judge with his wig and that one is the foster carer with her big hair. If you know a little bit you could probably tell. And another thing she did was these are pockets from trousers that Emily wore and then William wore and these were trousers I really loved so she just sewed the pockets on. It must have taken so long.

Alison rummages back in the bag and pulls out another quilt, covered in bright yellow embroidered flowers.

So thinking about beginnings and endings. I had another really good girlfriend, Mari, from years ago. Her sister died of breast cancer and when Emily was born, Mari's mum made this quilt and these sunflowers were for Mari's sister. She was just in her thirties when she died. At the funeral, I bought sunflowers to remember her and whenever Mari sews she sews sunflowers to remember her sister. It's funny talking to you because I feel a sense of things going round and coming around. I don't often stop and reflect. I suppose for us, why I wanted to actively stop and chat, because for us I feel we've reached a point where we've put a lot of work into building the family and it's like a sort of starting point. What do I mean? I think I feel a sense of layers and ebb and flow. I'm not sure what I mean. It's like those sunflowers. I can so picture Mari's sister's death, I can picture her being diagnosed. I can see the funeral and now looking at that quilt, there's a sense of things weaving on. Our family life never felt like life just going on, it felt like oh it's an almighty effort.

William grins at a birthday cake. A traditional, round birthday cake with white icing and three candles. No Spiderman face or other gimmicks. He looks slightly sweaty with messy hair, like he has been running round moments before the picture was taken.

Oh, look, he's so sweet. That's his birthday. So was he three? Oh yeah, yeah, he was three. Interestingly, we've just had a letter from birth mum and she said don't worry about me, everything is fine, I'm okay. We've written to her through the social workers but she's never written back, but she's just written back for the first time and it arrived on William's birthday, which it's not supposed to do. Apparently, the dad's back on the scene, which is not good news but apparently birth mum went to social services for help and then they supported her to write the letter. The letter arrived on his birthday and it was a signed-for letter so the doorbell rang and the kids ran to the door and it was this letter. The day was quite charged, so I didn't read it to William that day but I did read it to him later. I don't know what he really understands about being adopted but the main thing he says about it is I wish I was in your tummy and Emily was in Tracey's tummy. I don't mean this in a nasty way but I don't think I'd lose any sleep over her but I think it's quite good if her life is resolved in some ways. And then there's another mother out there in Cyprus somewhere. William's birthday is a loaded day for me and that whole word, 'birth,' you know. I felt that real, I don't know, rub, tension maybe. It was really weird on William's birthday this year but I don't feel it on Emily's birthday. I think Emily feels that William gets more attention because he's adopted so she says William's adopted and my egg was adopted. It's really weird talking to you today because I feel like everything finds a way, it's like water, isn't it? It's quite refreshing, that's what families are supposed to feel like. I mean, I want to say that things find their natural course but neither circumstances are very natural, are they?

'The sun will come out tomorrow'

1

Between the 1740s and 1760s the procedure involved a swatch of fabric being cut from the baby's clothes and then cut in half; one half was attached to the child's admission paper or 'billet' on which was written the child's unique admission number, while the other half was given to the mother.

2

[M]others also left an object unique to them – a token – as a means of identification. These everyday items range from found objects such as coins, medals and jewellery, to personalised items created for this purpose such as poems, needlework and inscribed medallions.

3

At some point in the mid-nineteenth century the billets were opened and some of the more interesting tokens were put on display in the Hospital however, no one thought to make a note of which tokens belonged to which baby, so the majority of the tokens are themselves orphans.

4

The Adoption Act of 1926…It was probably thought good that adopted children did not inquire too deeply into their background, as most were the illegitimate offspring of poor working-class women. The origins of many adopted children continued to remain shrouded in secrecy and shame.

5

The unmarried mother was a psychiatric case who needed treatment.

6

Token (noun)
    A thing serving as a visible or tangible representation of a fact, quality, feeling, etc.
    A voucher that can be exchanged for goods or services, typically one given as a gift or forming part of a promotional offer.

7

Mum leaned forward eager for the sister to know we were there to do the right thing. Then this mortal sin would be erased from my soul and hers, too. My penance would be to go to the home for unwed mothers. Absolution would come after I gave up my baby. Sister was telling us that I would forget everything. It would be as if it never happened.

8

Mary said to the angel, 'How can this be, since I am a virgin?' The angel answered and said to her, 'The Holy Spirit will come upon you, and the power of the Most High will overshadow you; and for that reason the holy Child shall be called the Son of God.

9

The Devil led us to the wrong crib.

10

My mum wouldn't pick another baby; she'd become attached to the idea of me in the months of ghost pregnancy, where she'd shadowed my birth mother in her own imagination, picturing, perhaps, her belly getting bigger and bigger. She already felt like I belonged to her.

11

My mum was crediting this other mother with exactly her own sensibility, her sensitivity, her outlook. Not for a single second was my mum thinking that there might be another mother somewhere who never bothered to think about me on my birthday.

12

Did she think of me? Had she wiped me from her mind, as Sister Dominic had undoubtedly advised?

13

I can never shake off the feeling that Trudy and Mike are not only part of our children's lives, but part of Rob's and mine too. They are like silent partners – infiltrating, influencing, blocking.

14

I have no claim, I say. I have done nothing – but I will do the next eighteen years and more. Probably Elena is most important as she has the genetics, but she's never touched Hope or seen her.

15

Both the birth mother and the adoptive parents are equally important to spirit babies. One must carry them over the threshold of life; the other must nurture and guide them down life's path. All are essential karmic participants in the spirit baby's destiny.

Sources

Title quotation: from the film, *Annie* (1982)

1: The Foundling Museum (n.d.)
2: The Foundling Museum (n.d.)
3: The Foundling Museum (n.d.)
4: Howe et al. (1997)
5: Howe et al. (1997)
6: Oxford Dictionaries (n.d.)
7: Schaefer (1991)
8: Luke 1:34–37
9: Winterson (2011)
10: Kay (2010)
11: Kay (2010)
12: Schaefer (1991)
13: Donovan (2013)
14: Jolly (2017)
15: Makichen (2005)

The creation of this quotation collage is analysed in Chapter 1 'Birthing the book', 'Collage as an evolution beyond narrative'.

Reference list

Annie (1982) Directed by John Huston [Film]. Columbia Pictures.
Donovan, S. (2013) *No Matter What: An Adoptive Family's Story of Hope, Love and Healing*, London, Jessica Kingsley Publishers.
Howe, D. et al (1997) *Half a Million Women: Mothers Who Lose Their Children by Adoption*, London, Penguin.
Jolly, A. (2017) *Dead Babies and Seaside Towns: One Mother's Journey to Surrogacy*, London, Unbound.
Kay, J. (2010) *Red Dust Road*, London, Picador.
Luke 1:34–37, Revised Standard Version of the Bible.
Makichen, W. (2005) *Spirit Babies: How to Communicate with the Child You're Meant to Have* [e-book reader], London, Dell Publishing.
Oxford Dictionaries (n.d.) *Definition of 'Token'* [Online]. Available at: https://en.oxforddictionaries.com/definition/token (Accessed 4 March 2019).

Schaefer, C. (1991) *The Other Mother: A Woman's Love for the Child She Gave Up for Adoption*, New York, Soho Press.

The Foundling Museum (n.d.) *The Tokens* [Online]. Available at: https://foundlingmuseum.org.uk/collections/whats-on-display/the-tokens/ (Accessed 27 February 2019).

Winterson, J. (2011) *Why Be Happy When You Could Be Normal?* London, Vintage.

4
CHARLOTTE'S STORY

The lady of the house

We're waiting on the corner by the pub, she says. *You can't miss us. Look for the big red buggy.* I am walking and talking to Charlotte on my mobile when they come into view. I wave at them from across the road and finally we are face to face. We shake hands; it's impossible to get close. Charlotte wears her sleeping son in a padded sling, his open mouth resting on her exposed breast; a metal scooter is slung over her shoulder. She wears motherhood like a suit of armour. She looks to be in her mid-thirties; her long, straight brown hair is tied back loosely, revealing amber earrings that match her necklace. *We're just on our way back from Tahlia's music class. She's got a friend coming for tea, later.* I'm introduced to Charlotte's fresh-faced au pair, Sabine, who pushes the buggy containing Charlotte's sleeping daughter, maintaining a subtle distance as we chat.

How was your Mother's Day? asks Charlotte. I tell her it was the first year I spent Mother's Day without my mum, who is in Goa, partying with ex-pats and locals. *How was yours?* She gives a non-committal reply and doesn't mention her own mother. Soon, we are outside a large period house where Charlotte collects a parcel from the recycling box. *Chia seeds from the Amazon courier; we're experimenting with recipes.* Inside, it is stylish and roomy, light streaming into an open plan living space through to huge windows. Maybe only people with big houses volunteer to be interviewed; perhaps those living in grotty bedsits aren't quite so keen to have strangers poking around in their nooks and crannies.

Tea? The fridge hums. Both children are still asleep. Charlotte leaves Tahlia in her buggy and the au pair disappears upstairs. I compliment Charlotte on her home as she busies herself in the kitchen, opening and closing cupboards, with baby Albert still attached. *Oh we don't own it; we're just renting. There's a really funny story about this house. I rented a room here years ago while I was at university and,*

DOI: 10.4324/9781003290179-6

you know, it was a shared student house, everyone with their own shelf in the fridge and everything. Years later, me and Alden were driving past when I was pregnant and there was a 'to let' sign outside and I enquired and the whole house was available to rent out so I ended up back here. It was really strange. Once a lodger in the house, now the lady of the house.

Charlotte is sitting opposite me on the comfy sofas now, Albert's head lulling at her breast. There is a silence while she sips water, waiting for me to start. I ask her when and how she first became an egg donor. *It was, what, about ten years ago. I was 26 and I'd just come out of a two-year relationship and I happened to be sat reading the family section of* The Guardian, *on a Sunday, I think it was, and there was a piece in there about a family who had their children through egg donation and I thought, oh, I've never really thought about egg donation. I'd heard about sperm donation but not egg donation, and I thought, how odd. I'd looked into becoming a surrogate, I think, at that point. Yes, about six months earlier. I'd even gone to a Surrogacy UK conference so I was already in the mindset of wanting to help in some way. And then next to this article was an advert that a couple had put there saying that unless they could find someone to be an egg donor for them, they wouldn't be able to have children. I remember exactly seeing the advert and having an epiphany and thinking this is my future. There was a number to call for the fertility unit so I called it.*

Albert starts to twitch and Charlotte inserts her nipple back into his mouth.

A counsellor called straight back and they invited me down to, kind of, chat to them about being able to help this couple. That whole process took about nine months. I think I went down and had two or three chats with a counsellor. Usually, they were looking for women to donate who had already had their families but, actually, I think they realised that was a little bit naïve because lots of women were leaving it later to have their children and they want you to be under 35, so they were cutting out a massive chunk of potential donors. As it happened, I think they'd put this advert in Woman's Own *and* The Guardian *and what happens is they always have a lot of people respond almost immediately and then they whittle down to one person but this time they'd whittled it down to two people, me and another woman.*

The counsellor said, 'This has never happened before and we don't really know what to do but we're gonna let the couple decide which of you they want to go with, so I need you to answer some questions for me,' which was quite unusual, so it was, like, what are your aspirations and what are your family like? And it was the most important CV you've ever written in your whole life. And suddenly it was, like, I know there are lots of other couples I could help if they didn't choose me but I was, like, I really want them to choose me!

Albert continues to squirm and Charlotte carefully removes him from the sling and resettles him on her lap, where he duly falls back to sleep.

You know, I'd been to the clinic and anyway, me and this other woman put our stuff forward and then they decided to go with me, which I was delighted with. Then there were a lot of delays and tests, you know, that you had to go through and some of the tests took ages to come back and then there was a delay because of health concerns on their part and then I was going to Australia. Finally, it happened so I was put on what I call a slow cycle, so I was down-regulated for two weeks where I took a nasal spray every day to suppress my ovaries, then injections for two weeks to stimulate and then a final injection to release the eggs to be collected. So it was all pretty straightforward, really. I had a friend who lived near the clinic so I'd go down and stay with her the night before my appointments. They always booked early morning appointments so I could get the train back to work and be back at my desk by ten, which was pretty good going.

She introduces her experience of egg donation as something she was excited about; going to the clinic sounds almost like a day excursion, something to look forward to. I imagine her packing her overnight bag to stay at her friend's house, carefully folding a silk nightdress, selecting her toiletries and jewellery and zipping everything into place in her holdall. I see her sitting on the train, sipping tea, looking out of the window at the trees and sky rushing past in a blur, smiling to herself. The chosen one.

MOT

Charlotte looks lovingly at Albert, still sleeping on her lap. I look for the family resemblance but it is hard to make out his features in his curled up position. *You know, I just love being a mum. We can't wait to have more children. We're planning one more next year and then we're gonna get married. Then we'll just see. We aren't gonna plan any more after that but if more come along that would be a blessing. My partner, Alden, already has two children from before we got together so he's already up to four. Everyone says, 'Oh what an altruistic thing to do,' being an egg donor, but I found the whole thing really fascinating. Every time I went, I learned a lot more. I mean, the kind of reason I wanted to do it wasn't altruistic, I really wanted to know at this point what my own fertility levels were like because at 26 … I mean now I'm like, huh 26, but then I'd just come out of a relationship I thought I would be having children in, so I wanted to know that by the time I was in another relationship and we got to the point of having children, everything would be okay. So I felt that doing this, I'd get something along the lines of a sort of fertility MOT so that was definitely a by-product that was very positive for me, so I was delighted when all the tests came back as they should.*

This first couple were anonymous so obviously I never knew anything about their circumstances but at Christmas time, maybe six months in, yeah cos it was May bank holiday weekend when I saw the advert, so yeah that would tie in, it was that Christmas, so they sent me a Christmas card and some chocolates through the clinic just before the donation went ahead. I was very surprised when I had to go to the sorting clinic to pick it up. It just said from your grateful recipients or something. And I sent them a card back through the clinic again. Erm, but, yeah, once the eggs had been collected and I'd kind of done my bit, I think they got 14 eggs that first time which is a brilliant number to get, I obviously didn't get to know anything about what happened afterwards. I wasn't involved in the process thereafter. I wasn't informed about anything.

I was told you could phone up in a year's time and find out if they'd had a baby but that felt like a long time when I knew in the next few weeks they would be trying with my eggs. That was a long time ago now. At 36, I'm too old to be an egg donor again but I'm involved in a charity that supports egg donors. Nowadays if you go through a reputable agency, you are kept much more in the loop. We really want things to be more transparent so that donors are kept informed and feel valued and validated. Sometimes, couples say they want to stay in touch with the donor and afterwards they don't want anything to do with them, which I understand but it's really difficult for the donor.

Charlotte's entire journey into motherhood, both as an egg donor and with her own pregnancies, is documented on her Facebook account. The first images I look at are from a private album that Charlotte set up for one of the couples she donated to. The caption describes it as a picture story of the first day of IVF treatment.

I knew I might do it again but I knew I wouldn't do it anonymously. Then really strangely, I was contacted by the mum of an ex from university, Fergus, who said your rugby top has been in our house for five years if you want to pick it up and I thought, Oh I love that top so I went to pick it up and I had a catch up with her and what they were doing. And just out of the blue she told me that Fergus's cousin, Sara, was having problems conceiving and was probably gonna have to go through IVF and I went, Oh, that's a shame. And she said, yeah it looks like they're gonna have to use egg donation, do you know anything about that? And I was like, yeah, I have just been through the process of donating my eggs! And it was a real kind of, what?! So I was, like, 'If Sara wants to talk to someone who's been through it …' and she was, like, 'That would be great'.

The montage opens with a photo of Charlotte wearing a pink tee-shirt in what appears to be a bedroom, against a backdrop of flowery wallpaper. She is holding up a box of medication in front of the camera and smiling.

We met for a drink and we were both wearing red, patent Clark's shoes and I thought … I'm spinning this story to you as though I'm a great believer in, like, destiny and fate, but there are so many points in the story that did feel very meant-to-be, so I immediately felt with Sara that, ah this is where we're going next. So I met with Sara and had a coffee and I loved her and I said to her, 'Look, I know you are waiting on an anonymous egg donor from the agency but if you wanted to go with me and it wasn't too weird for you and obviously I'd need to check with my ex, your cousin, then, you know, we could always look at that.' So she was, like, delighted. So I had to have a drink with my ex, Fergus, and his girlfriend at the time and I don't think they really understood the implications. Fergus was like, 'Yeah fine!' So I was like, 'You do understand your cousin's son or daughter would be from my eggs?' And he was like, 'Yeah fine!' And then I met him a few years later actually – it hadn't worked for Sara – and Fergus came up to me in a pub ranting at me. It turned out he had a hard time with his girlfriend who was, like, you know, 'I don't want your ex-girlfriend's genes in the family!'

In the second photo, Charlotte is wearing the same tee-shirt, sitting against the same wallpaper but wearing glasses and reading an instruction leaflet, looking very serious.

I got a good collection of eggs again with Sara, 11 eggs, but I think on the day, her partner's sperm wasn't great and I think they ended up with two or three embryos, which is a really bad fertility conversion, and I think of the three, they said only two were worth putting back but they weren't so good that they would recommend putting them in separately so they put the two embryos in at the same time. Oh, I feel emotional even talking about it.

It was so, so upsetting, like, we had a meal the night before she was doing the test and she knew she wasn't pregnant and I felt so desperate for them. And I think she blamed herself a lot because in her, like, twenties and thirties, she really, I mean, she must have been in her late forties, I think she's in her fifties now, she was fed that you can have everything, go to university, you can get your job, you can travel, yeah, and I think in some point in all that, she never said, but I kind of concluded she'd messed up her fertility somewhere, she felt she was to blame for the fact she couldn't have children. So I was just, like, 'Let's just do another cycle. We'll do it again.' But I was the last port of call for them, they couldn't do it again. So they went on and adopted and now they have twin girls. And I did think that they might drop all contact with me, just because it was a painful thing to have gone through but actually we've stayed in touch through the years and it's lovely.

In the third photo, Charlotte is grinning at the camera, holding open the box to reveal its contents: a clear vial with a green lid, a syringe, a rectangular packet and an indiscernible plastic item.

While helping Sara, I started giving information on forums and I came across a couple who really wanted a sibling for their daughter. They told me what town they lived in and I happened to be going to a funeral near where they lived and I thought we should meet up. So I said, 'Yeah, yeah, let's go for it.' Angela, that was her name. She would come and meet me and we'd go for lunch. She was really nice but the cycle was a bit of a disaster in terms of … It's difficult to remember the details of what happened but the clinic kind of messed up, I think, but they didn't realise there was a problem until maybe a week into treatment. When Angela phoned up to see what the embryos were like at day three, they weren't dividing as well as they should be. So by this point, oh no, no, they weren't my third couple, they were my fourth couple. I'll come back to them.

The fourth image is a shot of Charlotte's torso with her head and legs cut off. It reminds me of the sex education diagrams my son has recently been presented with at school – a dismembered body, revealing only the vital organs. But unlike the sex-ed diagrams, Charlotte is clothed and only revealing a section of her midriff as she pulls up her tee-shirt with a ringed hand to show her cleaning her abdomen with an antiseptic wipe. She wears jeans and is sitting on a wooden chair.

So with my charity work, I'd started going to national events to run the stands and talk to people about egg donation. So I met a woman called Eve at one of these events. She came up to the stand and started talking to me and she was in remission from breast cancer and I was really struck by her story. She was amazing, she was so warm. While she was pregnant with her first baby, Freddie, they discovered she had breast cancer so he was born early by caesarean section and she went straight into chemo, so that was all very traumatic. Then when I met them, they were trying to conceive a second child and she needed a surrogate and an egg donor and they thought it would be easier to go to America for treatment. I heard from the charity a few months later and Eve had asked to get in touch with me and I just knew what she was going to say. She said, 'We really like you and we can't get through the red tape in America and if we found a surrogate…' Ooh no, they actually had a surrogate. They said, 'We have a lovely surrogate and you're the missing piece.' Oh, I was delighted, absolutely thrilled.

In the next image, Charlotte holds up a loaded syringe, glasses perched up high on her head, eyes wide. She is about to start off a process to hormonally alter her body.

So their surrogate, Maggie, lived really far away from me so it was a bit of a logistical nightmare; we had to find a fertility agency in between us all. They were really pleased to find this clinic because three or four other clinics wouldn't work with Eve because her prognosis following breast cancer wasn't great. I was really surprised she was turned down for treatment, but this agency they found, they'd do anything for money, so we went with this one. So, yeah, good collection of eggs from me. They had some embryos frozen and they put two embryos back into Maggie, which I was really surprised at because there's a campaign for one at a time because of the amount of people going through IVF who have multiple pregnancies which is such a strain on the NHS and on the woman's body if she has twins or triplets. So anyway, they had two put back but Maggie didn't fall pregnant.

Next, a very artistic close-up shot of an incredibly long-looking needle, the hand and syringe blurred in the background, the focus on a drop of bright red fluid emanating from the needle, shining like a Christmas bauble.

The process could have worked without any of us meeting but we all got together and I got to know Maggie as well as Eve and her partner, Graham. It made it all very fascinating knowing the people. I didn't really think of any potential negatives, to be honest, because I'm quite a positive person; I just thought, Wow, that's amazing; we're gonna make this baby; Graham is gonna put his sperm with my egg that's gonna make an embryo that's gonna go in Maggie; Maggie's gonna give birth which is gonna be a little brother or sister to Freddie. I didn't think of the risks and stuff. I was just like, 'Yeah!'

Charlotte smiles out at the camera, holding up an empty syringe.

So after the first attempt didn't work, Maggie had another frozen embryo implanted. At this point, I was now working with Angela and Brian. So, at this point, I'd already had one cycle with an anonymous couple that I didn't know anything about, one unsuccessful cycle with Sara, and I was in the middle of the second cycle with Eve and Graham via Maggie, okay. And I had a phone call from Angela saying, 'I'm so sorry to have to tell you this but the reason none of your couples have got pregnant is because there's a problem with your eggs.' She said she rang the clinic and they told her. And I was like, 28, and like, totally devastated, thinking I am infertile. It was just awful. I was just so numb. But I did think it was weird, like, why am I hearing this from Angela? I still don't really know what happened. So then I went to see Eve and Graham and said, 'Look, I'm so sorry. Maggie's not gonna get pregnant with that frozen embryo. It's not gonna happen because there's something wrong with my eggs.' The next month, Maggie was pregnant with my not-working eggs.

In the final image, the syringe has been replaced with a cup of tea. Charlotte is still smiling.

I could not continue a friendship with Angela after that. They just wanted a 100 per cent guarantee that they would get pregnant and they couldn't bear it and they were so desperate that they just put the blame onto me. It was just a desperate move on their part. I didn't need that really. So we don't have any contact now, not since that phone call. So then Maggie was pregnant which was absolutely fantastic. Eve sent me a picture of the pregnancy test that Maggie had sent her. Eve's not one for talking on the phone really, she'll do a lot by email or text, she's not one for chatting. So yeah she sent the text and she just put 'pregnant.' Then I phoned Maggie cos she was quite a chatter. They'd already had many years with Maggie trying to get pregnant, using egg donors from abroad. They'd had a nightmare time. They had 15 embryos and they put them all into Maggie in two cycles. I mean, they put Maggie at massive risk if all the embryos took, she could have been carrying seven babies at once.

If you click through the photos quickly, they almost look like a video. I feel like an intruder, present in the room, witnessing a personal, intimate act.

I was absolutely elated, totally chuffed. I got this package of things together, like you would if it was a close friend, but I had to keep thinking of the next hurdle, like, let's get to the 12-week scan, let's not get too excited. Then it was like let's get to the 20-week scan and they found out they were having a boy. It was just so lovely. We did a piece in a glossy magazine and we all got together, they dressed us all up and took pictures; it was a really lovely day just kind of hanging out, feeling a bit like celebs, yeah we all got on really well.

A day at the races

Maggie phoned Eve and Graham when she started going into labour and I think they arrived within hours of the baby being born. I was sat up here in this house because I was a lodger in this house at the time and I was just going mad for information about what was happening. It was such a weird time. It was a Saturday and in the morning, I'd gone for a coffee with a gay couple called Stephen and Anthony who I was a donor for next – I'll tell you about that later – and I was telling them all about Maggie being about to have the baby with my egg. Then I remember for the rest of the day feeling really, um, not, er, what's another word for isolated? Quite, erm, disconnected, like separated from everything because I was so far away in miles and I was single, and I had no-one really to share this, kind of, massive event with. You know it was the birth of a child that was my biological child and there was no-one. My best friend was away on holiday and there was no-one to sit down and talk to about the gravity of the situation, and I felt really disconnected and quite, not vulnerable, but it wasn't a pleasant feeling at all. I don't have any contact with my immediate family so there was no-one. And I remember I just felt so alone in this house when all this was going on, this kind of big, big stuff in my life and I had nobody to share it with and I got in the car and went to the horse races to see my friend Josh, which was pretty random.

*

I imagine Charlotte waking in the early hours of Saturday morning, sitting bolt upright in bed and knowing, just knowing, something is happening. Instinctively, she reaches out for her mobile. There's a text from Eve saying that Maggie has gone into labour and that they are on their way to the hospital. Her heart pounds as she rereads the words. It's happening. She stands up, pacing the room, her eyes flicking from the floral wallpaper to the phone. She sits back down on the edge of the bed, still in her nightdress, and swipes onto Facebook to alert her friends that there is news. The sun streams through the windows.

She showers and brushes her teeth and slips into jeans and an organic cotton tee-shirt. She has time to kill until her breakfast date. She cleans the house and sorts out old letters. A few hours later, she's inside a coffee shop looking out for two men. Stephen and Anthony. She sees them before they see her, recognising them from the photo they texted. Both have dark hair and deep tans. Very groomed, sharply dressed. Stephen is slightly taller and thinner, a little older perhaps.

'Hi! Hi! I'm Anthony!' Anthony's face is flushed and Stephen steps from side to side. They order coffee and croissants at the counter before taking a seat. Charlotte fills them in on Maggie.

'It's happening! She's in labour! I'm so excited!'

Anthony looks at Stephen and squeezes his hand. And Charlotte knows.

Back at home a few hours later, the phone in the hall rings. She snatches it to her ear. It's Graham. The line is a little crackly but there's no mistaking the emotion in his voice.

'He's here!' A boy. 'We're calling him Jake. He's great! Maggie's fine. It's all gone well.'

A million questions run through Charlotte's head. What was the birth like? How long did it take? What did his first cry sound like? Does he look like me? She asks after Eve.

'She's good. Everyone's ecstatic.'

He says he'll send a picture and Charlotte's stomach flips.

A whoop of laughter on the other end of the line. 'Anyway I …'

'You go, Graham! I'll arrange to come visit soon. Thanks so much for calling. It's fantastic news! Give my love to everyone.'

She clicks the phone off and slowly lowers herself onto the bottom of the stairs before punching numbers into it.

'Hi Debbie! Guess what?'

The voice on the other end sounds cheerful but distracted. Charlotte's best friend Debbie is on holiday. She doesn't have children. The photo comes through on her phone. Charlotte's genetic offspring. A baby that is half her but belongs to someone else. She wonders what his hands look like – everyone in her family has long fingers – but she can't see his fingers under the blanket he is wrapped in. She can't see any of herself in his tiny squashed up face. She stares at that picture for ages as the afternoon passes in a blur. Charlotte is alone in the house. She updates Facebook with news of Jake's arrival, posting the photograph that Graham sent. She checks it repeatedly. After several hours of not speaking to anyone, she picks up the phone again.

'Josh? Are you all going to watch New Sensation race later?'

Charlotte is surrounded by a group of friends who co-own a horse. Josh gives her a hug and gets her a pint. She melts in his hug, tears pricking at the back of her eyes. She's missed physical contact but it's not enough. She feels faint as she looks round at the smiling faces. They walk to the paddock and meet the jockey; New Sensation walks around, his glossy, chestnut coat shimmering in the afternoon sun, the number six displayed over his saddle. His dark eyes seem to be watching her. Charlotte recalls a nature programme showing a foal being born. A whooshing of fluid, two front legs, the foal sliding out, slimy and limp. Somebody is talking. She's finding it hard to focus but looks up at the people standing in front of her. The men wear suits and the women are dressed up, faces painted, hair groomed like the horses' manes. Charlotte is still in her jeans. She tells one of the women about Jake.

'That's nice. Do you know what's happening in the 3.40?'

She watches as horses charge past, the jockeys bent over them in a blur of bright colours, whips moving through the air. Life moving quickly by. She watches the audience, enthralled by the chase. It's too fast. She can't breathe. She holds the phone in her pocket, thinking of the photograph, itching to check Facebook. The autumn sun is bright on her back but the air feels fresh. She wonders why she came.

★★★

Charlotte grips the steering wheel as she drives to the hospital. It's going to be different this time. She scans the car park before pulling into a space. The ticket machine is right over the other side of the car park; it's pouring with rain. She fumbles in her bag for an umbrella, slams the car door shut and trots across the car park, purse at the ready before realising that she needs her registration number. She can't remember it and has to dart back. Her breathing comes quickly. Helen is in labour; the baby could be coming any minute now. She can't miss it this time. She won't. She runs back until she can see the registration number and turns on her heel to complete the task. Finally, she is marching inside the automatic doors, down the corridors, checking the signs, finding her way to the ward.

And there they all are.

'Charlotte! I'm so glad you're here!' exclaims Anthony, rushing forward to hold Charlotte's hands. He bounces on his trainers.

Stephen stands slightly behind, watching Helen on the bed. Helen's husband, Rick, holds her hand and places a wet flannel on her forehead.

'And you are?' a stout midwife calls.

'I'm Charlotte. I'm their doula. And I'm the egg donor.'

The midwife checks her clipboard. 'Hmm.'

Charlotte goes over to Helen's side. Helen groans.

'Give her some space, love,' the midwife shouts in her ear. 'She's too far along to talk.'

'Yes, of course. Have you read the birth plan?'

The midwife raises her eyebrows in answer.

New dads Anthony and Stephen stand at the back of the room. Stephen's forehead is slightly furrowed. He runs his hand through his hair before putting his arm round Anthony.

'Is the baby okay?' asks Anthony, bouncing up and down like a small child in need of the loo.

Helen lets out another almighty groan. The midwife rushes over. 'I need to do another examination, okay, love?'

Rick squeezes Helen's hand as the midwife parts her legs and puts a gloved hand up her vagina.

Charlotte watches in fascination. This will be her one day, now she has found Alden.

'Don't push yet, love,' shouts the midwife as Helen moans. 'You're not quite ready yet. Won't be long.'

'Is everything okay?' asks Anthony.

The midwife frowns. 'There's too many of you in here. It's not good for mum and baby. I'm going to have to ask one of you to leave.'

Charlotte looks around the room. Rick strokes Helen's hair. Anthony and Stephen cling to one another. She stands fixed to the spot.

'Charlotte,' whispers Anthony, 'I think you'll need to step outside for a while.'

'Oh, yeah, sure, sure.' Charlotte wipes her hands down her jeans and leaves the room, looking over her shoulder through the window.

Another midwife shows her to the waiting room, a small, airless room with too many pot plants and a stench of coffee. She paces. A baby is being born, another baby who is half of her. She phones Alden. She phones her best friend, Debbie. She walks round like a caged animal. Within the hour, Anthony is at the door, his eyes shining.

'She's here. We're calling her Macey.'

Charlotte feels faint.

'Rick's popped out for some air. The baby's fine. Helen's fine. Do you want to come and see her?'

As she walks back into the room, she sees Stephen sitting on a chair in the corner, holding a swaddled baby in a white and yellow striped hat, feeding her from a bottle. Stephen looks up, flashing his teeth.

'She's beautiful!' gushes Charlotte. 'She looks just like you, Anthony! Congratulations, guys!'

Anthony joins Stephen's side. The perfect family unit.

Charlotte longs to see Macey's fingers. 'Is it okay if I take some photos?'

She can't wait to upload them to Facebook later. She goes over to talk to Helen. Her matted, sweaty hair is plastered over her face; her deflated belly wobbles under her gown.

'Well done, Helen,' says Charlotte quietly, moving closer. 'How are you feeling? Can I get you anything?'

Then the offer to hold her. Anthony stands before her, offering Macey in his arms. Her eyes are closed. Charlotte takes her in her arms. She feels surprisingly heavy. Heavy and warm. There are no sounds except the sound of Macey breathing. There is nothing to see except Macey's sleeping face, with the tiniest of eyelashes against her porcelain skin. Macey's milky scent fills the air. Everything is still.

★★★

A video plays on YouTube, a montage of black and white photographs, zooming in and fading out. A shot of Charlotte face on, hair tied back, elbows out, sleeves rolled up, leaning forward, as though she is about to get stuck in to kneading bread. A side profile of her standing in a dimly lit room, leaning into a wall, her hands placed above a radiator, her bump protruding through her floral sundress, or perhaps it's a night dress. Now Alden, in a baggy black tee-shirt and jeans, assembling an inflatable birthing pool, which resembles a children's paddling pool; he sports a beard and a serious expression. Charlotte and Alden squat together on the floor, gripping hands. Back to standing, hands in the small of her back, then on the wall, her face serene, other worldly. The lens focuses on the soft lighting in the background, heart-shaped lanterns emitting a delicate glow.

We cut to Charlotte in the pool, head resting on the inflated side, arms dangling out, Alden kneeling by her side, looking as though he is talking to her. I wonder what he is saying; the sound of Charlotte's guttural moans has been camouflaged with sentimental music, ebbing and flowing. As the image zooms in, the worry lines on Alden's forehead become visible. Charlotte bobs above the water; her dress has disappeared, replaced by a black bra top. The pool is set against French windows, looking out to the night sky. I see the stars in my mind's eye. Now she smiles with her eyes closed, an infectious smile, mirrored by Alden. A series of images of Charlotte in the water, her smile gone, Alden caressing her cheek. Pain etched on her face as she leans into his shoulder. I am in the room watching, willing her on. I feel I shouldn't be looking but I can't take my eyes off her. We cut to another close-up of the heart-shaped lantern. No! No! I want to see!

The camera pans up and down her back and into the water. A shot of her face, eyes closed, exhaling. Now there is another woman in the picture, dressed all in black, like Alden, holding Charlotte's hand over the side of the pool. Charlotte's doula; I'd forgotten about her. I am jolted out of the room and become aware of the hum of my laptop, of noise outside. I put my hands against my ears and focus back on Charlotte sipping water from a drinks bottle held out by Alden. Then her head rests on the side as though she is sleeping. No, not sleeping. Her face now screwed up in pain, perhaps screaming, perhaps roaring. Hands gripped. Exhale. Alden is in the pool, fully clothed, sitting behind her, holding her. The woman in black leans over the other side. Is anyone behind the camera now?

Back to the lanterns, reflecting against the glass in the windows, lights bouncing across the room.

We peer over Charlotte's shoulder into the water. Closer. Closer. A tiny hand reaches out of the water. An alien thing. Then the baby is in her arms, a shimmering creature coated in waxy vernix. I imagine her inspecting the baby's long, delicate fingers. It's different this time.

Holes

Charlotte meets me on the corner by the pub again, pushing Tahlia in the buggy, this time without Sabine; she looks less guarded than before. She wears bright pink jeans, a blue linen top, grey marl socks, brown boots and a brightly coloured baby Albert on her chest. They wear matching amber necklaces; I seem to remember something about healing properties. As we wander back to the house, Tahlia is agitated and wants Charlotte's full attention. *Hopefully, she'll fall asleep by the time we get back and we can have a long chat like last time.* She is not asleep when we get back but wants to show me her playroom, a room I've yet to visit. Tahlia opens the door and makes a beeline for the piano; she is not drawn by the music but by the three brightly coloured packets of snacks nestling on top. Organic balls of some sort. She opens them one by one and pops them into her mouth with a satisfying crunch, while Charlotte stays in the hallway, calling up the stairs to Sabine to hatch a plan, something to do with a walk to the post office to get ice-cream. *I don't really agree with bribing children with ice-cream!* protests Charlotte, as coats are rearranged and bags packed.

Once Sabine and Tahlia are out of the house and we are settled on cushions on the floor in the playroom with a crawling Albert, I switch the digital recorder on and thank Charlotte for sending over the Facebook links. After flicking through the IVF picture story, I was keen to see what Jake and Macey looked like. Charlotte sent me lots of pictures of Jake. The first set shows her first meeting with Jake as a newborn baby. *I remember that moment very well,* she says. *I remember being a bit taken aback at the outfit because it was like a miniature grown-up outfit rather than a baby suit, if you see what I mean.* In the picture, he wears denim jeans, a pale blue long-sleeve top and a blue and white striped tank top. He is draped in a matching blue and white polka dot muslin cloth. He is asleep in all the photos, his eyes closed, his head lolling back, his little hand outstretched as though reaching out for something in his dreams. In the first picture, he is ensconced in a carrycot, surrounded by cuddly toys – a pale green frog with multicoloured plastic rings attached to it, what looks like a fluffy purple ice-cream and a grey bunny, possibly a bear. In the next three pictures, a grey-sleeved arm is visible supporting his head. In the last two, the owner of the arm is revealed as Charlotte, first smiling down at Jake, then smiling up at the camera. The photos are taken in front of stacks of red and white boxes containing 'panetone cioccolato'. Are they in a restaurant? A shop? Somebody's house?

I tell her that I can see the likeness between her and Jake.

Really? I can't see it at all but I must say people say that Tahlia is my spitting image and I can't see that either so it wouldn't surprise me if you can see a likeness between me and Jake or me and Macey because I can't even see it with Tahlia. What about between the children? Can you see any similarity between my two, Tahlia and Albert? What about with mine and Macey and Jake? Really? Isn't that funny. Wow.

There are pictures of the day when Eve brought Jake to come and visit baby Albert just after he was born. Eve is holding Albert while Jake embraces him from the other side in a group hug. The brown hair from Jake's newborn photos has turned white blond and is worn in a pudding basin cut; he has bright blue eyes and a broad smile. His smile is just like Charlotte's. Another picture, taken outdoors somewhere, shows Tahlia wearing a peach-coloured anorak, sitting on her dad's shoulders, her lime green wellies dangling over his chest. Jake stands slightly behind, navy wellies firmly planted in the mud. It's a relaxed picture. Everyone looks like they are having fun. Next, a picture of Tahlia and Jake sitting at a toy strewn table in a restaurant, *The Gruffalo* picture book spread open in front of Jake. They have similar eyes; they look like siblings. Later, there is an evening picture of Tahlia wearing Gruffalo trousers, a present from Jake. A snap of Jake and his older brother, Freddie, looks like it belongs on a greetings card – two Labradors and two little blond boys share a huge dogs' bed. The older boy, wearing only one sock, has his arms wrapped tightly round the younger boy, in checked blue dungarees. He has choppy blonde hair like Jake. In another picture, Freddie is kneeling on the grass, wearing a school uniform, with his arm round Tahlia. One big happy family.

I can't help but notice that among all the Facebook photo albums Charlotte sent me, there are none of her with her own parents, no family other than the ones she created.

I haven't spoken to my own parents since I left for university. My mum's family has a lot of issues. Her mother, my maternal grandmother, had seven kids and she had a mental breakdown and couldn't look after them and they ended up in a children's home.

Charlotte looks away, her usually warm, smiling face turning blank. Albert climbs up on her lap and makes baby noises against her ear. Her smile returns.

I was always looking for the next couple to help so when I was helping one couple, I was looking out for the next. Reflecting on it now, it was probably serving to fill a whopping hole. I didn't have a relationship so the time I would have been putting into a relationship I was putting into being an egg donor. Obviously now it's completely different. I'm in a relationship, I'm a full-time mum, so it feels completely natural not to be doing it. I wouldn't have the time to do something like that anyway. I was also very involved in the Samaritans for many years and I couldn't keep up with that because of the night duties and I did feel a sense of loss giving that up but with egg donation, you know, it feels as though I gave my fertile years and now, I mean I'm not going to even go back to being an egg donor support network because I can't fit in the phone calls so I feel it has kind of come to a natural end. You know, the only thing is, I'd quite like to be a surrogate for someone and I'd like that to be a journey I do before I'm too old. If we want to have a third child, which we hope to next year, then I'll need a couple of years to recover from that, so how old am I now? I'm 37 this year. There are timescales, loose ones, but you can get around them. My friend's sister desperately needs a surrogate so I started thinking this is what I am supposed to do but then I thought no, I'm about to have a third child, this isn't the right time. But I wouldn't be surprised if at some point before I hit 43 somebody comes along who needs a surrogate and I feel the fertility thing will rise up again. I'll have a feeling if it's meant to be. So it's not quite the end of the chapter. I think I'd be a great option for somebody as a surrogate.

Charlotte stands in between two men. Both men have dark hair and wear shirts and jeans. Charlotte wears a lacy cream dress with tiny orange and green flowers, pulled in with a wide leather belt. It is the only photo of her that I have seen where her hair is loose, freed from its ponytail. All look happy and carefree.

I wouldn't want to do any more IVF. Because it took us 11 months to get pregnant with Tahlia, there was a time I thought I'd messed things up doing five cycles of IVF and I started considering using an egg donor myself. I already had someone in my mind who I would use as an egg donor. But I'd only do that if I thought my own eggs weren't gonna work. Obviously, you'd prefer to be biologically related to your children. Did I tell you about Stephen and Anthony's spare embryos? So they had two spare embryos and you have to pay for these to be kept in storage. So after Tahlia, my periods didn't come back for 18 months and Stephen and Anthony were aware I was incredibly twitchy and worried that my periods might not come back and we might not be able to have a second child and I was quite desperate. So Anthony got in touch and said that the storage date on the embryos was coming to an end but they couldn't afford to continue paying for it so they were going to allow them to perish. I really thought these two embryos might be my only chance of having another biological child, so I told them I felt really strongly about this. But of course this meant I was asking Alden if he would take on a child who was half me and half Anthony, you know. But I said to him, 'You've already got three biological children.' So he was, like, 'Okay.' So I told Anthony I was really keen to have this option and pay for the storage and Anthony was fine but then when he asked Stephen, Stephen said no. The baby would be a full genetic sibling to their child and I think Stephen just thought I don't want you to have my husband and my daughter's genetics; I think he just felt he had no control over it as he had no real part in it. When Anthony came back to me he said, 'I'm very sorry I should have checked with Stephen.' Then Alden said, 'Thank God because I didn't really want to have a child that was half Anthony's.' Then a week later, my period came back so it was all okay. I would have loved to have been a fly on the wall for the conversation that Stephen and Anthony had. I mean I could have vetoed them using the embryos at any time in the process by withdrawing my consent but I would have never done that to them but that's what they were doing to me. I felt like they'd pulled the ladder up once they got what they needed.

A Facebook photo of a newborn Macey, wearing a white and yellow striped hat, all swaddled up and resting on a hairy male arm. With a congratulations message addressed, 'To my dear friends Anthony and Stephen'.

We haven't introduced Jake and Macey to Tahlia and Albert as their siblings. They just think they are friends of the family.

Summer BBQ in Charlotte's garden, shortly after Macey is born. Macey is lying on a baby blue picnic blanket, wearing a pretty pink and yellow striped summer dress. Stephen and Anthony are in tee-shirts and navy shorts. Stephen's tee-shirt is plain blue and Anthony's has some sort of superhero picture on it. They look barely recognisable from the photo before Macey was born. Anthony is greying and Stephen balding. They smile baring their teeth, leaning over Macey almost on all fours, in a protective stance. In the next picture, Charlotte and Alden lean towards the camera, their heads touching, smiling, Macey just visible in the background. There is a jokey comment about Macey photo bombing. This was taken before Charlotte had children of her own; I wonder how she felt, being so close to baby Macey.

I would say Stephen and Anthony, and Eve and Graham, both raise their children in ways that are hugely different to how we raise ours. Do I feel any differently about it because the children are biologically connected to me? No, I don't really. I suppose the only thing I feel some responsibility for is the fact that Macey doesn't have a mother; I feel like there is a mother role that is missing, or maybe I am projecting that. But I feel a bit of a responsibility to her. I feel a bit uncomfortable about that. Because I know when Stephen and Anthony started conversations about that, I know we agreed we would be very open about it all and start a book for her about her journey. But Anthony's told me they are avoiding talking about how she was made. She's four and about to start school and already she's asking, 'Why don't I have a mummy?' And they just say, 'Some people have a mummy and a daddy, some people have two mummies, some people have two daddies' etc. But she's going to go to school and learn that two daddies can't actually make a baby and there is a mummy somewhere. I think it's gonna be a huge shock to her. It feels as though the years are going on and they are shrinking away from it, and I don't know what their plan is for what they are gonna tell her when she's older. I hope they don't just fob her off. But I need to know what their plan is because it affects what my plan is in terms of what I tell my children. I haven't told Tahlia anything. She doesn't know that she has half siblings because I can't tell her if they aren't telling Macey. When we have met up, we're just introduced as family friends. When I've seen her she doesn't know who I am. I think they see me as a threat. I haven't seen them for ages. Macey had a birthday party last month and we didn't get invited. I think they'd be quite happy never to hear from me again.

The next Facebook image is when Stephen and Anthony brought toddler Macey to meet newborn Tahlia. Stephen and Anthony both wear jeans and striped shirts. Stephen wears a subtle blue pinstripe, Anthony a lairy green and yellow stripe. Stephen holds their daughter, Macey; Anthony holds Tahlia, Charlotte's first child 'for keeps'. Their body language betrays their unease. They smile with lips slightly pursed, the children are held as far apart from one another as is possible.

I think the way they parent her is they just shut her down a lot. Anthony said to me, 'Oh I'm fed up with nursery saying she's been naughty and then I have to shout at her and make her cry.' They are certainly not into gentle parenting. I feel really sad that any child would be treated like that. I bet they left her to cry it out when she was a baby. A couple of days after she was born they put a jokey post on Facebook with a picture saying, 'Macey is really enjoying her buggy ride' and she is red faced and screaming and I hadn't had children at this point, not for another year, and I looked at that picture and I actually thought it was really funny. I laughed and I put a comment on it and I printed it out and put in inside my wardrobe along with pictures of my godchildren. I didn't think anything more of it. It was a wardrobe I didn't go into much but when I'd just had Tahlia, I went to get something in that wardrobe and I opened it up and I saw the picture and I immediately, I mean I feel upset just talking about it now, she was so distressed. I just didn't see that before. I didn't connect with it before. I was really upset. It was about a year and a half later and I couldn't believe the shift in me. I burst into tears and thought, how did I ever think that was funny? What part of me could think a newborn baby screaming in distress was funny? It was so odd. I hadn't thought anything about it when she was born despite her being my biological child.

If she gets to 18 and I haven't had contact with her for 14 years I would probably contact her which is probably against what we agreed at the beginning but then they have gone against what we agreed and I would jeopardise the friendship that I no longer had with Stephen and Anthony. That's just crossed my mind. I've never said that before. I think she needs to know who I am for her sake, not for mine. I'm not prepared to keep up sporadic contact without her knowing who I am. It's not fair on Tahlia to see her and not know who she is because it involves deceiving Tahlia but I can't tell Tahlia if Macey doesn't know because you know what children are like and she'll say to her, 'Do you know my mummy's egg made you?' If they don't contact me in the next two years, I'm going to have to contact them and ask them what they are gonna do about it. It won't go on for 14 years. It can't. The only way it can get that far is if contact is severed. But then maybe they won't wanna do that because then they'll think that I will be more of a threat when Macey turns 18 but if they've read any research at all they will know that that is not a good thing to leave it. I would hate for my role to be negative for her but if they don't do anything about it, and deny her that information, she might be really angry about that. It never occurred to me until speaking to you about it but they've said they won't have more children so she's going to be an only child and she won't even know that she has two siblings here living up the road. It's driven by fear that she will reject her two daddies and want this mummy who she doesn't know.

There is a commotion at the door as Sabine and Tahlia return.

Alden talks about Macey being a little bit like a dressing up doll for Stephen and Anthony. They are both comic mad, really geeky, so if she's not dressed like a pretty little girl then she's dressed as Wonderwoman and they take her to lots of sci-fi conventions dressed up as all sorts and post it on Facebook. That's their enjoyment of having a child but she very much slots into their world. Their life doesn't seem to have changed to accommodate her.

As soon as Sabine releases Tahlia from her buggy, she runs into the room and sits on Charlotte's lap. *Mummy! Mummy!* Albert has started banging a toy car onto the ground and shouting; I sense this conversation coming to an end soon. Now that Tahlia is in earshot, I have to be careful about how I phrase my questions; she doesn't know that Macey and Jake are her genetic half-siblings.

I'm a great believer in things working out the way they are kind of supposed to work out so if I am following that through, I shouldn't really have any regrets. I just wish I could recall the ins and outs of my original conversation with Stephen and Anthony, so if I need that information I could use it. No regrets. I am happy with how it all went and the path it took me in. If I hadn't been doing all this stuff it wouldn't have led me to meeting Alden, so it was all meant to be. I met Alden through a friend who was setting up a deli business just after I got made redundant and I said I'd help her set it up. I just thought it was what I was meant to do. I helped her for six months but she totally messed it up and blew the bank loan so she got involved in a scheme to find an investor so cue, in comes Alden, as an investor, and they hit it off and started a relationship. She took £20,000 of his money and pissed it up the wall. They split up and a month after it happened, Alden contacted me and I didn't like him at all. I thought he was an idiot. He asked if we could get together and have a chat about what had happened with the business. So we had a coffee and he'd grown a beard and I saw him in a different light and the rest is history. We moved in together within three months. It's funny because I was having my last injection for IVF for Macey on the day of our first date.*

Tahlia pulls on Charlotte's arm. *Mummy! Mummy! Come and play!*

It's been a really positive experience for me. I always warn caution if becoming an egg donor or surrogate for a family member. I remember reading a story about two sisters who were incredibly close and one sister became an egg donor to her sister who couldn't have children and then she felt she just couldn't live near her sister because she felt she was always watching her. So she ended up moving to Australia and breaking all ties. So the sister who just went into it to help ended up losing her sister. I always thought that was a poignant story. I always tell people to go through counselling first; clinics should insist that both sides have counselling first.

Tahlia has gone off to play with a toy garage and Albert has crawled after her. *Mummy! Albert's ruining my game! Mummy!!!*

Charlotte moves over the other side of the room where her children are and speaks in a calm voice. *I need you to stop shouting love, okay?*

You know the law changed in 2005 to end anonymity of donors and when those people born after 2005 turn 18, so from 2023, they will have the right to obtain details about their egg or sperm donor. I was at a conference and a counsellor was speaking and she said give it ten years' time and the egg donation world will explode with people trying to trace their donors and eclipse adopted people tracing their birth parents. It's going to explode.

For further information on egg donation and surrogacy, please consult the references below.

Reference list

Donor Conception Network (2022) 'Questions' [Online]. Available at: https://www.dcnetwork.org/who-are-you/donor-conceived-person/questions (Accessed 3 November 2022).

Surrogacy UK (n.d.) 'About Us' [Online]. Available at: https://surrogacyuk.org/aboutus/ (Accessed 3 November 2022).

5
SHANTA'S STORY PART II

I like mine with a kiss

I sit on the toilet peering down into the gusset of my faded black knickers, the ones that used to look sexy in a certain light but are now just worn, patchy material, barely held together by nearly snapped elastic. Apparently, it should be the colour and consistency of raw egg white. If you're ovulating. I prod and poke about with tissue, scrutinising the texture of my bodily fluids before pulling and zipping up my clothes, flushing and washing my hands with antibacterial soap. That night, I wake in a sweat. This is a good sign, I think. Raised basal body temperature is one of the indicators of ovulation. I pull on my dressing gown, slide my feet into my slippers and go to the bathroom to find the thermometer, stick it in my mouth and suck hard. Then I walk downstairs to the kitchen and consult the chart stuck on the fridge. Inside, the shelves are full of Chinese mushrooms, vitamins and homeopathic supplements. Later that day, I lie on a couch semi-clothed with needles stuck into my forehead, abdomen, chest and arms to improve my fertility. My back sticks to the couch. I close my eyes and listen to the sound of dolphins. Do they ever have trouble making babies?

'I can make you up a fertility tea,' says the acupuncturist-come-herbalist. 'It might help.'

> Ovulation occurs each month when an egg is released from one of the ovaries.
> An egg lives for about 12–24 hours after being released. For pregnancy to happen, the egg must be fertilised by a sperm within this time.
> *(NHS, 2019a)*

DOI: 10.4324/9781003290179-7

I'm back on the toilet peeing on sticks. Pregnancy tests, ovulation tests. It's all the same. I stare at the little windows so long and hard that I start seeing lines and crosses appear. Through the round window. I have a flashback of Play School from my childhood. Floella Benjamin is smiling at me from the TV screen. She hugs Humpty, while Big Ted, Little Ted, Jemima and Hamble sit by watching.

Within 24 hours of ovulation, the egg is fertilised by sperm if you have had sex in the last few days without using contraception.

> About 5 to 6 days after ovulation, the fertilised egg burrows into the lining of the womb – this is called implantation.
> You're now pregnant.
>
> *(NHS, 2019a)*

I grow my grey roots out on the underside of my head so that I can cut a three-inch section of hair off and put it in the post for analysis. Minerals. Chi. Something is missing. I have not seen my hair grey for years. I keep colouring the top and just leave the necessary patch underneath to grow. Every now and then I flip my hair up and stare at it in the mirror. I look like an upside down skunk.

> Three weeks after the first day of your last period, your fertilised egg moves slowly along the fallopian tube towards the womb.
>
> *(NHS, 2019a)*

My four-year-old son bounces up and down on the trampoline in the back garden, talking to his toy cat in lieu of the sibling that I have as yet failed to produce. The garden is in full bloom, nature's abundance fills the space. When I was four years old, our black cat, Pepsi, went into hiding. The next day, there were five slimy, pink kittens suckling on her. I remember worrying about their transparent skin. Two of them died a few days later. My mum wouldn't let me go in the conservatory to look until she'd cleaned everything away.

> In weeks 4 to 5 of early pregnancy, the embryo grows and develops within the lining of the womb.
>
> The outer cells reach out to form links with the mother's blood supply. The inner cells form into 2, and then later into 3, layers. Each of these layers will grow to be different parts of the baby's body:
>
> The inner layer becomes the breathing and digestive systems, including the lungs, stomach, gut and bladder.
>
> The middle layer becomes the heart, blood vessels, muscles and bones.
> The outer layer becomes the brain and nervous system, the eye lenses, tooth enamel, skin and nails.
>
> *(NHS, 2019a)*

I walk up and down the supermarket aisles, basket in one hand, child's hand in the other, looking at fresh produce. Spinach, sweet potatoes, onions, mushrooms. I consult the nutritional sheet. It's very important to eat and do the right things. My son, however, wants Coco Pops.

> At 5 weeks … [t]he baby's nervous system is already developing, and the foundations for its major organs are in place. At this stage, the embryo is around 2mm long.
>
> The heart is forming as a simple tube-like structure. The baby already has some of its own blood vessels and blood begins to circulate.
>
> A string of these blood vessels connects the baby and mother, and will become the umbilical cord.
> At the same time, the embryo's outer layer of cells develops a groove and folds to form a hollow tube called the neural tube. This will become the baby's brain and spinal cord.
>
> (NHS, 2019a)

I sit in the darkened room watching a man in a navy suit point to a chart on the screen, gesticulating. The tone of his voice rises and falls. The door swings open and a woman rushes to the back of the room, perching on the edge of the last available seat. The consultant coughs, smiles then carries on pointing and talking. There are a lot of numbers – percentages, statistic success rates. I have no idea what he is saying but the graph resembles a terrifyingly steep slide, an icy hillside that you might dare to attempt toboggan down only if you're feeling very brave. It seems it's all downhill after 35 years.

I am 39 years old.

> By the time you're 6 to 7 weeks pregnant, there's a large bulge where the heart is and a bump at the head end of the neural tube. This bump will become the brain and head.
>
> The embryo is curved and has a tail, and looks a bit like a small tadpole. The heart can sometimes be seen beating on a vaginal ultrasound scan at this stage.
>
> The developing arms and legs become visible as small swellings (limb buds). Little dimples on the side of the head will become the ears, and there are thickenings where the eyes will be.
>
> By now, the embryo is covered with a thin layer of see-through skin.
>
> (NHS, 2019a)

'Secondary infertility is more common than you might think,' says the doctor, staring at the computer screen. 'We can start with Clomid. It'll make you produce more eggs. If that doesn't work, we'll move onto IUI and then IVF and then egg donation. Spain usually. I can give you a sheet on the prices.'

A small giggle escapes from my mouth. Spanish omelette. I'm hungry now and I start thinking about what I might have for dinner when I get in. I'll need onions, potatoes. I realise the doctor is still talking.

'Sorry?' I say, staring into the distance. 'I'm not sure I want to … not sure I can…'

I open my handbag and rummage around for a tissue, embarrassed that I am shaking.

> By 7 weeks, the embryo has grown to about 10mm long from head to bottom. This measurement is called the crown–rump length.
>
> The brain is growing rapidly and this results in the head growing faster than the rest of the body. The embryo has a large forehead, and the eyes and ears continue to develop.
>
> The inner ear starts to develop, but the outer ear on the side of the head won't appear for a couple more weeks.
>
> The limb buds start to form cartilage, which will develop into the bones of the legs and arms. The arm buds get longer and the ends flatten out – these will become the hands.
> Nerve cells continue to multiply and develop as the brain and spinal cord (the nervous system) starts to take shape.
>
> *(NHS, 2019a)*

'You can still ovulate,' says the doctor, after they have removed my left Fallopian tube with my baby inside it. I stare up at her kind, lined face in a daze, still wearing my hospital gown, wincing as I try to move. How will the eggs get through?

I will never get over this.

> By the time you're 8 weeks pregnant, the baby is called a foetus, which means offspring.
>
> *(NHS, 2019a)*

'You can't replace one baby with another,' says the counsellor.

I shift in my seat and dig my nails into my thighs, imagining the marks I'm making on my skin.

'Adoption isn't an easy process. Most adopted children are older, they've been in care, they've suffered abuse and neglect and have special needs.' Her mouth seems to twist as she speaks. Her salt and pepper hair shakes as she moves her head to emphasise the point. Her bangles clash as she writes in her notepad. Then silence fills the room as she stares at me, her eyes searing my cheeks. 'You're at sea and you're fixating on adoption as a life raft. It isn't that.'

I look out of the window. Grey pellets fall from the sky.

I am drowning.

'You've experienced a terrible loss. You need to take some time out. You can still have IVF with one Fallopian tube.' She wears a lilac top in exactly the same shade as my childhood Care Bear.

The wall clock ticks. The session is over.

> An ectopic pregnancy is when a fertilised egg implants itself outside of the womb, usually in one of the fallopian tubes.
>
> The fallopian tubes are the tubes connecting the ovaries to the womb. If an egg gets stuck in them, it won't develop into a baby and your health may be at risk if the pregnancy continues.
>
> Unfortunately, it's not possible to save the pregnancy. It usually has to be removed using medicine or an operation.
> In the UK, around 1 in every 90 pregnancies is ectopic. This is around 11,000 pregnancies a year.
>
> (NHS, 2019b)

I light a candle for Baby X and sit with my head in my hands watching it flicker. The flame rises and falls under my breath.

In. Out. In. Out. In. Out. In. Out. In. Out. In. Out. In. Out. In. Out. In. Out.

In. Out. In. Out. In. Out. In. Out. In. Out. In. Out. In. Out. In. Out. In. Out.

I stare for the longest time until my vision is blurred. The flame blows up and engulfs me, filling me with heat and pain. I am in the ambulance, convulsing. Hushed whispers buzz inside my head. A screaming silence. I am on a hospital bed, waiting. Blood spurts from my arm over the white sheet as the junior doctor tries several times to get a line in. I am breathing into a mask, counting. They are cutting me, mutilating me, saving my life. One life for another. I let myself cry. Angry calm tears. I am drowning.

I wanted you. I loved you. I'm sorry you didn't make it.

The flame roars within me. Red. Orange. Yellow. White. Light swirls within me, filling every fibre, drowning out the noise. I open my eyes and blow out the candle.

The cuts in my abdomen have healed but the silvery white scars remain.

Reference list

Brodszky, N. and Cahn, S. (1951) *How D'Ya Like Your Eggs in the Morning*, Beverly Hills, CA, Sony/ATV Music Publishing LLC, The Bicycle Music Company.

NHS (2019a) 'Pregnancy Week by Week' [Online]. Available at: https://www.nhs.uk/conditions/pregnancy-and-baby/pregnancy-week-by-week/ (Accessed 28 June 2019).

NHS (2019b) 'Ectopic Pregnancy' [Online]. Available at: https://www.nhs.uk/conditions/ectopic-pregnancy/ (Accessed 28 June 2019).

6
RUBI'S STORY

Would you like something stronger?

Rubi leans out of the door to usher me inside the annexe where she and Sunni reside, a miniature version spawned by the grown-up house next door. The door opens straight into a compact open plan space, with a staircase running up one wall. She gestures for me to sit next to her diminutive frame on the red leather sofa, where she nestles, wearing a loose fitting, green and yellow patterned tunic over grey leggings, with a bandage around one ankle; I have yet to discover the significance of this. Her long, dark hair tumbles over her face as she talks. *Would you like something to drink?* It's an oppressively hot day in late August, and my legs stick to the leather sofa. *Do you want to come out, Sunni?* A rustling noise emanates from the corner of the room, which houses a well-stocked bar, complete with red leather bar stools.

Then a man pops into view like a Jack-in-the-box. A very tall, very smiley man. *Can you get us some cokes, please, Sunni?* Sunni clinks two glasses together, grins and asks me if I want something stronger, waving to a bottle of Bacardi. I decline. He brings the drinks over then retreats to the back of the room, where he sits in a cubby hole of a study, tapping away on his laptop. I take in the surroundings – a white shag pile rug covers white laminate flooring, a huge widescreen television blares from the wall, silk tapestries hang on the opposite wall, running up the staircase, dotted with blue spotlights. *Sunni! Can you turn the TV off please?!* Sunni sighs in a jovial manner and steps forward to attend to Rubi, duly turning off the television and placing a red leather footstall under her injured foot. *I've got him well trained,* she says to me with a wink as he returns to his cubby hole, always within earshot.

Oh, okay, you want our story? Okay. We got married in 1995 when I was 29 and Sunni was 30, and two years later everyone was asking, 'When are you gonna start a

DOI: 10.4324/9781003290179-8

family?' You know, it's a typical Asian thing. Family kept saying, 'Why aren't you pregnant? Why haven't you had a baby yet?' Then we went to see a doctor and he told me to see a gynaecologist. He just said, 'Oh there's nothing wrong, nothing wrong. You need to start doing IVF.' Then we had our first IVF. Sunni, where did we have our first IVF again?

Sunni pops his head back out to confirm the location and then pulls it back in again. I imagine him nodding away as Rubi speaks.

It was a bit daunting at first when they said you have to inject yourself. I thought, 'Oh my God.' So I always used to do it five minutes before Eastenders came on. My mother-in-law used to say, 'Eastenders is coming on!' It was quite painful. The first IVF attempt didn't work. The second time was a disaster because when they came to retrieve the eggs, there was nothing to remove so that was a setback. I was devastated. So we waited about six months before I could go for it again. My mother-in-law was saying, 'Why isn't it working?' It was getting a bit too much for us but we still carried on. Then the doctor suggested that we should get an egg donor and a surrogate and use my husband's sperm. In the UK, trying to find an egg donor and a surrogate was very difficult. Where do you find them? So we started doing some research. We put an ad in the paper. We joined an agency. That was a bit of heartache. There was a girl who was gonna help us but it didn't work out. My sister was gonna help us in the beginning but she found out she had endometriosis and had to go for a hysterectomy as well so she couldn't help us, so that fell through.

Two floppy-haired children run into the room, slowing down when they see me. First a boy, then a girl. They are beaming and out of breath. Both children look remarkably like Sunni.

Prince say hello! He's the youngest. And then erm, we went to the surrogacy agency, we went to their meetings. Dawn say hello! She's our eldest. Finish your drinks, kids! Sorry. So, we went to the meetings and we couldn't find anyone so I actually started looking online. We found this lady online who said she'd consider being our surrogate. She lived quite a way away but we drove to meet her and her partner, and the first impression he gave us was you need to have a BMW and gold chains and rings to be somebody in life and we were like, 'We've only got a Sierra, we can't do anything like that.' We went out and had a meal and everything and he started saying, 'Look, let's just do everything with ourselves, rather than getting agencies involved moneywise.' It felt a bit odd but obviously we chatted. The next day, she rang us up and she said, 'Send me £5,000 and I'll help you.' And I thought, 'Why do you want money up front? We haven't signed anything, you haven't had the tests or anything.' You know in this country, you can't pay a surrogate, only their expenses. She said she needed it to get tablets and maternity clothes, so I said, '£5,000? Um, no.'

Prince appears at the top of the stairs, rubbing his eyes and asking if he's allowed Lucozade.

No Lucozade. So she said, 'Then I'm not going to help you.' So obviously we're desperate but we're not that desperate we're just gonna hand over £5,000 to a pair of strangers. So that fell through. That night, we felt there's no point going on in life. All the time, we were having family falling pregnant. I didn't mind; I was fine about that. It's when people stop telling you. You know, when they have the baby, they stop inviting you because they think there's something wrong with you. I felt that. Everyone was saying to my mother-in-law, 'You know, they've been married for seven years now, why aren't they having children?' My mother-in-law didn't wanna tell people that we were going for IVF and I was like, 'Look, Mum, I'm having to listen to everyone every time we're going to parties, so let's just get the family over and get it over with cos I'm not gonna go through this trauma every time.'

We know quite a few couples that lie about it, even to family. If you've been trying for a baby for ten years and suddenly you're pregnant, especially with twins, you know, come on! They say, 'Oh I took this special medicine.' They put a pillow under their clothes. You know! People don't wanna hear about IVF and everything. I say, 'What's the shame in it? What's so wrong in saying it?' A lot of them don't understand, when I talk about surrogacy, they think Sunni would go sleep with these ladies. Even my best friend, to this day, I've known her for 12 years, and she still can't get her head around it all. I say, 'I'm not gonna tell you anymore.'

Prince is back at the top of the stairs, again pleading for Lucozade. He's taken his top off and stands there bare chested, his hands in his jean pockets. His sister giggles behind him.

No, I don't care if Dad said you can have it. Kids, I'm trying to talk to my friend! Sorry about that. Kids, eh! So I said, 'Look we've been having IVF, we tried for seven years, it's not working.' People were saying to Sunni, 'Why don't you get married again to someone who can have kids?' Even my family said, 'Look if you want to get married again, we're happy. We'll take our daughter back tomorrow.' Sunni said, 'No, if I'm gonna have babies, I'll have them with Rubi but I won't have them with anyone else in my life, no way.' So we carried on going through our journey. Sunni started a blog online and someone was following our story and they phoned us up and said, 'Look there's this clinic in Mumbai. We went there and my wife had IVF and now she's carrying twins and they do surrogacy and egg donors there. Why don't you try over there?' And we thought, 'Oh good idea.'

Passage to India

We didn't know where to start in India, so we advertised for a surrogate in the Times of India *and this young girl replied and said, 'I'm willing to help you. I'll be your surrogate.' So we talked about it because it would be giving up our jobs and going abroad for about six months. And then, she fizzled out of our life as well; she stopped replying to our emails so that was another setback. When I turned 40, I said to the family, 'That's it. It's not meant to be. I can't do it anymore.' Sunni quit his job and went into a depression mode for two years. He didn't leave the bedroom, he stopped going to wedding functions, he stopped going out. He focused on running his website, telling our story, what we were going through and people would read it. Everything revolved around that for him. He told me to give up my job but I wouldn't do it. I said, 'I'm still going out, I'm going to work, I'm going out with my colleagues. Life still goes on.' But he didn't give up. He carried on. Then I can't remember what happened but he said, 'Oh my God, that lady that contacted us before, she had a motorbike accident. She broke her arms and ribs and she's been in hospital and that's why she stopped replying to our emails but she said she's getting better and she still wants to help us.' So it took us three months to decide. Look, we're going to India to see this lady to see if she can help us and we're also going to go to the clinic to see what they can do. So I packed up my job.*

Sunni comes out of the study, carrying his laptop; he's keen to show me his website, says it will help me to understand their story. The home page is busy and full of graphics and links. A slideshow: 'Meet Dawn' shows a curly haired preschool Dawn, sitting on the floor, wearing a white tee-shirt and white leggings, holding a toy doll and babbling into a mobile phone; 'Meet Prince' shows a baby Prince sitting laughing, putting a ball in his mouth, before cutting to Prince on a red and blue toy motorbike. There is a lot to take in. My eyes flick from image to image.

A shot of a windscreen at the back of a car, displaying a classic 'Baby on Board' sign, with a piece of card with the word 'No' written on it stuck above it with masking tape; to the right, a piece of A4 paper with the words, 'Surrogate needed to carry our baby. £10,000. Please visit our website.'

A flowchart of the different routes and costs involved in rupees. Eight white rectangles on a grey background connected by arrows. Insemination by syringe apparently costs a thousand rupees per attempt; a 'test tube baby with drugs' will set you back by Rs. 40,000 plus Rs. 20,000 per month of pregnancy; all followed by an additional Rs. 20,000 on completion of a live birth. There is some mention of a 'bonus payment'. Rubi ushers Sunni away so she can carry on talking. He retreats back to his study; I can just see his back through the archway. His body language suggests he would rather be in the room with us.

We went to India, and we went into the hotel. This girl came over and she introduced herself and she said she was willing to help us. I think she was very young as well and we sort of, we really didn't know what she wanted either. She hadn't been a surrogate before. It was her first time. I think she wanted money; she wanted a good life in India. You know, she was very young. She was using her own eggs, so we started doing artificial insemination with my husband's sperm. First attempt failed. The second attempt, we started having a lot of problems with her. Her father passed away. She stopped responding to our calls, our emails. For two months, we didn't hear anything, we were just living like in a prison cell in the hotel, waiting.

So we got in touch with the clinic and asked if they can help us using the same lady as a surrogate but using a separate egg donor, but she wasn't happy with that. Said she wanted to use her own eggs. Okay. So we took her to the clinic. But she wasn't doing the injections. She didn't like doing it through the clinic. About four treatments we had to abandon. The clinic couldn't get hold of her for three or four days at a time. It's understandable that she was mourning but it was difficult for me too. So she didn't respond for two weeks then she sent us an email saying, 'Sorry I'm going through a tough time.' And I said, 'Look, I'm going through a tough time.' I said, 'Look, you said you wanted to help us; if you don't want to help us, just let us know.' So she says, 'Give me one more go.' Same old, same old. She said she couldn't find the nurse to get her injections. When the doctor did egg retrieval, she was half sedated, so the doctor said to me, 'You're making a very big mistake using her eggs because the eggs we've got from her are very bad quality because she didn't take her full medication.' So I went in and told her. You know, we named our daughter after her even though things didn't work out with her because she was the start of our journey, and my mother-in-law liked that name, as well; her name was Dawn. So I said, 'Dawn look, we've given you all this money, you didn't take your medication on time, and the doctor said your embryos are so poor it's worthless us putting them back in you as well.' She said, 'I'm sorry, I'm sorry.' I said, 'Let's just leave it. We can be friends but that's it.' So she was very upset. She said she didn't like the way I spoke to her. She didn't speak to me on the four-hour cab journey back. It's understandable. But we did it about five times with her and the amount of money we spent with her.

In the meantime, while we were in India, we got a phone call from Mum, that's Sunni's mum, saying she's not well, then we got a phone call from my sister saying she's expecting a baby. I kept saying to Sunni that we were gonna get news. I knew it. And it was Diwali. I just closed the curtains and we just wanted to die. I thought, why us, what have we done? And while we were in Mumbai, we saw a woman sitting down with a newborn baby, half-clothed; we even went to the shop and bought clothes for this child, hoping it would be an omen that we would be blessed with a child and everything. We tried everything. We went to temples.

Sunni hangs out of his cubby hole to remind Rubi that she's only told me half of the story.

I'm getting to that, Sunni. I just told Shanta we had the call that Mum was ill. I said to the clinic, 'Look we're going home because Sunni's mother's very ill.' So I said, 'Let's put us on hold for a while and let's concentrate on Mum.' While we were in India, she was diagnosed with cancer. Sunni was crying his eyes out. Mum's got cancer, we can't have a baby. It was killing us. So he flew back to India to carry on surrogacy without me while I stayed at home to look after Mum, taking her to hospital for her cancer treatments. During the attempts with Dawn, Mum was dying of cancer, so Sunni came up with an idea. He said to the doctor, 'Can you give us a scan, somebody else's scan, to say that we were gonna have a baby?'

Sunni races out from the back of the room, his face animated. He blurts out that the doctor gave him someone else's scan but his mother died before he could show it to her. He says he persuaded Dawn, the surrogate, to phone England and give the good news, to lie. His mother died thinking they were having a baby.

Sunni, I'm telling it. So, yeah. We had a few falling outs with relatives. Also, my sister-in-law had a little girl. We brought her up. It was her first baby and she didn't know how to look after her. So for the first year we looked after the little girl, while I was looking after Mum, working full-time, doing her treatments. Our life was on hold. Sunni came back for the funeral and then we started up again six months later.

Sunni sits on the edge of the footstall, clearly not prepared to leave during this vital part of the story. He nods and murmurs, uttering words here and there in agreement or disagreement.

He crammed in five attempts in one year with five different surrogates. I was at breaking point. I got to the point where I said to the doctors, 'If Sunni comes to you, shut the door on him. Don't let him have any more attempts with any more surrogates.' He's breaking inside, I'm hurting and each time we find out it's failed again. I begged the doctors, 'Please don't take Sunni anymore, just turn him away, say you can't help him anymore.'

Our daughter was conceived on the seventh attempt. Sunni took me for a meal and said, 'The surrogate's pregnant.' But I didn't believe it. I just sat there. I didn't believe him. He said, 'Have a look at the scan.' I said, 'No.' He said, 'Don't you wanna know the sex?' I said, 'No.' We never told any family members until the surrogate was seven months pregnant. Two months before I left work, my colleagues, they killed me, they said, 'Oh my God, every day you go to work, you look so down, you say all you wanna do is die, your life is worthless, there's no point going on and look what you're telling us now! Why didn't you tell us earlier?' Then I started packing to go to India and I thought, 'What if she doesn't wanna hand the baby over? What if there's something wrong with the baby or she wants the baby back?' There were still so many hurdles. It's so funny cos we thought we'll go a couple of weeks early and we'll go touring and we'll be there in time for the delivery, and within five days of booking our seats we got a phone call from the doctor saying, 'Congratulations, you've got a baby girl.' She was four weeks early. Sunni sent me a message at work to tell me and I was like, 'What are you talking about?' I was looking at this email and I was thinking, 'Is this real or is it someone downstairs winding me up? My friends were all jumping for joy. Sunni said to me, 'That's it. I've got to phone the travel agents cos we're not touring anywhere, we're gonna go to Delhi, go straight there, get a connecting flight and go to Mumbai.' We were five days late for our daughter. What Sunni?

Oh, okay, no eight days late. And you know, that journey on that plane is never ending. We just threw our suitcases into the hotel and we went to the hospital and I said, 'I want to see my baby girl.' And they said, 'Who the hell are you then?' And we said, 'We're Sunni and Rubi.' So the woman at the hospital, she said to me, 'Sorry but you need to go through the formalities.' And I said, 'What formalities?' And she said, 'You have to be admitted into the hospital.' I said, 'But I didn't have the baby.' We were in this posh hospital and they made me walk around in a gown and have four meals a day. The nurses were asking me if I'd fed a baby before. Of course, I've fed a baby before – I brought my nephew up and nieces. So they took me to see my baby in the intensive care unit. She was so tiny. And the nurse says, 'Your husband can't come in with the camera.' He was there taking pictures, yeah, so she said, 'He can't take it in.' And it's just tears and I said, 'I'm your mum.' Oh my God, it was true. I said to the nurse, 'Can I pick her up?' It was feeding time and they were feeding her through a syringe. Then I brought bottles and you know, it was like a dream. I thought, 'She is my daughter.' Sunni asked to come through and they said, 'No, you can't go through.' It was so funny. He said, 'It's not fair, my wife is holding the baby.' I thought, 'No, I'm not gonna let her go.' I was like, 'Yes, a miracle has happened. She is mine and I need to get her out of hospital.' I didn't want the nurses telling me what to do, I knew what to do, but they said, 'No, she's got to stay in ICU for two days, you've got to do the paperwork.' So the doctor said, 'Look, the baby is ready to discharge but we can't discharge because we haven't had your final payment.' Two days, Sunni was running around, trying to sort it out while I was bonding with our daughter. We named her Dawn because she was the start of our journey and my mother-in-law always liked that name, as well. We also had a newspaper reporter following us, when we were in hospital, she was following us all the time.

The surrogate? Oh, eight days in, she was gone. We didn't see her. The agency would have handed her the money and she would have signed the paperwork and she would have gone. Trying to do paperwork in India, it's so slow. Trying to get the birth certificate was a nightmare. We had to take Dawn backwards and forwards everywhere; no-one was gonna take hold of my baby. The paperwork killed us. The visas and everything, it was really difficult trying to get the clearance. I think they had a problem with us because we were British. I thought they were going to stop me at immigration and say, 'That's not your baby, take her back.' At immigration, they looked at baby's date of birth, and looked at our arrival date and were, 'How comes you weren't here when your baby was born?' And, you know, we had to explain it all over again. They don't really know what surrogacy is. A lot of people don't really understand.

I tell you when we got on that plane and shut the door, I thought, 'I've done it now. The plane door's shut, I'm not going back to India again.' And when we got back, this one says to me that we want another one. The second time we went to another clinic. Sunni said, 'I'm sure the clinic in Mumbai is not gonna take me again.' So off Sunni went to this other clinic and had three attempts there. I thought, 'Oh no, I can't do it again!' Dawn was going to turn two when the little one would be born and going back to India for all that time with a two-year-old! But yeah … Prince was born a week early. This time we were five days late. When we saw Prince, he was crying, it was in Gujarat, it was raining. It was totally different. When I saw Dawn she had this lovely smile and she was happy and this one was a cry baby. And he was wearing pink and I said, 'I thought it was a boy?' And they said, 'Yeah we'd run out of clothes.' Dawn loved it in India. She loved Prince. She thought he was like a little doll. We looked after both babies in a little village and there were power cuts for eight hours a day and it was a thirty minutes bus journey to the shop. Prince was a bit finicky at first. He wouldn't feed. Then because our visas were running out, me and Dawn had to come back. Then I got ill, I got abscesses on my legs so I had to come back home.

It took three extra weeks with Sunni running around until he could bring Prince home. I was ringing him up every day, asking, 'Did you feed him? Did you put his hat on?' People were like, 'Oh my god, why has your wife gone back?' But my visa was only for six months. Then they messed up and they had to go to the police station and bribe them with whiskey bottles to get out of the country. In India, money runs out fast. We lost count of what we spent in total but I'd say at least a quarter of a million. We used all our savings up and if you consider loss of earnings, I keep saying we could have had two houses by now. Two empty houses. When I see a little baby now, I do feel broody but I wouldn't do it again. I'd never do it again. It was a very long daunting journey.

Later, clicking through the website, I can still hear Rubi's voice, still feel Sunni's presence. I imagine Sunni hunched over his laptop, curtains closed, uploading images, typing letters furiously, desperate to tell their story.

The wedding photo. Both dressed in white, a formal pose in front of purple and green foliage. Sunni, tall, dark and handsome, towering over Rubi, her eyes hopeful and expectant.

Sunni wearing a grave expression, standing in front of a white tiled wall, holding a scan photo. The first time I have seen his face without a smile. Behind him is a shelf, stocked with bottles and a hook, hung with gowns.

A young-looking Rubi, wearing a shiny sari and armfuls of bangles, sitting on patterned, carpeted stairs, her chin resting in her hands, staring into the camera, looking for answers.

A tiny, newborn baby lying prone on a white hospital sheet, a tube taped to her nose, wires attached to her chest. Under the image, her date and time of birth is listed. Her birth weight 2.55 kg.

The text of emails, faxes, letters, contracts ... paperwork of all varieties, all in the public domain on the website Sunni created. Sunni and Rubi's story.

It all started with my legs

I am back on the sofa with Rubi. The weather has turned; it is raining outside. Today, she wears a thick woolly jumper and leggings. There is no sign of the bandage on her ankle. *Yeah, it's better at the moment. What do you wanna ask me today? Oh, Gosh, where Rubi started? You need warming up. Let me just call Sunni to get us some coffees. Sunni! He'll be down in a minute.*

So, okay. I was born on the other side of London in 1965. I have four sisters and a brother; the oldest sister died. She was 18 so we were quite young to understand what happened because of the age gap and everything. So it was like the normal Asian community, close family, all the kids play together, all the neighbours' doors were always open. I became very ill, quite young. I got rickets when I was aged 12, so I was in and out of hospital because I was also anaemic and they couldn't figure out why and was losing a lot of weight. It was because of the wheat. I had a gluten intolerance and they couldn't figure out what was happening. Then I became bulimic as well. So I was going through all that in high school but you still carry on. My dad used to have to carry me because I couldn't walk because of the rickets and because I was under three and a half stone. A ten-minute walk home would take me an hour. My brother and sisters used to laugh at me, saying, 'We can tell it was you coming down the street from the way you walk.'

The sound of footsteps overhead. Doors slamming. People milling about upstairs. Voices of adults and children.

As we got older, you know, my sisters were in nice dresses and with me, I had to stick with long skirts, you know because of my legs, so I went through that phase. The doctor said, 'Do you want surgery on your legs to straighten your bones out?' They kept saying 'yes' or 'no' because I was anaemic, the bones won't heal properly. 'We can't do this leg, this will have to wait a year.' So it was a lot of hurdles I went through and, erm, then I got rushed into hospital and I was in there for about six months when I was 16. Sunni, coffee!

Sunni calls out from upstairs and then appears with a tray, which he duly lays on the coffee table in front of us. He is quieter than last time and interrupts less, perhaps because he is not part of this story, not part of Rubi's childhood. Still, he lingers in the background, fussing, shuffling. I sense him waiting for his moment.

I don't know what triggered the bulimia but, you know, at high school all the girls were wearing nice little skirts and I was the odd one out cos of the rickets; none of the uniform would fit me. I used to say to my sister, 'Yeah, I'm going home for dinner.' It was a 20-minute walk back. And then I'd say, 'Yeah, I've eaten.' The body gets used to it.

Because obviously I didn't want to mingle with the girls in the playground because they were wearing nice skirts and I was wearing the trousers to hide my legs. I used to wear about four tee-shirts so no one could figure out how thin I was. So I used to go and sit in the library and say, 'Yeah, I went home for my lunch.' My sister was getting tall and pretty. All these girls picked on me for being small; I remember we had school plays and it was like because you're the miniature one you can be the baby in the pram and I was like, 'Okay, fine.' I used to have to use safety pins on my uniform because nothing would fit me and my blazer was literally falling off, then I got taken into hospital again. So I missed quite a lot of school.

Rubi is picking up speed now, speaking very quickly. I dare not interrupt to ask questions.

My eating problems started when I was about 12 and it got really bad when I was about 15. It got really bad. And that's when my sister found out as well. She said if I carried on, she would tell Mum and Dad. But I carried on discreetly. One day when everyone was out, I felt really ill but I needed to go to the bathroom so I slowly struggled to go to the bathroom, I sat on the toilet, all I saw was blood and I don't know what happened after that. I woke up in hospital three days later and the nurse said, 'You're lucky to be alive. Any later and you'd be six foot under.' And she brought this great big jug of milkshake and I just threw it across the wall. I'd been constantly making myself sick so I'd ruptured myself inside. That was what all the blood was. I came out of hospital and the doctors said, 'We're still going to have to monitor your weight.' I thought, 'Yeah, I know, I'm the smart one. I know what I'm going to have to do. I'll just have to drink water before the appointment before they weigh me.' I always think back and ask, 'What made me do it?' My sister always says, 'If you hadn't done that to yourself, you could have been tall like me.'

Rubi's head tilts to one side as she looks into the past. She's no longer in the room.

I finished college, I didn't want to go to uni, so I thought, 'Okay, get a job.' It's funny because my first job is what helped me get better. I don't know why on earth but being bulimic, I went for a catering job. So I went in there, and the lady interviewed me and said, 'I think you've got a lot of potential but I won't put you in the catering section. There is a market research department here and they need people.' So she offered me the job and I started the job a week later and there were about 24 women there. Oh my God, all different shapes and sizes and there was one woman, she was very young, and she said to me, 'You're not eating; why don't you come to the canteen?' She was the one that helped me. She said, 'We'll start off slowly.' So she took me to the canteen and I had a cheese roll, okay, I had that. And she said, 'You're not going to the bathroom to be sick. You're just going to sit here. You had a cheese roll and that's it, I'm not going to push you to have a slice of cake.'

The words gush out of her, tumbling over one another.

She was there for me and she goes to me, 'Why don't you put a bit of weight on? You'll look nice.' And my hair was very thin and brittle, so she said, 'Why don't you get your hair cut?' so I came home and Asian families are very strict about hair cutting but my sister cut my hair and my dad said, 'Why do you keep tying it up now? Leave it open.' So I carried on going to work and things started changing. I started to build my confidence and one of the girls said, 'Look we go to the pub on a Friday night.' And I was like, 'Pub? Oh my God!' But I started going to the pub. But then there were times when I would go, 'Oh my God, I am eating too much.' So I would go out at lunch time to make myself sick and I had put on weight and when I went to my sister's, my brother-in-law said, 'Oh you've put on weight since you've been working.' And that hit me, so I didn't visit my sister again for weeks after that. She had her own flat and everything and she kept saying, 'Why don't you come over?' but I went into my old way of constantly exercising and when she saw me again, she said, 'What have you done to yourself?' I said, 'Yes, I heard that day I'd put on a lot of weight.'

Her face is expressionless as she forces the words out, as though trying to purge herself.

My parents used to say, 'Do you want to get married?' and I'd say, 'No, no, no.' You know, I worked hard so they let me get on with it. I used to go to night classes. My sisters got married and then they said, 'It's time to get married.' And I said, 'Oh, do I have to?' My mum said, 'Okay, there's a couple of people asking.' And I said, 'I don't mind if the guy's ideal.' But meanwhile, I met Sunni as a pen pal out of the newspaper. I said to my mum, 'Look, I'm not doing anything wrong, I'm independent and if it's meant to be, it's meant to be.' But I had my heart set on moving to India to teach children English. My parents were happy with that. In the meantime, I was writing to pen pals. I'd get the paper every Friday night and read it. People looking for friends. You'd get the odd one, you know, when you meet a few you can tell if they're not genuine.

Out, out it all comes. Rushing out.

I'd booked to go to Canada on holiday and before I went, I got a letter from Sunni and he asked to meet up so when I came back from Canada, I met him. He sent his mates to have a look where I worked but they saw the wrong girl and told him I was fat with a tight perm. He wrote to me saying, 'Look, you're not my ideal girl but we can meet up.' So I said, 'Okay.' I was happy with that because I was going to India to teach children anyway. So he started popping down, we met up a few times and one day, my sister said, 'You can't go to work today because Sunni's coming down.' And he proposed to me. Within four months, we were engaged. I had to be approved by all the aunts; I was taken to all the houses and we met all the family on both sides. Seven months later was the registry office wedding. Then it was just a normal married couple enjoying life, then the questions started, 'Oh why aren't you having a baby?' Then it all started.

An elderly gentleman comes down the stairs and nods hello. Rubi pauses for a moment to speak to her father-in-law. He says he is going to the shop and asks if she wants anything. *Lemon and ginger please, Dad.*

Sorry. Yeah, so I was still underweight when I got married; I was only five and a half stone. I told Sunni about it all, yeah, he was aware of it. The hospital said my infertility was unexplained but I think my bulimia had a lot to do with it as it messes with your hormones. I think all my insides are shrunk and damaged. I didn't have any periods until I was 22 and then they were erratic, so I think that was part of it. My friend's daughter is going through anorexia and I say to her, 'Look at what it's done to me. Tell her not to put herself through all that.' I think I've been through a lot. After the fourth attempt at IVF, I broke down and said, 'I can't do it anymore. I can't carry on.' After that, I started making myself sick again. It started again.

I am distracted by the sound of Sunni chatting to his father. They walk through the sitting room and up the stairs. Sunni is back downstairs within minutes, back on his chair in the man cave, his legs swinging in an out of view.

When my sister-in-law had her first child, she didn't know how to change nappies or breast feed. She wouldn't bond with her. When we came back from India, the baby was seven months old, and she used to sleep in with us, we used to bottle feed her. So, I'd wake up in the middle of the night with the baby and for my mother-in-law, then I'd get up in the morning and go to work on two hours sleep. She got pregnant with her second baby when the first was three months old. She threw it in my face. The baby was very close to us; if she couldn't see us, she'd scream the house down. It went on for over two years. Then when mum passed away, the family came and said to my sister-in-law, 'You need to take your daughter and put her in your bed.' They said to me, 'You need to break away. It's her daughter; she's got to bond with her.' But I was getting attached so it was very hard. I could hear her screaming through the wall. She didn't want to go with them. She got sick. She wanted us. She's 11 now. Then the other girl was born.

I am waiting for Sunni to interrupt; this is his sister that Rubi is talking about. I picture Rubi sitting upright in bed, listening to the baby's screams, Sunni's hand on her back, his low voice telling her to go back to sleep. He stands up and sits down again. Rubi carries on.

My sister-in-law tells them not to talk to me. She doesn't accept my kids either. She doesn't agree with surrogacy. We had a big argument this weekend at a family party; two nasty comments were made about my kids and I walked out. My niece came up and gave me a great big hug and said, 'I still love you. I don't believe what Mummy's saying but she told me not to come to you.' I don't care where my kids came from; I brought them up; I love them and they love me. I am their mum. Sometimes in the Asian community, it happens. Dawn was a bit upset. I said, 'As long as you've got Mummy and Daddy by you, don't worry about what the world says.'

Rubi speaks very loudly, with an eye in Sunni's direction.

They have disowned me because I couldn't have children. So what? There's no shame in it. One of my proudest moments was when I took Prince to get weighed for the first time and he'd actually put on weight. I was so pleased. The doctor said I was a typical Punjabi mum! And I am a typical Punjabi mum; I just did it differently. So what? I tell the kids, 'Mummy was too small, I couldn't carry a child.' Why lie about it? Some people asked my sister-in-law if she would have a child for us. She said, 'No, I can't give my baby away.' When she had her second child, Mum said to her, 'Let them have your first daughter to bring her up.' But she said, 'No.' But she was happy to let her sister back home in India have one of her children, her sister who couldn't have children. So she did it for her but not us. Not Sunni and me. There's a family sleepover next weekend but we're not going. I said to Dawn, 'I know they're cousins but we can't go.'

Rubi's father-in-law drifts back into the room. He has not yet been to the shops. *Dad! You wanna just go and eat? Dad, they've just been to the park. Okay I'll see you later.* There is something of a commotion at the back of the room. Several people coming and going from different doors. Sunni moves into view and prompts Rubi to tell me about taking the children back to India.

So yeah ... We took both the children to India to explain about their roots. We told Dawn how she was born, we took her to visit the clinic, and she met the doctor. We took Prince to Gujarat to the clinic. At the clinic, they said, 'Oh, the surrogate that carried Prince in this clinic is in the area and she wants to see Prince.' We said, 'Oh, okay, no harm in it, no hard feelings, we don't mind.' The surrogate came over to the hotel and we had afternoon tea. Oh my God, when she walked in with her daughter, straight away, Prince's face just lit up and he kept hiding behind me and you know, he felt that, and she gave him a hug and said he was cute and everything and she said to the little girl that she carried Prince and I said to her, 'It's okay, you can call him your brother and everything.' The little girl gave him a pink teddy; he still has that pink teddy. We gave them a bit of money and everything. But Prince kept hiding; there was something there. In a strange way, we knew as soon as we went to Gujarat that he felt something there and when we took him to the hospital, we sensed it and the hotel we stayed at, we had the same room that we stayed in when he was a baby. I think he had a memory of it. Even when the surrogate walked in, Prince's face! I think he knew. Dawn's surrogate, she worked in a bank, didn't she, Sunni?

He's back in from the cold, moving towards us smiling.

Oh, a call centre. Yeah, once she had her money, she was long gone. I don't think there'll be any contact. They haven't got our contact details but I don't think she'd want to. They're getting on with their own lives; they do it for their own reasons. Okay, they get the money, the equivalent of about ten years' salary. It's life changing for them. So they're not gonna think, I want the baby. They think, okay, I've helped someone who couldn't have a baby and now I can help my own family with this money. They use egg donors so they're not giving up their own baby. Often the baby's a different colour from them so they wouldn't want to take it back to their village anyway. People talk about exploitation but I don't think of it like that. In India, once the surrogate falls pregnant, she gets taken to the surrogacy home and gets well looked after for nine months and she learns a new skill, needlework or whatever so when she's finished, she goes out and she can do better things.

Rubi explains how surrogacy has been banned in India unless you are an Indian national; Sunni clarifies that the court has ruled but there will be an appeal. They unite. Talk as one.

All different nationalities and ethnicities were going to India; we knew people from America, Japan, Canada. As long as they had a baby at the end of it, they don't mind. One English couple we knew, they had a beautiful little baby. They brought her here for Prince's first birthday party, didn't they, Sunni? She walked in, blonde hair, blue eyes; you would never know she was from an Asian egg donor. British can't go there now. They say it's because of the exploitation of surrogates but wealthy Indian nationals can still use the same surrogates so how come that's not exploitation? There's a lot of people here at the moment, thinking, 'What do we do, where do we go?'

Sunni nods and lets Rubi lead.

I felt okay meeting Prince's surrogate, you know. I've always told them, 'Mummy's been ill and Mummy couldn't carry so we got two special ladies; we helped them with their children and to buy a house and they carried you for us.' They both had egg donors too, two different surrogates and two different egg donors. The day they were doing the egg retrieval, Sunni got to see the egg donors because he was doing the sperm on the same day, you know. I never saw them. I was in the UK. But Sunni saw them all. In total, with all the surrogates and all the egg donors we went through, there were, what was it Sunni?

He cracks jokes. Calls them Rubi One, Rubi Two, Rubi Three …

Yeah, about 15 women. A lot of people don't understand. You know, my niece told Dawn I wasn't her real mum cos that's what my sister-in-law told her. We don't get on. They told her, 'Your real mum's in India.' I goes, 'Who feeds you? Who clothes you? Who looks after you and who gives you the kisses and hugs?' She said, 'You do.' I said,' I've always told you mummy couldn't carry you so we had a special lady who carried you, we gave her the money and when you were born, she gave you to us to keep and then she was gone so I'm your real mum.' So now, I keep telling her, 'Whatever anyone says, I'm your real mum.'

Rubi ignores the knock on the door. She carries on talking as Sunni greets the visitors. She seems oblivious to the comings and goings, determined to finish her story. I sense we are coming to the end, one way or another.

You know, Dawn's always asking me, 'Mummy tell me about when I was little.' I tell her about the hospital and she says, 'Did you see the special lady?' She asks what she looked like. I say, 'No, I never saw the lady.' My friends say, 'Oh you're so brave telling them. What if when they turn 18, they go and look for them?' I say, 'What 18? What they gonna look for? She just carried them.' We haven't gone into anything about egg donors. We don't need to tell them that. We just need to tell them, 'A special lady carried you.' They can see the surrogacy agreement and it's got the name of the lady on it. That's it. It would be too much for them to think about the egg donor, as well. Plus the donor was anonymous so we don't have a name or anything.

I always say to them, 'Say "thank you" every night.'

A good life

They've been married for seven years now, why aren't they having children?
I just closed the curtains and we just wanted to die.
Send me five thousand pounds and I'll help you.
She wanted a good life in India.
Why don't you get married again to someone who can have kids?
I started making myself sick again.
Can you give us a scan, somebody else's scan?

Wisdom

This womb is wizened not wise.
It holds no ancient intuition.
Knows nothing of what it was made for.

This body deceives.
The curves are an illusion.
An allusion to woman. Still he believes.

This woman doesn't function.
She's not fit for purpose, she's worthless.
How long until he trades her in for a working model?

This marriage is empty.
The space between them widens every month
she doesn't conceive. They look into the abyss

together.
Hang on.
This family can still happen.

The beds in my head

I line up the beds in my head,
the beds of the surrogates sleeping in the dorms, their bellies swelling.

I line up the beds in my head,
the beds of the babies born to the sisters and cousins and aunties and friends.

I line up the beds in my head,
the beds of the hospitals and hotel rooms I stayed in along the way.

I line up the beds in my head,
the beds of the women who've had my husband's sperm inside them.

I line up the beds in my head,
the beds in my childhood dolls house, where miniature people live happily ever after.

I line up the beds in my head,
and count them one by one, with my eyes wide open.

In her belly

When you were in her belly,
I thought, at least you'll look like me,
It made me feel a little better knowing that.
Just a little better, you see?

When you were in her belly,
I told myself you were coming home with me.
I might not be carrying you now,
I thought, but I knew I soon would be.

When you were in her belly,
I often found it hard to breathe.
There was a pain in my chest just under
my heart above the space where you should be.

When you left her belly
and flew through the universe to me,
your dazzling wings made the earth spin
now mine for eternity.

Everything can be fixed

As soon as it drops from my hands,
my heart goes into freefall,
I cannot save it as it smashes on the kitchen floor.
The line runs all the way round its girth,
cracking it wide open.

'It's okay, it's okay,' I say as my daughter
rushes in, eyes wide like the saucers
that go with the teacups that go with the teapot
that's lying there broken, the teapot she gave me
for Mother's Day, the teapot she hand painted

just for me.
'It's okay, it's okay. It can be fixed.'
And we walk hand in hand to the corner store
to buy super glue, trembling as we go,
daring not to think the unthinkable.

Back in the house,
my daughter and I sit and stare
as I gently run the glue round the wound, smiling
at her all the time, pressing it back together.
'It's okay, it's okay.'

She watches as I pour hot water into it,
careful not to reach the break line.
'See? It's okay.' She doesn't move.
'You have to pour,' she says, 'to be sure.'
We hold our breath

as we look, waiting to see if it leaks,
if the crack cries. Exhaling,

> she runs out to play. Only then do I
> let myself fill it past the line
> anticipating its tears,
> the ooze from its wound.
> But it doesn't cry.
> The tears are all mine.
> It's a miracle, this Mother's Day present,
> an everyday miracle.

The poems "A Good Life", "Wisdom", "The Beds in My Head", "In Her Belly", "Everything Can Be Fixed" were first published on the author's website at: https://shantaeverington.wordpress.com.

For further information on surrogacy, please consult the second two references below.

Reference list

Everington, S. (2022) '"A Good Life", "Wisdom", "The Beds in My Head", "In Her Belly", "Everything Can Be Fixed"' [Online]. Available at: https://shantaeverington.wordpress.com (Accessed 14 November 2022).

GOV.UK (2022) 'Guidance: Surrogacy Overseas' [Online]. Available at: https://www.gov.uk/government/publications/surrogacy-overseas/surrogacy-overseas (Accessed 10 November 2022).

Surrogacy UK (n.d.) 'About Us' [Online]. Available at: https://surrogacyuk.org/aboutus/ (Accessed 3 November 2022).

7
ROBIN'S STORY

Drama queen

Robin opens the car door, pulling a face at the passenger seat, which is covered in dog hair. *Hello, hello. Sorry about the mess and sorry I took so long to get back to you yesterday too. I didn't stop till really late.* She continues chatting as I climb inside. *I've got three jobs – I'm a single mum so I have to pay the bills – I work as a hypnotherapist, a dog walker, and now for four afternoons a week, I'm working in a hippy shop that sells crystals and wonderful stuff like that. It's my ideal job!* We drive past street upon street of unremarkable looking semis until we end up parked outside Robin's house. Inside, an engraved wooden plaque in the hall reminds visitors to 'Enjoy the little things in life because one day you will look back and realise they were big.' The cosy living room is furnished with a mishmash of furniture draped in soft fabrics. I sit on the sofa opposite Robin, who perches next to a wooden sculpture of a pregnant woman with a feather in her hair. Shelves display a plethora of trinkets and pictures. A striking photograph of four girls with bobbed brown hair looking over the back of the sofa catches my eye. Two of the girls look identical, the other two very similar; rosy cheeked and laughing. Energy leaps from the picture.

So how did I end up becoming a surrogate? I suppose it was my mum who first planted the idea in my mind. A lot of people are told when they're teenagers, when their menstrual cycles don't come in evenly, a lot of people are told you might not conceive because you're not ovulating. So my mum, being a drama queen, took me to the doctors at 14 saying she's not regular, her period might be every two weeks, it might be four weeks. Now I know that that's quite normal when your hormones are out of balance. I know that now but I didn't know it then, so I was put on the pill to supposedly regulate my cycle, told I might not have children, told I was not ovulating. All I ever wanted was a monkey, you know, like Michael Jackson and Bubbles, so that didn't really bother me. But I started to think as I got a bit

DOI: 10.4324/9781003290179-9

older and got involved in my first relationship. I remember when I was 17 thinking, 'Yeah, I would like a family one day and what if I can't?' My mum had said, 'Don't worry. I'd always carry for you if you couldn't.' And it kind of planted a seed. I thought, 'Oh. I didn't realise that was ever an option.'

Robin speaks calmly but urgently; her voice has a hypnotic quality. The quiet is interrupted by the sound of a dog whining; perhaps it's the owner of the hair that now decorates my black trousers, although I haven't seen any dogs since we arrived. Robin pauses, as though considering getting up but instead carries on talking.

You know, before I became a surrogate, I had pondered, what's the motive for being a surrogate? Are they all attention-seeking people or weird people or baby making machines or … I was a bit concerned about what surrogates were like and if I wanted to be associated with that. And actually when I met surrogates at events, when I was researching the process, they were just really normal – although there were a handful of attention seeking people that I thought were doing it for the wrong reasons – but mostly normal, people. Nice. So it wasn't such a scary thing.

Interviewing Robin is quite unlike any of my experiences of interviewing other women for this book. She sits and delivers her story from beginning to end in one three-hour stint, over peppermint tea and macaroons. When she is finished, she leans back in her chair, spent, and I know I won't get any more out of her. There will be no going back for two, three or even four meetings, building up the trust, eking a little more of the story out at each turn. She is totally in control of the process; I do little more than the Dictaphone that sits between us on the coffee table. Her story is well rehearsed, ready to perform. And what a story it is.

The farm and the full moon

Let's fast forward to being 24 with my then husband, now ex-husband. We decided to start a family and I did not expect it to happen first time. I came off the pill, had two months off, and said, 'Right, let's try for a baby.' And it worked. Then when I had my second baby, it worked again. Then there was a bit of time. I wanted to have a third baby. I always knew I'd have four and after my second was born, I was ready to go straight away. I wanted a big family and I wanted it now. And he said 'no,' and it was the most devastating blow. We'd discussed it all those years before when we talked about having a family. I'd said, 'Look, I'm from a big family and I'd love a big family.' And he was like, 'Okay.' And I said, 'Four is a really good number. I'd like to have an even number of children, I think. Two doesn't seem enough. I want four.' So I was quite blasé about it at the time, not even knowing whether I'd even be able to conceive. But after I'd had two, I knew I'd have four. It took me two years to convince him to go for a third, and one night he agreed. Oh, it was the most magical night ever. We lived in a farmhouse on top of a hill and it overlooked a whole load of fells and it was just amazing.

The dog has simmered down, but Robin's attention is diverted by her phone bleeping. She picks it up off the arm of the chair.

It's probably the maths tutor. We homeschool. I'll have a little look just in case I have to get it but I won't reply if I don't have to. No it's fine. So, yeah, he agreed we'll have one more but on the condition that it's just one more. I knew I wanted four. I knew I'd have four. So one night, there was a full moon, an absolutely massive full moon, curtains open. At that point, we didn't really have much of an intimate life and sex was just about keeping him satisfied for another week, or two or three maybe if I was lucky; I wasn't really that interested. But that was a great night. A really good night.

When I play back the tape, I can hear the smile in her voice.

The curtains were open and the full moon was blasting in. And the next morning, he said, 'I don't know what came over me. I don't want any more. I don't know why I agreed last night.' But I knew already that something had changed. There was something chemically different with my body and it was too late. And the embryo split and became twins. So I got my four! And all of his friends used to call me Mrs T and they all used to say, 'What Mrs T wants, Mrs T gets.' But it's not something you can really make happen unless it's meant to be.

The room is quiet now but something about the stillness distracts me. My attention is drawn to the empty green chair between us. With its high, rigid back, it looks out of place next to the squidgy, battered sofas. I can't imagine her children sitting on that chair. It's not a snuggly place. It looks lonely.

Actually, let's back track ever so slightly in the story to the day we moved into the farmhouse. There was a particular person who was pivotal in my story and he's sort of slotting in the middle somewhere. There were several hours before the removals van arrived and we didn't have the keys yet and we had my eldest daughter, Sky, she had just turned one. And the guy next door came out and he became one of my best friends. I got to know Ian when he broke his thigh bone in three places and ended up staying at home; they pinned it and put a full body cast on. So his wife Jenni – I didn't get to know Jenni quite as much – she'd set him up on a morning and his mother-in-law would go in at one point in the day and I would go in at one point and the neighbour at the other side would go in. So we had a rota of Jenni, mother-in-law, me, neighbour, then Jenni was back from work. So we did that for about eight weeks and in that time I got to know him really well, we became really good friends. He was a fireman, a football coach and a taxi driver. One day he asked, did I want to have my tarot cards read. So I said, 'Okay yeah.' And he said, 'Ah, you're going to have another baby in the next 12 months.' At that point, I just had one baby. Sky was born in December and I really wanted a spring baby next so I didn't have to have those long dark nights. I told him I wanted a spring baby and he said, 'You can't just plan for things like that.' And, I was so... even though I'd previously been through not knowing if I could have children, I'd forgotten all that. As soon as I had my baby, I was like, 'Great, it worked. I can do this!'

The sound of dogs barking starts up again. This time, more than one dog. It gets a bit difficult to concentrate. Robin fidgets in her chair. I try to block out the sound.

I had no idea at that point that he and Jenni had been trying for a baby for 11 years. So what I said was a really cutting remark. I had no idea; I was so lost in my own little bubble. And as it happened, after all those years, they did fall pregnant at the same time that I fell pregnant but they lost it, and Jenni died a couple of years later. My experiences then changed my views about a lot of things. They didn't know at that time that Jenni had cancer. But the issue was all his, apparently because his sperm. Well he had pretty much a zero-sperm count and the odd one that they saw was swimming in circles, so the mobility and the morphology of the sperm was really poor. So that was a really pivotal point because they told me at 11 weeks that Jenni had fallen pregnant and they'd lost it. And they told me that when I was like, 'Jenni! Ian! Guess what? I'm pregnant!' and they'd just got the news. Ian was an incredible support while I was pregnant because I was really sick and he'd walk my dog and take Sky with him. He'd knock on the door and say, 'Does Sky want to come and wash the car with me?' So Ian and Jenni had to watch my pregnancy go on whilst they were going through, 'Why hasn't it happened? And what is that being flagged up here?' and then they got the cancer diagnosis.

The dogs get louder and louder. My head starts to hurt.

Sorry about the dogs. In the time when Jenni was going through this journey, they both trained in hypnotherapy because that helped Jenni to calm and prepare herself for the next step. Because, what happened if things weren't to heal? And Reiki. So they were both trained in Reiki so they used that because it made a big difference to them. So I then started training in these methods myself, so I'd do swaps with Ian and just try and help support him through that. Jenni died when I was about seven months pregnant, and I actually didn't go to the funeral because I didn't think Ian needed my massive bump shoving in his face whilst he was going through all that grief. So I kind of did the supporting from afar and told him I was there. And, I mean, we've still got our friendship now from afar.

Robin stands up as the dogs reach a crescendo.

I've just figured out why the dogs are barking so much because the kitchen window's open. Erm, yeah I might close it. It might help them quieten down a bit.

The air changes when she leaves the room. I hear Robin talking to the dogs, the clunk of a window closing, the patter of feet. I look again at the pea-green chair, sensing it has a story or two of its own to tell. And she's back.

To cut his story short, and he won't mind me sharing his story, but about ten months after Jenni passed away, he got together with one of his first loves from when he was at school. She was in the middle of divorce, had three children already and one night and one night only resulted in a positive pregnancy test. And he was like, 'But it can't be. We tried for years. It was all to do with my sperm.' When the baby was born, you could see it was definitely his. I think they did do a DNA test as well because he was like, 'No, I can't, it can't be right.' And then they subsequently had a second one. As to how and why is open to lots of different potential. A different person? He says he thinks it's to do with all the healing that was done while he was doing everything that he was doing with Jenni. And that Jenni sent the babies down. That's his viewpoint, he thinks Jenni is part of the journey, you know, he didn't have the babies with her but she's part of the journey. That's where his belief lies. And it led me to the belief that, wow, anything is possible.

So, fast forwarding a bit, I ended up where I was trained in hypnotherapy, neuro-linguistic programming, emotional freedom technique, all sorts of different types of mind–body practices. I was working with war veterans and people with all sorts of Post-Traumatic Stress Disorder (PTSD). Then, somehow, even though I wasn't going to, I ended up working with people with birth trauma, because they were displaying typical PTSD symptoms just as people who were coming through war had. And it's really hard to say that a man who has been blown up and shot by the Taliban and a woman with birth trauma are displaying the same sort of symptoms. You think, errr. But actually, for them, you know the shell shock of being in the hospital, and typical hospital births that go on nowadays when all control is taken away from the woman, forceful vaginal examinations are done and the baby is pulled out by one way or another and it's very traumatic. So I ended up working more with women with birth trauma and then I ended up getting a lot more people with secondary infertility, classically following birth trauma. And before I knew it, I was working with more and more people with fertility and issues to do with conceiving or being terrified when they are pregnant. So I ended up working with people whose babies had died. I work from home so that chair is the client chair.

She nods at the empty green chair. Green for growth, freshness and fertility. Green for jealousy. Green for grief.

To listen to women just heartbroken because all they want is that baby, it got me thinking of how I felt when I already had two and I was heartbroken because I wanted that third and I wasn't allowed it. And I just couldn't compare how I felt to these women who didn't even have any babies, that heartache, that instinct that is just so painful. I just kept thinking I can do so much to help women, whether it's to ease off stress, you know whatever it is, even if they are going through IVF, you know, walking that path alongside the women going through IVF but what if a woman can't do that? So a woman who's had breast cancer can't risk the oestrogen rise in the body or a woman who's born without a womb. There are loads of women born without a womb; it's more common than we realise. So no amount of trying or no amount of IVF is ever going to turn into an embryo to implant into a womb if there's nothing. So there's no hope without an extra person. So it got me thinking about people like that. And gay dads too. I pondered over it for ages and then I spoke to my daughters about it to see how they felt about me becoming a surrogate. That picture there is the age they were when I decided I wanted to do this.

Robin points to the picture that caught my eye when we first walked into the room: her daughters hanging over the back of the sofa, giggling.

The photographer who was taking the picture said, 'Make them laugh.' So I bent over and wiggled my bottom. So they're laughing at me wiggling my bottom. So that was the age they were when I decided that I wanted to be a surrogate. Currently, Sky is about to turn 16, Rain's 13 and Willow and Ivy are 10. So they were 6-year-old twins, that makes Rain 9 and Sky about 11, I think. When I spoke to them about it, their responses were just so classically them. I said to them, 'I'm thinking about helping a mum who can't carry her own baby by carrying her baby for her until it's born and then the baby goes back to mum.' And then Sky said, 'Oh yeah, that's a good idea. Great.' She really is very gung-ho, do now, and reap the consequences later. She's getting a bit better now with age. Then Rain was like, 'Well no because what if it looks like me? What if it's a boy?' Because I've got four daughters. 'What if ...? What if ...? What if ...?' And she was like, 'No, I definitely don't want it to happen. Absolutely not.' I thought I can't do this if everybody's not on board. It has to be everybody. Willow and Ivy were like, 'Yeah, okay, can I go and play now?' and disappeared.

Robin picks up the packet of biscuits from the coffee table between us.

Do you want one? Chocolate macaroon. You're welcome. I was single at that time. I separated from my husband when Willow and Ivy were one and a half. I've had relationships in between but never for any prolonged period. My priority is the children. And you know, when I get involved with people, it's awkward. I've got to work, I've got to pay the bills, I've got to look after the children, I've got to have enough energy. If I factor in another person, maybe it would ease the load a bit but you know, it takes up time and it takes up energy. When they were younger I thought it would be easier to date when they got a bit older but actually as they've got older, it's got more difficult. Having four daughters, two in their teens, it doesn't feel like the right time for dating because I feel they are more vulnerable. I date men or women, it depends on the person, not the gender and for some reason, it feels so much safer dating women. I've gone on to dating sites before and there are so many men in their forties who are looking for women aged 18–45 and you know, 18 is only 2 years older than my eldest daughter so alarm bells are ringing. I'm just too, I just feel uneasy about it. So there was no partner involved to discuss my surrogacy plans with. It made it easier in one respect but there was no-one else around to support me through the pregnancy. So I asked Rain if she would not make up her mind fully until she had met some people who'd been through surrogacy. I asked her to come to a surrogacy conference with me.

Yes, no, maybe

Nine-year-old Rain plays with her loom bands in the car on the way down to the conference, making rainbow-coloured bracelet after rainbow-coloured bracelet. She slips them on and off of her wrists, then starts on her ankles. She thinks about when her mum was pregnant with the twins and imagines how it would have been if they belonged to someone else. Mum said it was up to her. If she says no, Mum won't have a baby for another family. She says the word inside her head, quietly then loudly, 'n-n-no', 'NOOOOO!' Then she thinks about the word, 'Yes', the sound of it, the hiss of it. She likes it when Mum says 'yes' to her and not no. 'Yes' you can have an ice-cream. 'Yes' you can watch television. 'Yes' you can have a friend for a sleepover. 'No' you can't have an ice-cream. 'No' you can't watch television. 'No' you can't have a friend for a sleepover. Yes. No. YES. NO. Y-yes. N-no. Yessssss! Noooooo!

'Ta da! Here we are!' Mum turns off the engine as they park up outside the hotel. It looks like a castle. 'What do you think?'

Rain opens the door and steps out into the car park, boots crunching on gravel, shielding her eyes from the sun as she gives the place the once over. Yes. 'It looks posh. Will they have those little bottles of shower gel and shampoo like that other hotel?'

Mum laughs. 'Probably.'

The car park is busy with people arriving for the conference. Rain breathes in exhaust fumes. No.

'Is that a surrogate baby?' asks Rain, pointing to a car seat being lifted out of a car a few metres away by a pale woman with shiny black hair and a denim jacket.

'Maybe.' Mum pulls their rucksacks off the back seat and slams the door shut, holding out her hand for Rain. Maybe. Yes. No. Maybe. Yes. No. Maybe.

'It's been a long drive, hasn't it? Are you thirsty?'

Rain shrugs, still holding her mum's hand, her bobbed hair swishing around her thin neck. Yes. No. Maybe.

'Come on. Let's go in and get checked in and then we can get a drink.'

'Ok-aaay.' Rain walks slowly through the reception, dragging her trainers along the floor. Her head whips this way and that as she stands waiting for her mum to get their room key. 'Mum, did you see those twins? They …'

'Robin!' A woman with greying hair and a purple silk scarf rushes towards them. 'So glad you made it. And this must be Rain.'

Rain looks at the old lady and bites her lip. Her stomach lurches as Cynthia introduces them to people.

'This is Sara and Pete. They've just joined the association as Intended Parents. And this is Yasmin and Joe, who have a wonderful new baby, Sampson, through surrogacy.'

Everyone fusses over Sampson, who is cooing in his cream-coloured carrycot.

'I saw you in the car park,' says Rain, reaching out to touch Sampson's foot.

'What would you like to drink?' asks Cynthia. 'Some orange juice, dear?'

Rain looks at her mum. Yes. No. Maybe.

'Maybe a little glass of wine,' replies her mum, screwing up her nose with a grin, as Cynthia flounces off, her scarf flowing behind her.

Rain is allowed crisps with her juice. Yes. She chats to Sara about being home-schooled, having twin sisters and how she loves canoeing. Pete tells Christmas cracker jokes. Her mum is laughing as though they are the funniest jokes she's ever heard.

Rain rolls her eyes. 'You're getting a bit loud now, aren't you, Mum?'

The next morning, they make their way into the conference hall, joining the queue of people filing into row upon row of grey plastic chairs. Rain hiccoughs from bolting her cornflakes down too quickly at breakfast, after they woke up late. Her yellow Alice band is on at an angle, the back of her hair matted. She takes a deep breath. Rain's head moves from side to side as she scans the room. She spots the couple they chatted to last night, the back of Sara's blonde head leaning next to Pete's messy red hair.

'Mum, look. Shall we sit with them?' Yes.

They creep through the crowds to the two empty chairs next to Pete. A panel of people sit at the front of the hall on a makeshift stage, their chairs arranged in a horseshoe shape. One of them, a boy with a black baseball cap and a Star Wars tee-shirt, bends down to pick up a bottle of water. The teenager, called Ed, tells the audience he's always known that he was not carried in his mum's tummy. Yasmin and Joe share their story of finally welcoming Sampson into their lives after years of trying and fertility treatments. Mum has explained things like this to Rain. Rain knows that Mum helps people who have lost babies. People come and sit in the green chair and give Mum money. Marianne, a woman with a complicated looking hairstyle, who has acted as a surrogate four times, will explain why she has babies for other people. Rain imagines a baby in Mum's tummy, a baby that doesn't look like her, that belongs to someone else. No.

Yes. No. Maybe.

Rain sits quietly and listens to people talking on the stage. She listens to Mum talking to Pete and Sara. There is a lot of talking. She is getting tired and wants to lie down or watch television. She wants an ice-cream. She wonders what her sisters are doing. Mum is nodding with a serious look on her face. Pete isn't making jokes now. Rain hears him saying he's worried he'll never be a dad. He sees Rain looking at him and smiles. It's a sad smile. The kind you do when you want to make someone else feel better, she thinks.

When it's time to head home, Sara hugs Rain goodbye. They get in the car and set off on the three-and-a-half hour journey home. Mum turns the radio on quietly.

'What did you think?'

Yes. No. Maybe.

Rain picks at a scab on her elbow, then pats her knees. She's silent for a moment. The sound of the radio fizzes between them. Someone talking about the chance to win ten grand prize money in a new phone-in competition. Yes. Rain pulls her Alice band off and turns it over in her hands. 'I know you're gonna do it. They're the ones.'

Half a kiss

When I started to research surrogacy, I came across organisations that looked good and organisations that I wouldn't touch with a barge pole. The organisation I chose is based on the principles of friendship first. How it works is, when you meet people you like, you phone up the support worker and tell them you'd like to get to know the people. The getting to know stage is three months and in that time, you are expected to meet up at least once a month, communicate at least once a week. Sometimes you can be at opposite ends of the country so it can be quite hard work but you need to get to know each other and preferences. For example, what if the baby had Down Syndrome? From my perspective, there was absolutely no way I would consider having a termination. If the baby they got happened to have a quirk or interesting fact about them, then that's what they're meant to have, that's what's chosen to come into their lives. That's how I see it. So I couldn't be a surrogate for someone who wanted so-called perfection because there is no perfection. We're all different and that's how it's meant to be. So, yeah, things like that and I'm very much of the home birth viewpoint. Yeah, so we spent that time getting to know each other. When I met up with Sara and Pete again, it was kind of like going on a first date. It's really weird. It's like, 'What if they don't like me or I don't like them?' It's just really odd. But as soon as we got together it was fine.

Robin pulls a white iPad out from behind the sofa. I lean forwards in anticipation.

Do you want to see them?

She fires up the iPad, tapping and swiping, her expression changing every few seconds, the corners of her mouth twitching, eyebrows rising and lowering.

This is Sara and Pete. I peer at the image on the screen of Robin standing in between a couple, their arms draped around one another's' shoulders, smiling at the camera. The woman is exactly the same height as Robin, with blonde shoulder-length hair, wearing a nondescript navy tee-shirt and dark jeans; the man towers over them, in a bold striped tee-shirt, with ginger hair and a ruddy complexion. *I set up a secret Facebook group to chart my surrogacy journey. I can add you if you'd like.*

They came to our house – I lived in a different house at the time – and I introduced them to my other children. Then we met up again without the children to talk a bit more and then we met up with the children a lot. Sara had 13 embryos frozen, this big batch of embryos created at the same time I feel pregnant with my twins. Everything was planned. So it had to be host surrogacy for me. Do you know the difference between host surrogacy and straight surrogacy? So, yeah, not using my egg. I know other surrogates who are straight surrogates and they go into it with the viewpoint that their egg is flushed down the toilet each month. I couldn't bear the thought of artificial insemination, just putting someone's sperm up there. The whole thought of it disgusts me. Plus I would find it hard if the baby was genetically mine. The bond is with the parents not the baby, but at the same time, if the baby looks like you, it must be hard, especially if you have children and the baby is their genetic sibling. So we started off with 13 embryos that Sara and Pete created with her egg and his sperm, when she was 24. At that point, the embryos had been frozen for seven or eight years; it's a long time. Sara had spent all these years worrying: what if the embryos never survive when they are defrosted? Then it's game over. Sara had medical problems, and she had to have a kidney transplant after the eggs had been taken, so she was on auto-immune medication and she wouldn't really be able to have any more eggs taken.

She flicks through post after post of lighted candles – tealights, lanterns, melting red wax, stars and moons – symbols of love and support from Facebook friends.

When Brexit was going on, I was grumbling to the girls and saying, 'There's no hope.' I'm normally so positive. Willow said to me, 'Think about what you are saying. Think about what you would say to us. Hope isn't a thing you hold in your hands; hope is a belief. You've always got hope if you want to have hope.' I considered myself told. Hope is everything. So while her embryos were stored, Sara had hope.

There are photos of mince pies and beaded bracelets, letters and cards, positive affirmations and Facebook mottos. Words of friendship, courage and strength on candy coloured backgrounds. An abundance of gifts.

When we were going through the IVF, I didn't fit the protocol of what the doctors thought was good because I had a short menstrual cycle and they said, 'We'll have to regulate your cycle because you'll never fall pregnant with that cycle.' I know, I know. I'd had four children. So I said, 'Let's try it a natural cycle first and if it doesn't work, then we will try it your way.' So that first treatment day, they said they would defrost three embryos. Sara called them Itsy, Bitsy and Ditsy. And then she texted me to say that only one survived the defrosting process. So they said to Sara, they were going to take another two out of storage. So she said, 'Okay, they're the professionals; they must know what they are doing.' But the extra two didn't make it, so of the five defrosted, there was just little Ditsy left fighting. And you know, out of those original 13 embryos, that's 5 gone, that's a big chunk gone in one go, taking it down to 7.

Another photo of Robin standing in between Sara and Pete; this time they all wear medical gowns, blue caps covering their hair, a clinical setting visible in the background. I stare into their faces, trying to imagine what they are feeling. But I can't see beyond the masks.

The one drug I took was Follicle Stimulating Hormone (FSH) because we had to align my cycle exactly with the embryo's age, to ensure the right environment in the womb, so it involved endless trips back and forth to the clinic. At eight o'clock in the morning, I had to take the children where they had to go, then go to the clinic. It was really hard work. I did six cycles. Yeah. I continued to work all the way through. So that first trip, I had the FSH injection but I had a really yucky reaction, but we had this one embryo that had survived out of the five that had been defrosted so they said we might as well do it. So they put it in me but it didn't work. It was just so devastating. I had to phone Sara to tell her that my period arrived. And we'd lost five of the embryos. She kept saying, 'We've only had one go. It'll be third time lucky, I'm sure it will.' She just kept putting her hope somewhere a bit more distant. She felt a bit safer. She didn't dare allow herself to think it could work. So she parked her hopes over there.

As Robin flicks through a montage of photos, my eyes settle on a selfie taken in a mirror. She wears a black bra top and a patterned wraparound skirt tied just below a very big baby bump. She stands in front of a window draped with pink and black curtains, a clunky old-fashioned radiator fixed to the wall.

We went again and that time, I researched the different types of FSH and I asked for a more natural product, a lot more expensive. So you do the injection once and it makes you ovulate the next day. My egg just floats around and gets reabsorbed, it's all the good stuff in that follicle that we need for the womb lining and for the hormone balance. So, on the third go, we put two embryos in. This time, Sara said to the doctors, 'You are only defrosting two. If they both survive, you put both in; if one survives, you put one in; if none survives, you can get one more out.' So this was her taking control. But when we were going through that it got me thinking, 'What if none of her embryos work? Do I offer to use my own eggs? Do I offer to go straight?' And I did. We were having lunch and Sara was talking about her worries and I said, 'You know if we try all options and we get to a stage where we've used all your embryos, I won't just stop. I'll happily donate an egg.' And she cried. She cried for two reasons. One, it was a great offer. But two, she was acknowledging that it was a possibility that it might not work.

There are images of baby scans – the classic kidney bean on a black and white screen, and a later scan showing a massive head and a tiny body stretching out what appears to be an arm or a leg. To the radiographer, a scan is a routine procedure, carried out umpteen times in the working day. Just one more to do before lunch. But to the expectant parent, the vision of a brand new person growing in utero is nothing short of a miracle, regardless of whose body it's growing inside.

I was so emotionally involved, I couldn't have just walked away. I suppose it would have been a possibility to use an egg donor but for Sara it was more about the roots; she wanted the children to grow up knowing their story. But on the third time, it worked. The official test date is four or five days after my period would arrive anyway because my cycle is so short. But I did a pregnancy test early and I saw the line. I had to be sure I'd got this right. I spent a fortune on pregnancy tests. It was ridiculous but it becomes an obsession. It's very all-consuming because you are carrying somebody else's hopes and dreams.

Images of pregnancy tests – a cardboard dipstick photographed on a stripy cushion, its two bold red lines leaping out from the lines of the fabric; three white plastic tests, with red lines glaring; and a digital test displaying the words, 'Pregnant 1–2'.

They came over, we collected the children from school, I went upstairs and weed in a little bowl, and we went into the kitchen, all of us. Sara did a digital test; she put it in the bowl and the word, 'Pregnant' came up. In the meantime, Rain had got her hair in the bowl and everything. It was just incredible; it's a moment that sits here. (Points to her heart.) *It's one of my best memories ever. After all that effort, such a wonderful feeling that it had worked. There were lots and lots of happy tears and squealing. It was really wonderful but at the same time, Sara didn't want to get her hopes up. She thought, 'Right, first hurdle over.'*

I'd moved into this house while I was pregnant but I'd never actually set up the dining table because it was a planned home birth. Sara hates hospitals with a passion and she was fully on board for a home birth. But the baby wasn't coming so we ended up changing our plan and going to hospital and being induced at 43 weeks and it was my first caesarean and it was horrible. I knew my body and I knew it wasn't going well and after two days, I asked for a caesarean. Nothing was working, nothing was changing. I was told, 'No,' by a really horrible obstetrician. Her words were, 'I hear what you're saying but here's what you're doing. We're going to get you on a drip and get that cervix open and you can push that baby out. You've got all those other babies out. You can do this.' But I said, 'I know how my body works and the baby's stuck. It's not going to work. I need a caesarean.' Even though the baby wasn't my own, I had mother's intuition, I knew my own body. I was doing everything I could. I was in a birthing pool and I'd get out and walk about to help. I said, 'If you are going to put me on the drip, can you give me an epidural for when you are going to need to do the caesarean?' The obstetrician didn't like me at all because I was pretty verbal about what I wanted. She spoke to Sara separately all the time. Sara has a really different version of that story because the obstetrician would go really nicely with her.

A shot of a baby's foot, criss-crossed sole, wrinkled like an old man, ankle wrapped in a plastic hospital bracelet. I wonder for a moment if there are people who read soles of feet like palm readers read hands. Parents of stillborn babies can have their baby's footprints taken in the hospital. There are companies that produce baby memorial footprint jewellery, some people even get footprints tattoos. I stare at the patterns of the baby's sole, the lines scoping out triangles and squares, the puffy skin resembling a quilt.

I ended up 12 hours on the drip, so I was absolutely exhausted. We call it The Lost Thursday because we don't remember anything of it at all. Sara was so scared because I was a single parent and she didn't want me to have a caesarean, looking after my own children because of the recovery time. When they finally said, 'Okay, the only option is a caesarean,' even though I asked for it, I still broke down in tears. It was a really traumatic situation. When the baby was born, they said, 'Oh, no, she was never going to come out.' They got the baby out; the baby went straight to Sara. In the meantime, my cervix, because it had worked so hard, just would not stop bleeding. So they said, 'Okay, we need to clear the theatre now because we're going to do a hysterectomy.' There was so much blood loss. Sara just stood there crying saying, 'What have I done? What have I done?' Look, now, I'm crying.

I start crying too. For a minute, I forget where I am. I am in the theatre watching Robin bleeding to death. The beeping from the machines is deafening. Sara's mouth is wide open in a silent scream as she is pulled away. Pale blue medics swarm over Robin's body. I let out a gasp. Then we are back in Robin's living room, the green chair vibrating between us. I gulp a swig of peppermint tea.

Sara's feeling selfish that her desire to have a baby is about to leave four children motherless. I was in total shock. We were aiming for a water birth and for Sara to catch the baby. It was not what we expected at all. What they did was they pulled my uterus on top to try to stop the bleeding so Sara and Pete could see it all. So the moment for her to finally meet her baby was hideous. Once the doctors got the bleeding under control, they said I didn't need a hysterectomy after all but it was so traumatic. They put Sara and the baby in a different ward from me. Sara always said she wanted us to be on the same ward. The obstetrician and everybody went to see Sara and nobody went to see me. They wouldn't even let her come and see me with the baby. On the chart, it has your name and details and on the board, under my name it said, 'No baby'. So nobody wanted to come and see me. I was a leper. The woman without a baby. They hardly ever came and the buzzer was out of reach. I hadn't had a shower after that bloodbath. They just came in and said, 'Right we have the form to sign you out. Who's coming to collect you?' And I was just crying saying, 'I've got nobody at home. I've only got my children. They're with their dad today. I can't go back to an empty house. I haven't even had a shower, I've still got a catheter in.' But there was no wee coming out into the bag so they kept pumping me with fluid but it was blocked. I don't know how I didn't pop. There were so many mistakes. They just wanted me out and gone but I refused to leave. I stayed in for three days. At least there I had a mechanical bed to help me get in and out and food was being brought to me.

A picture of Sara wearing a tiny new baby under her tee-shirt, a baby with a face so small and smooth that at first I think it is a doll. The camera angles pans down on the top of Sara's head, the baby's face snuggled at the top of her breasts. Sara's face is not visible in the picture but joy radiates from the top of her head; every strand of hair is dancing in that picture.

I asked Sara and Pete not to tell me the baby's name while I was pregnant because when the baby was born, I wanted them to introduce me to their baby. Sara actually discharged herself early so she could bring the baby to see me. They called her Rose. When she passed Rose to me, Rose started rooting in, as though to breastfeed, but I was so poorly, I just didn't want that at all. I don't know if it was me protecting myself or I didn't want to confuse Rose. But Sara didn't want me to either. She not only had to deal *with the fact that she couldn't carry her own baby but she also had to deal with the fact that she couldn't feed her baby. All the milk that I expressed just sat in the freezer doing nothing. Sara just said, 'No.' She wouldn't use it. So I felt quite a rejection at the time because initially she'd agreed to using my milk, so I was a bit put out. But with hindsight, I completely get it. It was such a blur, that time after the birth. I stopped expressing a few weeks after the birth.*

Photos of breast pumps and bottles, a half full bottle of expressed milk, standing in front of a cup of tea, on a kitchen worktop, the milk a beige colour, like someone has poured the tea in there.

Sara was very involved throughout the pregnancy; I'd send her pictures all the time. Sara just loved being with me and holding my bump. We'd see each other every two to three weeks. She used to talk to the bump and she read to it. Through the pregnancy I didn't bond with the baby at all. I felt that the baby was hardly there at all. Sara felt that the baby was with her all the time. But when the baby was born, I hit rock bottom. There was lots of PTSD stuff going on. I just slumped. It was almost as if my head was on the page that the bond is with the parents not the baby but my body was not on the same page at all. It was as though my uterus and my hormones were like, 'Hang on a minute, you didn't tell us.' I had this big belly still. I imagine it's like when somebody loses a baby. I had a really amazing tribe of women though. They came over with food, tidied the house, helped with the children. I had somebody here every day. I was always one for, 'I'm fine; I'll do it myself.' But I was in a position where I had to accept help and realise that they were really pleased to help.

One thing I haven't told you is that I can see people's babies. When I work with people fertility-wise, I know how many they are going to have. I'm working with this woman at the moment who's had one baby and I know she's going to have four; I can see them all. I see them as little ovals, like a greeny-orange oval. I always knew I was going to have four. I could see them all. I thought I was going to end up carrying twins for Sara and Pete because I could see two ovals but rather than side by side, one was behind the other. This is the bonkers stuff but it's just the way I've always been.

A photo of Pete sitting on a hospital bed holding a sleeping Rose, dressed in a yellow baby suit, his arms stiff, holding her like she might break. A precious china doll. Sara behind him, wrapped in a fluffy blue dressing gown, leaning on his shoulder, looking on in wonder.

I felt so guilty to my children because they sort of lost me in so many ways. Soon after having my own twins, I was straight back into size eight, I was doing parachute jumps, climbing mountains. But after the surrogacy, I turned into this fragile, overweight woman that needed help with everything. The twins were only about six and a half. My mother decided to bring my children to see me in hospital. I looked like a train wreck. It was just awful. Willow and Rain said they didn't want to come. My eldest and the youngest of my twins came over. The two that were a bit bolder. I was such a mess that when Sara's mum came in, she went faint and had to sit down. They went to see Sara then she came to see me and brought me flowers. She pretended it was just hot in the room.

Toddler Rose sitting between Robin's twins on a step. Floor to ceiling marble – I wonder where they are. All three girls hold cuddly toys – a cow, a gorilla, a character from *The Night Garden*. The twins look at Rose; she holds out what looks like a packet of raisins with her spare hand, as though offering them one.

So fast forward a bit but I phoned Sara and said, 'I keep having these dreams and I think we should have another baby because I can see you with two and it won't go away until I do something about it.' Sara was laughing and she hung up the phone. Then she rang back five minutes later and said, 'I've just spoken to Pete and I think you just said you want to have another baby for us. Did you really just say that?' We went through two cycles of IVF again and there are two years between the two babies, so it must have been about a year afterwards, we went again. I had no choice. My head was saying, 'Not again.' But something in my body – my heart, my womb – was just saying it's the right thing to do. There were small glimpses of huge panic but they would pass quickly.

Robin puts the iPad down for a moment and stands to take a picture frame down from a shelf. We look at a picture of toddler Rose holding newborn Charlie, children born two years apart but conceived at the same time and put on hold, their lives restarted one after another, hauled out of deep freeze. Rose has Sara's round cheeks and Pete's thick eyebrows.

The second time round it was very different. Yes, Sara was scared about the birth, but she could believe it would happen and she could see what her baby would look like. Carrying Rose and Charlie, they were totally different babies. I felt that Charlie was there with me a lot more than Rose was with me and Sara felt that Charlie was there less than with Rose. Personality wise in the womb, really different. Rose kept me at a distance, but I was a little bit scared, really, because I'd bonded with Charlie in the womb and developed this relationship. I think it's because I'd allowed myself to bond because Rose was okay, so I trusted more in the process. The birth was really different with Charlie too. Charlie is a girl by the way. Yeah, lots of people think that.

Back on the screen, a courtroom scene, three official looking people sitting suited and booted behind a table, piles of paper and a jug of water, Sara cradling Rose on her lap, in a white top and pink tights, Robin and Pete on either side. She's made it to the centre of the photo now.

Sara chose gender-neutral colours for the clothes. She's a real feminist and she was never going to dress her girls in pink. Pete chose Rose's name and Sara chose Charlie. She chose a gender-neutral name. She thought if the name Charlie is on a CV then no-one will know if it's a man or woman, it's just a person called Charlie. It was a really big thing for Sara to let Pete chose Rose because they couldn't agree on names at all. Sara said she wouldn't have chosen the name Rose but it really suits her.

An image of Sara holding Rose, now wearing tee-shirt and toddler jeans, a shock of strawberry blonde hair, her chubby hand placed on Robin's swelling tummy. Pete stands to the side. He looks relaxed, filled out a bit from the previous pictures, no longer gaunt and angular.

The girls call me Auntie. One of the things that was really important to all of us was to know your roots. I've got friends who've been adopted who know nothing about who they were born to, about what happened and there's that craving. There's always that need to know your roots. Sara never wanted it to be news for the girls that Auntie Robin carried them. She told me about the day she verbalised our story to Rose when Rose was

18 months old. Sara pointed to the cross where she had had keyhole surgery to get the egg collection, and she said, 'That's my kiss where the doctor's took my egg out of my tummy. And Auntie Robin's got half a kiss' – because I've got a caesarean scar – *'because she carried you in her tummy.' And Rose went, 'Oh.' She's a very bright little one. That was before she was really able to talk about things but she was pointing at things and being told about them and she was taking it all in. So Rose has always known and she says to me, 'I grew in your tummy, Auntie Robin!' For Rose to see my tummy grow with Charlie helped her to understand her own story. Rose kept touching my tummy and saying, 'My baby's in there!'*

Sara again stands in the centre of the picture, Robin and Pete on either side, Pete in a navy shirt and blazer, Robin in a navy wrap-over dress. Sara, the star of the show, shimmers in a floral tea dress, beaming from ear to ear as she holds baby Charlie on her hip. Charlie wears a formal white christening dress, a miniature bride, and stares at her sister, Rose, balanced on Robin's hip, in a full-on pink frilly bridesmaid number, with chubby fingers stuffed into her mouth.

I'm not religious but Sara is and so I am one of the godmothers. One day Sara asked me, 'If something ever happened to us together, I need to know that my children would be looked after and I know it's a really big thing to ask.' Normally a surrogate wouldn't do it but for me, it goes without saying. I'm so close to them all and I always will be and of course, I would. When you're pregnant, you have to have all your wills set up because let's say, I died in childbirth, you have to have a will to say that the baby would go to them because I'm the legal mother until the parental order goes through. The intended parents pay for life insurance in case the surrogate dies. It doesn't make it any better but there's peace of mind that some of those things are sorted out. My children would be provided for in the event of my death. And Sara has peace of mind that her children would be loved and cared for in the event of her death. In her head, if something happens to her, she's got me and Pete married off!

'She's got it'

1

Ever wondered what it's like to be famous? Well, you're about to find out. Having a bump tends to put even the quietest of wallflowers in the spotlight. Okay, we can't promise there'll be paparazzi hiding in your rhododendrons … but one thing you won't be short of now you're pregnant is adoring fans.

2

The images of the prepatriarchal goddess-cults did one thing; they told women that power, awesomeness, and centrality were theirs by nature, not by privilege or miracle; the female was primary.

3

With that, the image of the young girl dissolved into the green oval and the spirit began to move away. As she disappeared, I could discern the oval outlines of many spirits shining in the distance. The spirit babies began to move toward me.

4

She is dark red, bony, beautiful. Her soul is visible under her skin. Her face is feline, eternal. It has the serenity of an Egyptian mask. Every detail is complete – fingers, toes, eyebrows, the perfect globe of her head, marked by a mesh of veins, the fan of her tiny ribs. She's warm in my arms and surely only sleeping?

5

Then a thing occurred to me about ghost children. They don't age, unless you make them. They don't age, so they don't know it's time to leave home. They won't, without a struggle, be kicked out of your psyche. They will hang on by every means they know; they won't agree to go, until you make your intentions very clear.

6

The truth is that people with infertility issues are often gullible, desperate and mad. They need protecting from themselves. I can say that because I was one of those people.

7

It was like being hooked on drugs, my desire to have a baby. I was addicted, obsessed, it was a habit I needed to feed. Like most drug habits it was great at the beginning. I was infused with hope.

8

I remain convinced that none of this can possibly work because surely there are no women who want to have babies for other women?

9

In the Daily Mail, gestational surrogacy is referred to as 'rent a womb', and reports suggest that in India, the Ukraine or Kazakhstan it costs only £8,000.

10

Intended Parents should budget approximately £20k for straight surrogacy and £30k for host surrogacy – this includes all expenses for the surrogate, insurance, wills, and clinic costs (for host). A surrogate's expenses can be from anywhere between £7k and £15k, depending on her personal circumstances e.g. loss of earnings, rate of childcare, no of children, distance from IPs etc.

11

Childbirth is probably the most intense physical and emotional normal experience in a woman's life. It is recalled with terror or with joy, but most often its vividness is forgotten. For one woman it is a time of frightening loneliness; in this strange and aseptic hospital setting, she imagines the worst. She feels abandoned, prey to strange sensations and excruciating pain; nobody cares, nobody will come if she screams for help.

12

In Europe and many other places, postpartum women were once considered polluted and therefore dangerous to men; so new mothers were not allowed to prepare or cook food for forty days.

13

In south-eastern Nepal, people believed ghosts could invade the open 'sore' of the birth passage and cause madness or infertility; so women there stayed in a shuttered room for six days.

14

In the nineteenth century (and earlier, of course) no poor woman could afford to pay the fee required by a doctor for the delivery of her baby. So she was forced to rely on the services of an untrained, self-taught midwife, or 'handywoman' as they were often called. Some may have been quite effective practitioners, but others boasted a frightening mortality rate. In the mid-nineteenth century, maternal mortality amongst the poorest classes stood at around 35-40 per cent, and infant mortality was around 60 per cent.

15

Two years later, I decided I would like another baby. But after four months, not seeing a doctor or anyone of course, I miscarried and was very ill in hospital for three weeks. Enough is enough, I decided. I never tried again.

Sources

Title quotation: from the song *Venus*.

1: Douglas and Michaels (2005)
2: Rich (1986)
3: Makichen (2005)

4: Jolly (2017)
5: Mantel (2010)
6: Jolly (2017)
7: Lowe (2001)
8: Jolly (2017)
9: Jolly (2017)
10: Surrogacy UK (n.d.)
11: Breen (1989)
12: Cassidy (2007)
13: Cassidy (2007)
14: Worth (2008)
15: Barlow (2007)

The creation of this quotation collage is analysed in Chapter 1 'Birthing the book,' 'Collage as an evolution beyond narrative'.

Reference list

Barlow, Y. (2007) *Quick, Boil Some Water: The Story of Childbirth in Our Grandmother's Day*, Cambridge, Bookline and Thinker.
Breen, D. (1989) *Talking with Mothers*, London, Free Association Books.
Cassidy, T. (2007) *Birth: A History*, London, Chatto & Windus.
Douglas, S. and Michaels, M. (2005) *The Mommy Myth: The Idealization of Motherhood and How it Has Undermined All Women*, New York, Simon & Schuster Ltd., Free Press.
Jolly, A. (2017) *Dead Babies and Seaside Towns: One Mother's Journey to Surrogacy*, London, Unbound.
Lowe, M. (2001) in Sumner, P. (ed.) *The Fruits of Labour: Creativity, Self-Expression and Motherhood*, London, The Women's Press, pp.42–53.
Makichen, W. (2005) *Spirit Babies: How to Communicate with the Child You're Meant to Have* [e-book reader], London, Dell Publishing.
Mantel, H. (2010) *Giving up the Ghost: A Memoir*, London, Fourth Estate.
Rich, A. (1986 [1977]) *Of Woman Born*, New York, W. W. Norton.
Shocking Blue (1969) *Venus*, Blaricum, Pink Elephant Label.
Surrogacy UK (n.d.) 'FAQs' [Online]. Available at: https://surrogacyuk.org/faqs/ (Accessed 16 September 2019).
Worth, J. (2008 [2002]) *Call the Midwife*, London, Orion Books Ltd.

8
LORRAINE'S STORY

Damned if we do, damned if we don't

People mill around me in the foyer of Great Ormond Street Hospital. A thin, grey looking man pushes an overweight boy in a wheelchair. A teenage girl walks with a frame, an older woman in a pink tracksuit by her side. Another wheelchair, another girl, head lolling, tube stuck down her throat. A mother and son strolling along, holding hands, swinging arms, chatting. I keep looking, wondering. It's hard to make out whether the chirpy girl galloping towards me, all fringe and freckles, gappy teeth and gangly legs, is a patient or visitor. The fair-haired woman behind her rushes forwards to introduce herself as Lorraine. She has travelled here with her adopted daughter, Elsa, and her friend, Chloe. They set out early this morning to get to Elsa's appointment with the consultant; now, it's all over and they can relax. We go to a local café to chat over cappuccino, while Chloe takes Elsa shopping. They return later with a whistle. 'You're going to love that on the way home, aren't you?' laughs Chloe to Lorraine.

Do you remember that really long form you had to complete during the adoption assessment when you go through that process of what you would accept – HIV or one leg and it's just so horrible? I think you got to tick 'yes', 'no' or 'more information' and I think we ticked 'more information' for most of them. Ironically with Elsa, we ended up adopting a child who ticked all the boxes of what we said we wouldn't accept. I remember having a discussion with the social worker one day and she said, 'Why do you think we have so many children up for adoption with special needs? Because so many parents can't cope with it so don't beat yourself up if you don't feel you can take that on.'

Actually Elsa did not fit any of our yeses but because she was a full sibling to our first adopted daughter, Ana, it kind of overruled all our preferences. The minute we were offered her, we were kind of damned if we do, damned if we don't, I felt, because how were we going to explain to Ana that we rejected her sibling and made her grow up somewhere different?

DOI: 10.4324/9781003290179-10

But equally, we were presented with a child who was everything we said we probably couldn't deal with. And that was hard. We spent a long time trying to decide if we would go ahead with adopting Elsa and the social workers were quite horrible about it. They took quite a lot of time to unravel what was going on for her, which is fair enough, but they didn't want to give us the time to consider. I had to work out whether we were the best parents for her, whether it was fair to Ana to bring Elsa into our household. We were going on holiday for three weeks, and we said we need to take that time and space to think it through and they said, 'Right, we'll need to start advertising her to other couples.' I said, 'Right, go on then.' Don't tell me you're going to fix up an adoption in three weeks. They'd made us wait for the best part of a year by then so is another three weeks really going to make any difference? It shouldn't have to be like that.

Both Ana and Elsa were drug babies; they were placed in care as soon as they were born. Their birth mother was in prison for some of the time she was pregnant with Elsa, and Elsa went through withdrawal in utero then and at the time of birth, which resulted in additional needs. She has vision problems, developmental coordination disorder, ADHD and epilepsy, and is severely dyslexic. We take her to Great Ormond Street regularly and she is closely monitored.

Some adoptees I know would not adopt a child, they absolutely wouldn't but for me, it wasn't an issue at all. I remember when I was about 20 and I worked for NEXT and I was in a training session and for the life of me, I can't remember how it came out but it was in a group discussion and this girl said, 'If I can't have children, I'm going to get a surrogate mother' and I've always felt quite strongly against it because I think if children are already born that need a family why are you going to go and create one? I can remember getting really irate with her and saying, 'Surely you could adopt a child who needs a home rather than go to all of that effort to create one?'

Summer of love

I was adopted aged three months. I'm the classic adoption story. I'm a baby of the summer of love, conceived in 1969, born in Scotland. My mother was respectable – she just got caught out. She didn't tell her mother she was pregnant. Her employer – a bank – told her she could only keep her job if she gave up her baby. So she was whisked away and I was put in care and then given to adoptive parents in London. I always knew I was adopted. Everything we're told to do in adoption training nowadays, Mum and Dad did it instinctively. They adopted my brother – who has different birth parents – two years later, but we're not in contact any more. He hasn't dealt with being adopted at all well despite having the same upbringing as me. But he came from a different birth family.

I traced my birth mother when I was 27 and met her the following year. We have, I'd say, a cordial relationship. There's no animosity. We explored a load of stuff in the first few years and then it felt like there was not much left to say. I haven't seen her in eight years. She still sends birthday cards to my daughters and things like that. I think there are stages to coming to terms with being adopted. Up to say seven, it's like a fairy tale, you are a princess, the special chosen one; then you have a reality check and realise it's not all good. In my teens, I went through a difficult time and struggled to get to grips with being adopted; then as I was entering relationships aged 17–18, I got why it happened. I came to the conclusion that it could have been me – if I got pregnant, I wasn't ready for a baby. I didn't have a beef with any individual but with society for not supporting my mother to keep me. It took me a long time to come to terms with things. Being adopted is part of me but it doesn't define me. You have to be content with yourself.

I gave a talk to the Natural Parents Network, it was a group of women in their fifties and sixties, birth parents who would have been mothers around the time I was born. I was there in a dual role as an adoptee and adopter so I was liked and disliked in equal measures. I saw how painful it was for these women. Adoption leaves a mark on everyone. At the same time, I consider myself lucky because if my birth mother had kept me I wouldn't have had the life that I have had. She got married within 18 months of having me and I have two sisters very close in age to me. She tried to get me back as well but was told it was too late. But when you look at the time lines, it wasn't.

When I tracked down my birth mother, Jeanie, it was very random the way I found her. All my records were in Scotland where I was born, and we were actually up in Scotland for a month on our honeymoon. One of the things I remember growing up is knowing that when I reached 18, I would have access to information about her and in that build up to turning 18, tracing my birth mother seemed like a really important thing to do. I can always remember the point of turning 18 and thinking, 'Oh, oh, I can do it now but I'm not sure I'm ready' and actually deciding that because I had no idea of what I was going to find, I had very little of the background story, being very worried that what if what I actually found was awful or what if she didn't wanna know me and what if I was rejected again and in my mind, would my world fall apart? Then I stood back and took what I think now was a very mature decision that I needed to wait until my life was in a better place and then I went through my twenties thinking, 'I think I'll know when it's right to do it.' So, I think subconsciously the decision to go to Scotland for my honeymoon was, maybe at the time I hadn't actually thought of it, but maybe it was that actually I feel secure enough now to return to the scene, as it were. We ended up staying in a hotel in the street I was born in, just by fluke.

So all the dates were set and when I went to look for a hotel every single one was fully booked and I ended up going down the list until I was at bed and breakfasts, and I remember telling this guy on the phone my sob story, and he said, 'It's okay, I can fit you in.' And then I said, 'I'm sorry, I've rang that many places I don't know where you are,' and he told me the name of the road and I said, 'Oh, I was born in a nursing home in that road,' and he told me that the nursing home I was born in used to be the building next door and I was Whoa! I remember turning up and thinking for the first time in my life I knew I was in the place that she would have been. I mean, I was standing looking at flats but I remember thinking that one day, she had walked through that gate to the nursing home, pregnant with me and that was really powerful.

So we were halfway through the trip when I said to my husband, 'Do you mind if I go off to the records office?' All I knew was her name and roughly how old she was but she had quite a distinctive name and because Scotland's a small place, there were not that many records to look through. And they had a very good system, which bearing in mind this was 1995 so wouldn't be as it was now, but I put her name in and within two hours I had traced her, her parents, both sets of grandparents, the fact she was one of five and the fact that she had married and had two daughters and with the daughters, I found the marriage certificate of the older of the two and she'd only been 20 getting married and I thought hmm, 20 getting married, she'd probably still been living at home. And in Scotland, some of the certificates had a bit more detail so I went and found the phone book for that area and there was the address. It was ridiculously easy.

I'd set a time to meet my husband, Will, and he was at the front door and I was absolutely in shock and he was, like, 'Well, what did you find?' and I was, 'Her name, her address, her telephone number.' And he was like, 'Oh my God!' And I remember saying, 'I think I need a drink' and we went to the pub and I downed a vodka and it was like, Oh My God. But then with my sensible head on, I also thought, I can't go charging in here because I don't know what her life's like etc. And also, I found that very overwhelming so I contacted the post-adoption centre and went to see a counsellor. I think I had four sessions with him. The first one I just cried so much, he probably barely heard a word but oh boy, did I need to let that out. But he was really good and he acted as an intermediary and he wrote her a very bland letter along the lines of somebody who thinks they may be related to you is looking for you, written in such a way that only she would know what it was about. It was really well done. And off he posted it, and I waited and I waited and three weeks went by and I was getting so stressed out and it turned out that the day before the letter arrived, she had gone on holiday for three weeks. So when she returned she contacted him within 24 hours so it was fine.

And then partly because of the distance, we started writing to one another and that was really fantastic because we got to know each other and we got to ask lots of questions that if we'd met in person, we might not have felt able to ask. So there wasn't the pressure, you could consider what answer you wanted to give. And I've still got all those letters and they mean the world to me because it was like, that was our introduction. We wrote about once a month but we didn't actually meet until coming up to a year, so it was the time coming up to our first wedding anniversary. I remember one letter arrived on the Saturday morning and it came quite early and I was in bed and Will brought it up and she'd enclosed a photo of one of my sisters and I was absolutely overwhelmed by that because we really looked alike and I'd never had that. We had exchanged a picture of each other but in the next letter, she sent the picture of my younger sister, Carol, and we are two peas in a pod, we couldn't look more alike. The picture was taken in her flat and she had posters on the walls of bands that I liked and it was such a connection.

Then I arranged to meet Jeanie one afternoon in a hotel in Scotland and we arrived the night before. I remember the hotel manager rang the room and said, 'I have your mother on the phone' and that was the first time we spoke and it was really weird. It was quite formal; she said, 'Oh hello, I just wanted to check the arrangements for tomorrow' and I said, 'I'm really looking forward to meeting you.' It was very brief. I can remember that morning I changed my clothes about five times, I couldn't decide what to wear, it was worse than a first date. The actual meeting was in a beautiful old country hotel – we knew the owner so we asked if we could have a private sitting room – and they came up to the door and we just gave each other a big hug.

Sorry, I'm welling up now. After all these years, it still gets me emotional. It felt like the most natural thing in the world. Yeah, absolutely fine. But what I also remember is that I was very aware that Will was standing behind my shoulder and her daughter was standing behind her shoulder and they were kind of looking and thinking, what do we do now? And Will made the first move and broke the ice and it was great and within minutes we were chatting, we were laughing, lots of questions, you know. I remember we went and sat out in the garden because it was a lovely day and I remember he brought us out a lovely jug of lemonade and we just chatted.

And we were out there for a week, so I think it was the following day, she came and took me out, just the two of us, and we went to a local castle and we just wandered around and talked. There were all sorts of things, just suddenly noticing that we had very similar fingers and it was like, Ooh who are you? Sizing each other up. But absolutely from the moment we met, we just got on. We were very jokey. I said something about music and she said, 'What are you musical?' and I said, 'No,' and she said, 'Oh thank God for that because you wouldn't have got that from me.' And stuff like that. I think a couple of days later, her husband came to meet me and he is just the loveliest man because in my mind, out of all of them, he had no reason to want to get to know me. I was the cuckoo in the nest, I was the one who might upset his family and his grown-up daughters who had only just found out that they had a half-sister but he was the most welcoming. I'll always remember that, he was just so lovely.

Actually, as it turns out, he was a sailor in the merchant navy and my mother already knew him before she met my birth father – I think it was a fairly brief relationship – and by the time he came back, I was born and gone because she only had me for a few days. So I was in foster care and they approached social services together and said if they married could they have me back and were told no, which actually was a complete lie because I was still in foster care, the adoption hadn't gone through so they could have. They just said that. He ended up being a fisherman. I could have ended up growing up with a fisherman, such a different life to the one I had.

Do you remember when you were a teenager, in magazines, they used to do those pieces like 'How to read your palm'? I remember looking and actually there is a split in my lifeline and that's probably just coincidence. Look, that one is your lifeline. And mine has these two forks at the bottom and I remember being absolutely convinced that's what it was. Probably absolute rubbish.

When I met her, I think it was our second meeting, I went to stay with her when her husband was away at sea and she brought up the subject of my birth father. She said, 'Look, he didn't really know I was pregnant.' I said, 'Well, he either did or he didn't.' But she said she told him she thought she might be and she never saw him again. In the days before mobile phones or whatever, they lost touch and she'd not then sought him out, he never sought her out. But she had kept tabs on him and she knew exactly where he was. He's quite a wealthy man actually, which for me is almost a bit of a complication because he would question my motives for wanting to get in touch. Anyway, what she said was, if you want, I will contact him and let him know of your existence and I agreed. I didn't really hear much and finally I said, 'Okay, what's happened?' I knew she wasn't being straight with me, I think she wanted to spare my feelings but basically he didn't want to know. He said, 'Why are you telling me this?' From what I gather he never married and I don't think there are any other children because my younger sister, Carol, has also done a bit of detective work and he is a very wealthy man who owns large swathes of property. So that was about 14 years ago, so it was a long time ago. Jeanie sent him a recent photo of me and said, 'if you ever want to get in touch' but we never heard. So I just thought, 'Sod you then.' But every now and then, I do think of him. I actually put his name into Facebook to see what I could find and that's how I saw his picture.

Some people trace birth parents and find out they are living round the corner and that's really different. Having that distance between us made it easier in a way. I would say we were made to feel very welcome until we had the children. So for a good eight years, it was great. The difficulty arose when I had the children. Because Jeanie lives in quite a small town and is quite well known, one of the things I found hard when we went up there was that we could be walking down the high street and people will stop and say, 'Hello, how are you?' and it's just like I'm invisible, I don't get introduced. I've always stood back a bit and she was never directly asked who I was but I'm sure if she was, she would have said a niece or a cousin or something to explain away the family resemblance. And I get it but I did have to say to her one day, I'd taken my eldest daughter up there just once and I said, 'The thing is, you know, you want them to call you Grannie, that's lovely, so if they're running down the high street calling you Grannie and one of your friends hears and says, "Grannie? What's this all about?" How are you going to explain it?' Hardly anybody knows. It's a secret and she can't come out with it. She's of that era, you know, where only bad girls did. Even her closest female friends don't know. Her husband always knew but I don't think it was really spoken about. She's the middle child of five and her younger brother who would have been 15 when I was born, he didn't even know. I brought shame on the family.

I think part of my journey was reading stuff to actually understand where she was coming from. I thought, don't judge her, this could be anyone. Once I'd met her and realised that the story wasn't one of rape or incest or anything that was gonna be really hard to fathom, I made my peace with it. I thought, it happens. It wasn't personal. I think you do still process it. When my maternal grandfather died, I remember her ringing me and telling me and, obviously, her father had died so I had empathy with her for that but I didn't know how to feel because he was my grandfather but he had never said a word to me; I'd met him once and he couldn't speak to me. I met the grandparents and two aunts and he couldn't even look at me. I went to their house for tea and it was awful and it was so not what I was expecting. Having been invited, I thought it was because they wanted to meet me but it was the most awful hour of my life. We walked in, sat in the lounge, tea and biscuits came and were passed round. Grandfather sat there, Grandmother sat there and they looked everywhere in the room but me. Small talk was made about the biscuits or whatever and I said a couple of things but nothing. They said 'hello' when I arrived and 'goodbye' when I left and that was it. They didn't touch me or anything. And I had to make my peace with that and they came from the previous generation so that was even more deeply buried for them than it was for my mother. I was the cause of a great deal of shame and heartbreak for them. They just didn't know how to deal with it but weirdly from that point on, I got Christmas cards from them every year until they died. I still get a Christmas card from my aunt who never writes anything more than 'Best wishes'.

Jackie Kay got it right when she talked about it being like a cul de sac, you get to the end and you think, well, what now? It's been eight years since I last saw Jeanie. It all *stopped when I had the kids. She never forgets a birthday. She sends the kids lovely presents and we talk on the phone but it's whittled down to about twice a year. I'd always ask about meeting up and say, 'We could come to you, you could come to us' and she'd say, 'Oh yes, that would be lovely' but then the excuses would start to come so I sort of stopped asking as it felt like another rejection and as anyone who's been adopted will tell you, we don't do rejection very well. So, you know, I've just given up asking. It's just locked away and it's eaten away at these women for years and that's the burden they carry, which is awful.*

Ironically, this Sunday was my birth mother's seventieth birthday and I sent her a message on Facebook saying, 'Happy Birthday. I hope you are having a lovely day.' And she sent me a message back saying, 'Jenny – who's the older of her two daughters – is bringing me down to London for a few days.' So I was like, 'Oh okay. What a coincidence. I'm in London on Tuesday. Anyway hope you have a lovely time.' Thinking, 'Would she say anything?' No, I just got a thumbs up. And today, I went on Facebook and they'd tagged in at Covent Garden so it would have been easy to arrange to meet. But no. And you know, I kind of get it because it's a mother–daughter thing. She wouldn't want to upset Jenny who's obviously gone to great lengths to plan a lovely trip for them, so I get that. It's not for me to crash their party, as it were. But it's a little bit hurtful. It would have been easy for her to have said, 'Oh, are you? Is there any chance of meeting for a quick coffee or something?' But no. Jenny found it very hard because she'd grown up thinking she was the eldest daughter and she wasn't. Yeah. It is what it is. What I really realised once I'd met them all and a few years had passed is you cannot become part of a family at that point. I'm on the periphery, you know. You can't suddenly be included in stuff, it's not gonna happen. And actually, you know, I can't keep putting myself up to be rejected. There comes a point when you say, 'Enough is enough. You know where I am. If you want to see me. Your choice.'

It did occur to me, if anything happened to Jeanie, would I get invited to the funeral? Because I'm not sure that I would because not even all the family know about me. If something happened suddenly, would I even be told? Where they live, it's quite a small place and say there is a funeral and there's all friends and family and I walk in looking like family, am I introduced? Do I get passed off as a long-lost cousin? Because I am still a secret.

When I traced Jeanie, I didn't tell my adoptive mother, who I call Mum, at the time because I didn't know how it was going to work out. It's really interesting because at the time you think it's just about the two of you but it's really not; it's about everybody involved. So when I told her, there were a few tears; everyone was a bit upset. Despite the fact that Mum had always said, 'Oh if you want to find you birth mother in the future, that will be absolutely fine.' When push came to shove, she didn't like it and I totally understood that. I'm sure I'll be the same. The first time I went to Scotland to stay with Jeanie – I arranged it for a weekend, all fine – stupidly didn't realise it was Mother's Day. So it was … but in a way, it was lovely because it's the one and only time that my birth mother's had all three of her daughters together on Mother's Day and I don't think it'll ever happen again. But my mum took it really badly. It was almost like, 'Oh well, you've found her now, you don't need me now.' So we ended up having quite a frank discussion along the lines of, 'Do you know what? You've had me for every Mother's Day. Isn't it nice that she got me for one? And you don't mean any more or any less to me because of this. You are my mum. This is just the person I need to connect with and actually,' I think I said to her, 'Isn't it nice that I've got so many people in my life that care about me. You shouldn't be jealous of that.'

So, of course, I arranged for my mum and dad to meet my birth mother and have lunch because at that point I thought we need to break down the myths and the Bogey Man because each set of them are perfectly lovely people and there's no reason why they shouldn't get on and they've both got my best interests at heart so what could go wrong? It was one of the Queen's Jubilees. Yeah Golden Jubilee. Because I just remember that Jeanie and my younger sister came down to stay with us in London. I remember it because we went up to London and stood outside Buckingham Palace the night before, you know, because it was quite momentous. Ever the optimist me.

Perfectly polite

3rd June 2002. Of course Jeanie remembers it. Carol stands on her right and Lorraine on her left as they watch. Two of her daughters together to celebrate this important day together. It's a warm evening; they both wear floral summer dresses and sandals, making them look girlish. Like sisters in the playground. 'God Save the Queen' is projected onto the facade of Buckingham Palace in coloured lights. They change again: '1952 to 2002'. Important dates. It's important to mark dates. It's important to remember. Of course she remembers. Buckingham Palace is the backdrop to a spectacular laser and firework display to mark the Queen's Golden Jubilee. When she gets back home, she'll see the bunting left over from the street parties. Mrs McCann will have baked fairy cakes decorated with tiny, edible, golden baubles. Union Jacks will be dangling everywhere. She is good at remembering dates. Lorraine is smiling; she squeezes Jeanie's hand, walks arm in arm with Carol.

She doesn't remember what happens after that. Yes she does. They go back to Lorraine's, of course, where she is putting Jeanie and Carol up in her spare rooms. A lovely house. Soft beds. Lorraine has a lovely husband. Jeanie is so pleased. The next day, they watch the telly. On 4th June, the Queen arriving at Thanksgiving at St Paul's in the Gold State Coach, pulled by eight horses. What a spectacle that gold carriage is. So ornate. Beautiful really. It makes Jeanie think of Cinderella's coach. They took Carol and Jenny to see the pantomime one Christmas. It made her think of Lorraine. She hoped she was being treated well. She hoped she got her happy ever after. And she did. She had a good life. She got good parents. She got her Prince Charming in Will.

She watches the procession but she can't concentrate. Not really. She can't stop fidgeting. Lorraine asks her if she'd like a drink before they get here. She sips some water. She wonders what Mum and Dad would think of what they're doing, here altogether, meeting Lorraine's adoptive parents. 'Why would you do such a thing?' That's what Dad would think. It's better left in the past. But Lorraine asked her and she couldn't very well say no, could she?

'You okay?' asks Lorraine and she realises her fingers are in her mouth. A disgusting habit. It's disgusting. She moves her hand away and puts it on her lap.

It was always her hands that got her in trouble. She sees her 17-year-old hands, slightly plump and with bitten down nails. Writing letters. Opening a door. Holding his hand. She pushes the images away. Some things are best not remembered. She focuses on the Queen instead. How regal she looks. How proper. She bets her hands have never got her into trouble.

Lorraine's husband, Will, wanders into the lounge, wearing an apron with a picture of a woman's body on it. In underwear. The joke kind. Who would think that was funny? Why would anyone wear that while cooking? It makes Jeanie's head hurt just looking at it. The doorbell rings. Jeanie jumps.

'I'll get the door,' says Lorraine. Bright and breezy. Just like that. Like this happens every day.

They're here. Jeanie's heart pumps. She is falling down a hole. Back, back, back. She is screaming on a bed, a nurse leaning over her. Her skin is clammy, cold. She shouldn't have come. Dad was right. She shouldn't have done it. Her bitten down nails dig into the bed. Dig into the armchair.

'Mum, Dad, this is Jeanie. Jeanie, this is Sarah and Bob.'

A tall woman stands before her, offering her hand. Her nails are smooth, well-manicured. Plain varnish, nothing tacky. Well groomed. Classy. This is her daughter's mother. She stands up and shakes her hand, somehow finds herself enveloped into some kind of embrace. She wants to pull back but it's important to be polite.

She doesn't remember much of what happens next. They are seated in the dining room. Carol sits on her left and Lorraine on her right. Food is passed around. She remembers pictures. Pictures of Lorraine as a baby. Pictures in a photograph album. Pictures in her head. It's important to remember. But some things are best forgotten.

★

Sarah fiddles with her bag in the passenger seat while Bob drives. Nearly there.

'I hope this wine's okay. Do you think it's okay? Maybe I should have got fizz but that might seem a bit… a bit…'

'It's fine, love,' says Bob, eyes on the road.

'Hmm. Lorraine said Will's cooking. I should have asked what we're having. Maybe I should have got red. One of each.…'

'It's going to be fine.' They pull up outside the house and Bob turns off the engine.

Sarah smiles weakly, checking her lipstick in the overhead mirror. 'Just give me a minute.'

She unclips her seatbelt and reaches over to collect the flowers from the back seat, examining the bouquet.

'Martha did a really, lovely job with those,' says Bob. 'Lorraine will love them.'

'Oh my God, they're lilies, Bob! Sympathy flowers. We can't give those! Why on earth did she do lilies?'

'I think she was a bit short because of the street parties. They're fine, love. It's not just lilies, look.'

'Anyway, we should have got two bouquets, one for Lorraine and one for Jeanie. We've got nothing to give her!'

Bob bends inside the car to pull out the Waitrose carrier bag containing the photo albums. 'We have these.'

'I don't know if she's going to want to see those.'

'Oh course she will, love. Come on.'

Lorraine opens the door, wearing a floaty green cocktail dress and flushed cheeks.

'Hello, love. You look lovely,' says Bob, crushing her into a hug.

'Hello, Dad, Mum.'

Sarah kisses her daughter's cheek, breathing her in, just like she did when Lorraine was a baby.

'Do I look okay?' she mouths to Lorraine, handing her the flowers. 'These are for you.'

'Beautiful,' mouths back Lorraine, holding her. 'Come through.'

'Mum, Dad, this is Jeanie. Jeanie, this is Sarah and Bob. And Carol, there you are!'

'Hello,' says Sarah, rooted to the spot, staring at Jeanie, taking in her features. She looks like Lorraine. Same eyes.

'Nice to meet you, love,' says Bob, holding out a hand.

Same hands, same long fingers.

Sarah steps forwards and puts her arms around Jeanie, feeling her eyes well up. *This woman gave birth to my baby, carried her inside her for nine months.* She smells like Lorraine. She sees Carol, standing awkwardly to the side, looking like Lorraine's long-lost twin. Will appears in his funny apron, God bless him, and Bob hands him the bottle.

'Would you like a drink? Dinner will be ready in a minute.'

Sarah doesn't remember much of what happens next. They are seated in the dining room. Food is passed around. Carol is laughing over something Bob says, something about Lorraine not being able to play a tune or hold an instrument. Knives and forks clatter and crash, like Lorraine's attempts at playing the triangle in infant school.

'Lovely dinner,' says Bob. 'Let's raise a glass. To families.'

'To families,' they all chime.

Sarah drinks a little too quickly, the wine catching in her throat, giving her heartburn. She notices Jeanie hasn't eaten much. Maybe it's all too much for her.

'Thank you all for coming,' beams Lorraine. 'It means so much to have my two mums here. And my sister and you, Dad, of course.'

Then Bob brings out the photo albums. Pictures of Lorraine as a baby. He lingers over one of him holding Lorraine on a beach, in a white and yellow striped dress, rosy cheeks and chubby pink legs dangling over the froth of the sea.

'Do you remember that, Sarah? That was Lorraine's first trip to the seaside. Look at this one, Jeanie …'

Sarah watches Jeanie the whole time, watches the way she barely touches the photos, handling them with care? With fear? Like Lorraine poring over old newspaper cuttings of her school on a visit to the local museum, looking at the pictures of the children who came before her. That had fascinated Lorraine, seeing boys and girls stand in the playground where she played hopscotch with her friends, staring out of sepia images with solemn faces. Now Sarah watches Jeanie's face as she looks at the pictures of the baby she never got to take to the seaside.

It is what it is

Some weeks later, Lorraine is back in London for a work conference and agrees to meet me afterwards for a coffee. I wait outside Holborn station, hoping we don't miss one another as commuters knock into me, peeling off coats before they disappear down the escalators into the hot depths of the underground, wrapping scarves round their necks as they head out into the cold evening. Everyone in a hurry, desperate to be somewhere else; homes to go to, friends to meet, drinks to down, plays to watch, suppers to eat. Then she appears through the ticket barriers, wearing a smart black jacket over a patterned dress, blonde curls bouncing. She's ready to talk some more, tells me she thinks it's important to tell her story. We head to a tiny local café, where we are the only customers, and try to ignore the waiter pacing back and forth. Lorraine speaks into the audio recorder in hushed tones.

If you've relinquished a baby, then you are doing it to give them a better life, but in modern-day adoption, the women who've had the children taken from them, like my girls' birth mother, often they just go on to have more and more kids. I remember getting the details about Ana and I can remember very clearly getting emailed a photo of her and I can remember taking about an hour to open it because I was petrified that I wouldn't like the picture, that I wouldn't feel any instant something for this child, knowing pretty much it was a done deal. And, of course, the moment I opened it, I was like, 'Oh, oh, ah, oh, she's so gorgeous.' But really being quite scared what if I just don't like this child because you don't like every child you meet. Some of them are horrible, let's be honest. Some of them you just think, urgh! Then the first meeting was just delightful. We've got a video of it. Will made a little DVD called 'Here comes Ana' and he sent it to the grannies for Christmas because at that point, they hadn't met her. It's footage of our first hour with her and I'm lying on the floor with this Peppa Pig toy playing Peppa's in the box, Peppa's out of the box. It's lovely and she's just delightful. I remember both of us leaving and practically flying home, it was absolutely amazing. She's 13 now, yeah.

It was very different with Elsa, the foster carer was a very different person, very protective. It wasn't handled at all well. In fact it ended up feeling as though we'd taken Elsa from her mother. Ana's foster carers were very experienced and brilliant but I didn't bond as well with Elsa, I think because the foster carer, she made it very hard and also because Elsa was quite sickly, so immediately we were thrust into this endless round of hospital appointments and she has some severe behavioural issues. I mean, nobody else really sees the Elsa that we see but when she came to us at 12 months, if you said no, she screamed for 40 minutes and banged her head on the floor and she's pretty much been like that ever since. She has a terrible temper and she can fly off the handle with you and scream and froth at the mouth. She's getting better as she gets older but, you know, this weekend, we had a really shit weekend of major tantrums. One of the psychologists once said to us, 'Being Elsa is hard work because mentally processing things is difficult for her.' She holds it in until she's comfortable to let it out. And that's me. That's home. And it's tough. It's really tough.

The girls' birth parents were totally opposed to the adoption. A planned meeting with them fell through because they didn't want to meet us. We met two other birth relatives – there was a paternal aunt who had wanted to adopt Ana but by that point she was in her sixties and she was turned down and we met her very soon after we had Ana and she was an absolutely lovely lady. Absolutely salt of the earth type but by that time, she'd been diagnosed with terminal cancer, so it's really good that she hadn't adopted Ana because within two years, she was dead. When she was in the hospice, she asked if I would bring Ana and I did and she was really happy to know that the girls were going to be together.

When we'd had both girls for about two years, we met the paternal grandmother. We were doing letterbox contact at this point; our letter was distributed to the birth mother and father, his sister and mother and we used to get replies from grandma and the aunt and cousins but not from the parents, we've never had anything from the parents. To be honest, the letters aren't worth the paper they're written on. We never told them anything. 'All's well.' That's what we said. We said to Social Services, 'Look because there's not going to be any contact with birth parents,' that was obvious by then, we said, 'Would the paternal grandmother like to meet them?' because Ana and Elsa are the birth father's fifth and sixth children to three different mothers who have no contact with him. So I felt quite sorry for the grandmother because that was six grandchildren that she would have absolutely no contact with at all. So we arranged to meet her at the contact centre. Again, lovely lady but it just wasn't a healthy meeting for the kids because all she wanted to talk about was her son's – their birth father's – drug use. At that point, the children were two and four so they didn't really get what was being talked about but I just felt I can't. I felt dreadfully sorry for her but I left it for her to contact us and she didn't, so maybe she got what she needed from seeing that they were okay. The last time we wrote, I didn't get any replies so I didn't write again. At that point, I found it harder to write the letters and be positive.

At the beginning, I didn't mind sharing but the longer the girls had been with us, the more I felt they were mine and I didn't want to share. Plus we had a really hard time with Elsa and actually what I was gonna write was not gonna sound great. Actually this child has all these conditions, she has behavioural problems, you know, life is tough is what I needed to tell them. Part of me wants them to know that but where's the good in writing that. I didn't feel there was anything to be gained by that for anyone. I couldn't write a letter saying, 'Ooh we're having a lovely life' because actually what I wanted to say is, 'It's shit.'

We're in a better place now, but I think between the ages of four and eight, we had a really tough few years with Elsa – her behaviour nearly broke us at a few points. Because she's got ADHD, she's on the go the whole time, lashing out. You know, her vision is poor, she's got developmental coordination disorder, she's dyslexic and her behavioural issues are such that she's got a very short temper. Partly, we think that is just her inherited temper because that's certainly what we know about her birth father and partly it's her frustrations with everything else that's going on. It's usually the start and end of the day, it's only ever at home so for about three years, we had a paediatrician telling us it was our fault, we were bad parents. It's only when we were referred to Great Ormond Street and they said, 'Actually no, it's this, this and this …' There is definitely a question mark linked to the drug use. There are times we've felt quite angry with the birth parents. My husband finds it harder than I do because I'm quite philosophical because I think we knew what we were taking on and anyway, you could have your own birth child and they could have difficulties and at the end of the day – and I find myself saying this often – it is what it is and what's the point in getting angry about it.

We've got to deal with it and we've got to give her the best chance in life. And that's my worry really, what does her life look like in the future and what are her chances of a happy, balanced life? So part of what we're doing at the moment is giving teachers a hard time to make sure she's getting the support she needs. We've finally got there, she's now got a statement of educational needs. It's taken five years but she's now got 30 hours a week support at school. It's almost like the cavalry have arrived. I think when finally we got the right group of people together to look at it, they said, 'This child needs help.' I said to them, 'Are you going to give her the support she needs to achieve her education or are you going to continue to let her fail until around 15, you'll probably expel her and by that stage, I'm going to tell you, I'm not sure we'll be able to cope with her either. So what happens to her then? So do you spend the money now, giving her the support and education she needs or do you spend ten times the money in the future supporting an adult who can't support her?' I just kept saying this to anyone who'd listen – the educational psychologist, the head of education in our area. 'If at 15, you're expelling her from school and we're saying, take her into care because we can't cope with her anymore, what hope?' You know. It happens. An adopter I know, her 16-year-old son was beating her up.

I think you have to keep raising the subject of adoption with kids fairly regularly, that's what we do with our two. We always have a little thing on Mother's Day, I make a point of saying to the girls, she's thinking about you today, even if they haven't said anything. I'll say, 'Do you want to buy her some flowers or draw a little picture for her and put it away?' In terms of the future, I'm fully expecting them to turn around and say they want to trace, I'm fully accepting if they do. I think my biggest fear in this modern world is how they might do it and whether or not I'll even know they're doing it. If I know, I can support them but if they suddenly look her up on Facebook and there she is …. They have her name because they have their life story books with all the information. When you consider I couldn't get any of that until I was 18. Equally what worries me is if they talk to friends about it and they say, 'Oh, let's look her up.'

My brother's girlfriend just looked his birth mother up and phoned her. The first time he met his birth mother was at his wedding, which was a very bizarre day and they were all in the family photos together. You know, my mum and dad are very polite people and they just went with it but it was very weird. I think his wife just arranged it all and thought it was a great idea. It was fine but it was bizarre. They're not really in touch now so it's not like it was the start of a lovely, long-term relationship.

I don't have any memory of being told I was adopted. I've talked to my mum about it and apparently, she would talk to me about it before I could even speak. It's like I've always known. She would say, 'There was a little girl born and her mummy couldn't look after her so they needed somebody else to be her mummy and daddy.' There were some formal letters that I was allowed to see in my teens. Of course, in those days nobody had a phone, so there were letters from social workers saying, 'Can you please call the office on Thursday?' Or there were telegrams. It makes me sound ancient. It was only in 1968/69. There's a story when I was a toddler and I got a sick bug and my mum had been up with me all night and they got a telegram the next morning, offering them twin boys and my mum went, 'No way!' So I could have easily ended up with twin brothers but she said, 'No, I can't cope with that!'

For me, if you're living your life fighting against your history, then that's tough because it was not your fault and there's nothing you could do to change it and for me, that post-adoption work needs to support that acceptance. It needs to give children that chance to ask questions, get some answers and say, 'Ok, it is what it is.' If there are decisions that were made by individuals that I don't agree with but okay, why were those decisions made? And for me it's very much about accepting that a lot of those decisions weren't personal, they were what they had to do to get by and live their lives.

Ana and Elsa were their birth mothers' first two children. I don't know if she's had any more since. I think if Social Services knew, they would tell us because we'd be offered contact but if she's moved to another part of the country, they might not know. If she had more children taken into care, I think we'd probably be offered them. At one point, we made a joke because she was only 26 when she had Ana and we said, 'God, she could go on having babies for years and years. At what point do you say enough is enough?' I think if it had been quite soon after we had Elsa, I would have considered it. But not now, God no, I'm too old now.

I think after Elsa started sleeping through the night, which I think was about age three, I couldn't bear the thought of not having sleep again, it would have been too much and I think by then we realised what Elsa's needs were and I don't think bringing another child into the equation would have helped, so I think by then no. I'm quite glad that never came up. I must admit, I think if we'd been offered a little boy, having had two girls, that would have been very hard. I think I would have had to have persuaded Will, quite severely but I would have been tempted really. But I think, living the life they were living, I wonder whether they're even still alive. It wasn't good. She was in and out of prison. Part of me hopes she's cleaned her act up and she's living a lovely little life somewhere but you know, part of me thinks there's no reason to think she would and she's now living with the burden of having her two children taken away. That's hard. Yeah, that's really hard. That's the big debate I had with the therapist we saw last year because we've always said to the girls that they were and are loved by her and the therapist said, 'You can't say that.' And I said, 'Yes, I can because I know she wanted them and I know she thinks about them.' Her drug use was stronger than her love but it doesn't mean she didn't care and I don't want them to grow up thinking that.

What I've tried to get across to my girls is that their birth parents' life styles were just not compatible with raising children and that they were given opportunities to change their lifestyle but they just couldn't because they were ill. When they were very little and they asked, 'Why couldn't they look after me?' I would just say, 'Because they were ill' because they were because addiction is an illness. We were given quite a lot of information about their birth mother and her childhood; she was a looked after child herself, both her parents were drug users, it was a messy family. The grandfather had been in prison for kidnapping, after robbing an off licence while he was on drugs and hijacking a car and driving off with a child in the back, not realising it was there. Not somebody you really wanna have any contact with.

The other thing I have talked to the social workers about quite a lot is that I wanted some positive information if at all possible with some role models from the family and certainly on the father's side there seemed to be more of those. Because I know being adopted there were always questions like, 'Why am I good at certain things?' or 'Why am I not good at certain things?' At school, somebody would make a comment like he plays the piano well because he takes after his dad or something and so I was always like, where do my talents come from? So I was quite keen we got something I could tell them around that, and apparently I think it was a cousin somewhere that played for Liverpool so if they are a bit sporty or something.

His family seemed quite a nice family and when we met his mother, her view was, 'I don't know what happened to him. He wasn't like this. We're not like this.' He fell in with a bad lot. So only time will tell. One of the cousins was training as a nursery nurse so if there was contact in the future with that side of that family, that would probably be alright but the other side, I'm not keen really. Again, it won't be my choice, will it? It'll be down to the girls. But I see my role as counselling them with the pros and cons and equipping them with the tools. There was a thing on Facebook the other day and a woman had posted a photo of the child she gave up for adoption and she was trying to trace her and she was asking people to share it and it made me angry because that child might not even know she's adopted and might just see a photo of herself on Facebook.

I know someone who found out he was adopted at the age of 65. Where do you go with that? Nobody was still alive that he could still trace. I put the odd picture of the girls on Facebook but I never name them, I call them daughter number one and daughter number two. The photos I put up now are not the girls they would recognise because they haven't seen photos of them since they were two and four. I'm not overly cautious because we are living in the twenty-first century and I had this moment one day when I thought I'm not gonna live my life in fear and I'm not gonna tell the kids they shouldn't use technology. Part of the reason we moved was because we didn't want to be living near their birth parents and where we are now, it's very unlikely, we'd bump into them. But stranger things have happened.

At the end of the day, we can't stop them from contacting them in the future. The only thing we can hope as parents is that we've brought them up well enough and equipped them with enough thought that if it's right to be in contact they will and if it's not they'll walk away. We want to protect them but we can't. And actually, I'd rather they met them and had closure because what helped me was being able to ask questions I needed to ask and have some closure. I know where I fit into the jigsaw now. And that's probably the turning point for me. I think for me, wherever you start in life, it's important to get to the point where you can be yourself and not carry any burden or baggage about how you were created.

For further information on Adoption UK and Natural Parents Network, please consult the references below.

Reference list

Adoption UK (2022) 'About Adoption UK' [Online]. Available at: https://www.adoptionuk.org/Pages/Category/about-adoption-uk (Accessed 10 November 2022).

Natural Parents Network (2022) 'About' [Online]. Available at: https://www.facebook.com/NPNNaturalParentsNetwork/about (Accessed 10 November 2022).

9
SHANTA'S STORY PART III

No babies

It starts with a phone call to the local authority. Not my own local authority as their website informs me that they are closed for 'adopter recruitment' but a neighbouring authority advertised as being open for business. Of course, it started before that. It started in the counselling room. It started with the ectopic pregnancy. No, it started in the lecture hall for the fertility talk. It started when I thought, what if I can't have another baby? So here I am calling the local authority, aged 39 years, less than a year after one of my fallopian tubes was removed with my tiny bud of a baby inside it. I am married when I go through the adoption process; as this essay represents my story, and to protect privacy, I am narrating my adoption experience in the singular.

But let's rewind a moment. I'm in the park with a new mum friend, I'll call Sarah, who I met on my son's first day at school. Somehow in the space of two weeks, I have managed to find out that she adopted her son and daughter as toddlers. It's an autumn day and the kids are scrabbling up a climbing wall together, in fierce competition over who will reach the top first. As I watch them yelp and laugh, see the look of delight on my son's face as he revels in the company, I turn to my new friend and casually say, 'I'm thinking about adoption myself.' We sit on a bench, a flask between us. She sips her tea and nods, as if she's always known. 'How long did the process take? Being assessed and everything, I mean.'

'Six years,' says Sarah, not taking her eyes off the kids.

I nearly spit out my tea.

Theirs was a stop–start process, a long waiting list before they could even start the process, then more waiting for the preparation training, then getting halfway through the assessment with one authority only to get turned down and have to start again elsewhere. I can't wait six years, I think. I'll be 45 years. My son

DOI: 10.4324/9781003290179-11

will be starting senior school. I want a baby and I want a baby now. I shudder and wrap my scarf tighter around me. Her daughter reaches the top first. She is jubilant, cheeks rosy, dirty blonde hair swinging as she sings, 'I'm the king of the castle...' The boys moan.

'Can we get chips now, Mummy?' shouts my son.

> Prospective adopters had a range of motivations for choosing adoption. For 58% of respondents, being unable to have birth children was a motivating factor but, in almost a quarter of cases, adoption was a first choice for starting a family and 17% reported being motivated by a connection to adoption in their family.
>
> The Adoption Barometer *(Adoption UK, 2019)*

It seems that when you start looking for something, you discover it's been there all around you all along. One of my older cousins was adopted as a baby but I didn't know him well and we'd lost touch. I didn't think he would appreciate a contact out of the blue to discuss his family origins. Then I had a chance meeting in the street with an old school friend I'll call Mim. I hadn't seen Mim in over 20 years. The last I'd heard, she'd moved to Birmingham.

'Oh my God! It's so good to see you!' I exclaim as I bump into her outside the supermarket. 'Wow, two kids!'

She pushes a little girl in a buggy while a boy a little older than my son holds her hand, eying me suspiciously.

'Just the one for you?'

'Yes, yes. Just one,' I smile down at my son. 'For now.'

★

It turns out she moved back to London a few years ago.

'We live just round the corner,' says Mim. 'Do you want to come back for a coffee?'

We marshal the kids to her house, chatting and interrupting each other as we scrabble to catch up on two decades. On entering Mim's living room, her son leads mine across the room to look at his cars, while she plonks her daughter in her high chair and empties a packet of raisins onto the tray.

'That'll keep her quiet for a bit,' she laughs, the throaty, deep laugh I remember from school days. A series of memories flash through me. The geography field trip to Swansea where we shared a dorm and discovered that waterproof trousers are no good for wading waist deep in rivers. The seventies party at uni where she studied medicine; I turned up in brown velvet flares and a psychedelic pink and orange top to find barely anyone else had bothered with themed dress and she thought it was hysterical. It really is good to see her. She tells me about her husband, her work as a part-time GP. She talks about how her family came into being. 'It was a long road, yeah. So after going through IVF with him,' she nods in her son's direction, 'we adopted.'

My mouth hangs open. At that moment, I start believing in fate and miracles and people coming into your life when they're meant to and everything happening for a reason and all that horse shit. I tell her I'm considering it.

'You have to tell the social workers what they want to hear,' says Mim, matter-of-factly. 'They asked me if I'd been hit as a child, so of course I said no. My mum used to beat me black and blue yeah but you don't tell them that because then they'll think you've got problems or you'll hit your child. You just jump through the hoops and tell them what they want to hear.'

I'm not sure how one knows what the social workers want to hear but, like everyone, I have a few skeletons in my closet. The boys race round the room on plastic ride-on cars while the little girl squeals, banging her fists on the high chair tray.

'Whatever you do, don't tell them you want a baby or they won't even look at you.' She looks me deep in the eyes and my stomach flips. 'They'll tell you there are no babies but that's not true. The truth is that there are babies but babies are easy to place. No, the social workers want to find homes for their, quote–unquote, "hard to place" children.'

She makes finger marks in the air and looks at me as though I understand.

'You have to pretend you're not fussy, say you'll take any age, any ethnicity and any special needs. Otherwise, they won't take you on because they don't want to invest time and money in training and assessing you, only for you to go and adopt a baby from another agency. So you tell them what they want to hear and then after you've been approved, you just wait for your baby and turn down any children offered who you don't think are right for your family.'

I walk home holding my son's hand extra tightly, thinking about all those hard-to-place children and wondering if I am capable of being their mum.

> Adopted children are seven times more likely than their peers to have a diagnosis of autistic spectrum disorder. Adopted children are almost eight times more likely than their peers to have a diagnosis of ADHD. Adopted children in England were 20 times more likely to be permanently excluded than their peers during 2018.
>
> The Adoption Barometer *(Adoption UK, 2019)*

So I call the local authority advertising for adopters and try to say what I think they want to hear and it works, for now anyway, as they arrange for a social worker to come and view the house. The first stipulation is that you had to have a spare bedroom. I hastily tidy up the box room office and throw a few cushions on the desk chair in a vain attempt to make it look cosy, muttering to the social worker that the desk would be moved out of the room to make way for the bed. The second is that if you already have a child, there must be a minimum two-year gap between their age and the adopted child's age.

'So if you're approved,' says the smartly dressed, Black, male social worker, 'you'd be looking at a child of around three years of age. This is the average age for adopted children anyway. We don't take people on who are looking for babies.'

I swallow and smile. 'Would you like some more tea?'

> More than 4,500 children were adopted in the UK during the year ending March 2018. The majority of these children will have been removed from their birth families and placed into the care system. Most will have experienced abuse or neglect. All of them will have experienced the trauma of losing their birth family – and perhaps foster families – before finding their permanent home at an average age of three or four years old.
> The Adoption Barometer *(Adoption UK, 2019)*

The next step is to attend the preparation classes where we learn about attachment and trauma and loss and identity and bonds, about how parenting an adopted child might be different from parenting a birth child. There are ten or so hopeful people sitting round wooden tables arranged in a U-shape, facing a female social work consultant in a charcoal trouser suit with a purple, patterned scarf. The training is a blur of presentations, talks and hands-on activities, all carried out in the full knowledge that we are being observed and assessed throughout by both the trainer and a local authority social worker milling about the room. Two exercises stick in my mind: amputations and rubbish bags. We're given cardboard templates in the shape of a person and asked to write six words or phrases on them – one on each limb, one in the headspace and one in the heartspace – which represent different aspects of our identity. It's one of those exercises that you have to do quickly, intuitively, from the gut. We're then asked to place all our cardboard people on the table and walk round and read them. I don't remember the words I used to describe myself but I do remember heat creeping into my cheeks as I walked round that table with 'little me' exposed for all to judge. We're then instructed to pick up someone else's person and rip off one of their limbs. Perhaps it was two. I remember nervous laughter, the kind you hear at funerals. We're given back our amputated self and asked how we'd feel if we had to live like that now, with pieces missing. Next, we're each given a refuse sack of clothes and told to imagine that we were a child in foster care and this sack contains all our personal possessions. I remember walking round in circles, having to keep stopping and unpacking the bag only to pack it all up and move on again. I remember thinking: I don't want to play this game anymore.

> On 31st March 2019, 78,150 children were in the care of local authorities in England. 72% of children looked after were living with foster carers. 10% of the looked after children had had 3 or more placements during the year and 22% had two placements.
> *(Coram BAAF, Adoption and Fostering Academy, 2020)*

On day two, we have a visit from a single-mother adopter, who runs through her experience of adopting two older children, explaining the process and what to expect after the preparation classes. She's an unassuming looking woman with cropped brown hair, friendly and open, who tells it like it is: the social worker picking over the debris of her life – contacting her employer and her exes, interrogating her best friend and her ex-mother-in-law, examining her bank statements, her kitchen cupboards, her medical records, her deepest, darkest thoughts – *By the end of it all, they'll know you better than you know yourself!*; being interviewed by a panel of 15 people who could say 'yes' or could say 'no' – *Don't worry, they nearly always say yes!*; being handed a child's profile over a cup of coffee, reading how they collected ants and tore wallpaper from the walls with bare hands to feed a sibling because there was no food in the house, staring at their little faces looking out from staged photographs – *It's important to get the right match*; having to say 'yes' or to say 'no'; then being told that somebody else was chosen; looking at another profile and another, wondering if she can bear to see anymore and then … trying to convince them that yes, she is the right mother for this child; meeting her daughter for that first time, watching her child cling to the foster carer and slowly, slowly, come forwards and take the jigsaw puzzle she bought her with a shy smile; and finally, finally, bringing her home. I tuck my son in that night knowing how lucky I am.

> 92% of prospective adopters agreed that their training was informative and useful … However, more than half of respondents reported finding the process so difficult that they wondered if they could continue, timescales slipped, and half of prospective adopters experienced delays caused by changes of social worker, administrative delays, social worker absence or other reasons within their agencies.
>
> The Adoption Barometer *(Adoption UK, 2019)*

A freelance social worker comes to the house regularly for the assessment, a semi-retired Scottish man, wearing corduroy trousers and a rain mac, to ask questions about different topics. He has a chatty, leisurely way about him unlike the business-like local authority social workers. He asks to speak to my five-year-old son on his own; I sit in the conservatory and peer through the glass doors, watching my tiny boy jumping up and down, answering questions, thinking he's never looked so small and vulnerable. His school teacher is contacted to check if there are any parenting concerns. A number of written references are obtained. A file is being built. My line manager at work is contacted. (She breaks down on the phone to me afterwards, revealing her daughters' miscarriages.) My mother and my best friend of nearly 30 years are both interviewed separately in their own homes. My mum is a nervous wreck leading up to her interview: 'What shall I say?' My best friend recounts afterwards, 'Don't worry. I didn't tell them about the time your son cut his hand on the broken glass in the pub and had to be taken to the out of hours centre.'

> More than half of newly-placed adopters wondered in the early months whether they had done the right thing and whether they would be able to cope. 54% experienced stress, anxiety and/or symptoms of post-adoption depression.
>
> The Adoption Barometer *(Adoption UK, 2019)*

Once he's completed the assessment, the freelance social worker writes up his report and hands it over to the local authority. Then there is the Approval Panel to face. I remember the local authority social worker opening the doors and seeing 20 pairs of eyes looking up. Questions are fired from all sides, while the panel members take notes. I don't recall a single question they ask or a single word I say but I remember thinking this is the most important interview of my life. Our family is approved to adopt one child up to the age of three years, with the acknowledgement that a younger child would be an ideal match. Days pass. Then weeks. Checking the phone. Every day. Fielding questions from family and friends. Not yet, not yet.

> 420 was the average number of days between a child entering care and moving in with its adoptive family during the year 2017–2018. 171 was the average number of days between an LA receiving court authority to place a child and the LA deciding on a match to an adoptive family during the year 2017–2018.
>
> *(Coram BAAF, Adoption and Fostering Academy, 2020)*

Then.

The social worker rings. My knuckles are white as I hold on tight. She has a possible match for a sibling pair, aged two and three years. She talks about the possibility of fitting bunkbeds in the box room, or swapping my son's slightly larger room. Giddiness engulfs me. She's all for it, very persuasive. Yet ... my son is only five years old. Not only would he have to adapt to no longer being an only child but he would be outnumbered by two toddlers, moved out of his room, taken over. This is not giving birth to twin babies; the needs of the sibling pair would be complex. Don't let me look at the photos, I think. Just don't let me look.

> When considering possible matches, most adopters seem to be proactive in seeking out profiles of children waiting for adoption, with half of prospective adopters exploring profiles online or in magazines, 25% attending information exchange days and 16% attending activity days (where children are present). However, it was profiles selected by the adopters' social workers that were most likely to result in a confirmed match. 62% of matched adopters had been introduced to their child or children's profile by their social worker.
>
> The Adoption Barometer *(Adoption UK, 2019)*

My friend's words ring in my head, 'You just wait for your baby and turn down any children offered who you don't think are right for your family.' So simple to say, so difficult to do. Saying 'no' to children in need of a family; the siblings were not the only heart-breaking false starts. This is the hardest part. Agonising over decisions.

Agony.

And then.

> The report reveals that 79% of families would encourage others to adopt, despite the fact that 70% say they face a continual struggle for support.
> The Adoption Barometer *(Adoption UK, 2019)*

There he is.

A ten second video, played over and over.

There he is.

A tiny, beautiful baby laying on a baby mat, gurgling at the camera.

There he is.

Imprinted on me, like looking at my first son's 12-week scan.

There he is.

My baby.

Reference list

Brooks, B. (2019) *The Adoption Barometer*, Banbury, Adoption UK.

Coram BAAF, Adoption and Fostering Academy (2020) *Statistics: England* [Online]. Available at: https://corambaaf.org.uk/fostering-adoption/looked-after-children-adoption-fostering-statistics/statistics-england (Accessed 9 January 2020).

10
MARGARET'S STORY

Never forget

The first thing I notice as we approach the bungalow is the row of ornamental elephants lining the window sill: a large, pale, stone one with its trunk in the air; a small metallic one, trunk curled down; a multicoloured ceramic one; wooden ones in various shapes and sizes. Margaret is welcoming, making tea in the kitchen before leading us through to the sun room, to sit and look out through the large windows onto the rolling sea. She is welcoming but she doesn't smile; she is bare-faced, with piercing eyes, her white–grey hair cropped short, her thin frame clothed in black jeans and a red fleece over a tartan shirt.

★

Well, I'm a trained nurse and after I qualified, I did a couple of staff nurse jobs in London and then a friend of mine said, 'Oh, let's go and do something different.' [Laughs.] So we applied to a Butlin's holiday camp in Bognor. It was a very busy job. There were eight of us looking after thousands of campers. [Laughs.] Anything from birth to death. I delivered a baby and also coped with quite a few deaths as well, elderly people. So, I did that for one year and then I did some private nursing through the winter then I went back again to Butlin's the following summer. Then I started going out with a redcoat called Glen, so erm, we were going out for a few weeks then I got pregnant. I was 23 and he was about the same. This was a time when we didn't have telephones or anything like that. I wrote to my older sister; she's four years older than me so she would have been 27, yes. She came down with my mother to see me, to discuss the options, well, tell me, not discuss. My sister had been to the Catholic Crusade of Rescue it was called back then, it's now the Catholic Children's Society and said, 'All the arrangements have been made for you to go there and that's where you'll stay until you have the baby.' So that's what happened. My mother

DOI: 10.4324/9781003290179-12

kept telling me it would kill my father if he knew. I don't think it would. He was a very devout Catholic and he was a very kind man. I don't think … who knows … He never found out.

Abortion did happen. When I went to the GP to get my pregnancy confirmed, he wrote a prescription for a douche can. Do you know what a douche can is? It's a can, with tubing and a bit like a speculum. It's a glass tube with holes in the end and you had to put really hot water in it, which I did. Nothing happened. I know lots of women who did it themselves and did lots of damage.

So I stayed in this hostel as arranged. It wasn't a very nice place to be; obviously we had chores to do – cooking, cleaning, that sort of thing. I remember signing on at the sort of labour exchange then to get money. I don't know if that was unemployment benefit or maternity money. All a bit of a blur. [Coughs.] Obviously that would pay for our keep in the hostel. I can't remember how many of us were there but I remember a room like an old people's home with chairs all around the edge and a telly in the corner and all of us knitting, because we were asked to knit clothes for the baby. Yeah. Then it was arranged for me to go to a private hospital to have my daughter. I've no idea who paid for that. I vaguely remember that Glen might have been asked to pay for it but I don't know. I dare say if I was pushy enough I could probably find the evidence. [Coughs.] Sorry, I've got a chest condition that makes me cough. 2 March 1965 she was born. I was home by 9 March on my dad's birthday. He thought I was abroad all that time. I used to meet up with my mother and she'd bring airmail paper and we'd write letters for him. So within a week, I was home. When I was in the hospital, my younger sister came with my mother and took my daughter across the road to the Catholic Church to have her baptised. Why I don't know. You question these things much later. I never discussed it with my younger sister, I never asked the question of why she was there. Because she and my mother were much closer than I was.

I can remember waiting a long time for any pain control. I can remember waiting a long time to be stitched up. But otherwise it's just a bit of a blank. So home I came. My daughter went to a foster mother for a while before she went to the adoptive parents. I can vaguely remember having her for a week. I can't remember much. Glen wasn't there, no. Again, I can't remember his response. He must have been told. I can't remember. Being brought up a Catholic, obedience was the thing. You didn't question your parents at all, no. I can't remember any feelings, no. I don't remember any of the other women who were there, I never saw or heard from them again. I don't remember who ran it. So home I came and I had to find a job, so I found a job. I had three brothers as well and they didn't know, not until much later.

Half a million of us apparently, out there. Somebody somewhere thought that was alright to do that, not just society, not just an organisation, but somebody. There were 700 of these homes – some Catholic, some Church of England, all different churches. I think money changed hands, so the story goes. Obviously, blue-eyed blonde babies were chosen. I don't know how the babies and adoptive parents got paired together. I can't remember ever getting any court papers. I did go somewhere with a Justice of the Peace to sign something. I have a copy of the letter somewhere, the one they wrote to the adoptive parents to say that I was available, I came from a nice family. [Coughs.] And then, I wish I could get it out for you as the wording was very, if you'd like to take the baby, almost as if, if you don't like it, you can return it, sort of attitude. The adoptive parents were Catholic as well. Somebody said it was alright to do that to all these women.

I put it right to the back of my mind and just got on with things for many years. The job I took was quite near home, then the next job I took was near home as well. Then I got a job further away in London and then I stayed in London. The next contact I had with Glen was when I tracked him down after I met my daughter. Interestingly, he still had photos of me sitting on the bonnet of his car outside his house. Yes, he'd thought about me over the years. So, yes I must have told him about it, I suppose. Yes, I ... it's really annoying when you can't remember things. As I say, I didn't think about her at all for many years until I got to the menopause in my late forties and for some reason, I went into hospital to have a ... do you know what a D and C is? Yes, that seemed to unlock something in my head and all the grief that I hadn't expressed, it all came tumbling out and I was off work for three months. I was just crying all the time. I saw a psychiatrist but I don't think he really understood what I was feeling. I also wrote to the Catholic Children's Society to check that they had her records. I had a burning desire to know if my daughter was still alive. They told me about the Post Adoption Centre in London and I went there for counselling and they helped me so much. I was in a bad way. They understood. I also found out about the Natural Parents Network – they had a different name then but they were a support group. This was the first time I'd spoken to other women who'd been through the same experience.

I never had any meaningful relationships at all until after the menopause. I saw many of my friends having children, I saw my sister having her three children and it didn't affect me at all. I never thought about having more children, no. I didn't think about it. I don't know if you've ever read any of Evelyn Robinson's books where she talks about disenfranchised grief? I'll show you the books later. My younger sister went through the same thing; it was all arranged by my older sister. When I was tracing Penny, I said to my younger sister, I could help her trace her baby as well, which I did, I managed to track her, so they're in touch now but she doesn't seem to be ... she doesn't show it ... to have the same feelings as I did. She went to live with a Catholic family not the same place as I did, which was probably a nicer place for her.

When I wrote to the adoption agency, they told me that her adoptive parents had emigrated to Canada and they told me her mother was a school teacher, her dad was a nuclear physicist. So, I found them. I had their name and I had their marriage certificate. She was actually younger than me, her mother, so she must have had a medical condition or something, why she couldn't have children. I went to the Canadian High Commission in Trafalgar Square and asked if I could look in their phone book and there was only one entry with that surname, so I went upstairs to their library and looked to see if they have any support groups over there and found Parent Finder and they managed to do the contact for me. She was living with her father at the time. He wasn't best pleased with people ringing up. She told me that many years later. Her parents separated when she was 16 and her mother was back in England at that time. So contact was made. The agency relayed that she was pleased that I'd made contact and wanted to meet her – she was 24 at the time, the same age I was when I had her – but she didn't want to meet me. It was disappointing but because I'd heard similar stories from other women, it didn't surprise me. Once I'd made *contact, I used to send her a card every year on her birthday, through the agency. I put my email address in the card. She never wrote back.*

During this period, I got to know an adoptive mother very well; she had three adopted children, grown-ups. And she offered to write to the mother for me to ask why she thought Penny wasn't in touch. I found out the company the mother worked at and that she'd remarried. I can't remember how I found out. But my friend wrote to her. She just said I can't really interfere; she'll do it when she's ready. In fact, it took her 13 years to make contact. I got an email from her, saying she'd had a baby. That baby is now15. We corresponded for about a year via emails. It worked out that she actually met her birth father first before she met me. I helped her to trace him. She met him at Easter time and it wasn't until June that she came down here for the day. It was amazing. She's very demonstrative, bigger than ever in spirit, you know she's around. She just walked in the house with her little toddler and all the baby stuff like she felt quite at home. My husband was here. She was in her late thirties then, the first time I saw her since our first week together. We went down to the beach, it was a lovely day, we went to get an ice-cream, had a paddle in the sea. We had a few of those days. And from then on, we met up, not that regularly as she lives two hours away, and all during this year she was with this chap and it turned out he was physically and verbally abusive to her. Her mother wanted her to leave him but she didn't. She thought, as a lot of abused women do, he'll be better tomorrow. Eventually, he left her, thank God. She's still fighting him for maintenance, that's still going on. What was interesting about him, apart from the fact he was 13 years younger than her, he was Maltese; well, my dad was Maltese. It's strange, isn't it? Her daughter looks very Maltese, she's very dark.

Her husband comes in and offers more tea. *You'll be on tape, you know.* He smiles and mumbles something about not worrying, he's not saying anything he shouldn't. I suspect he's checking that she's okay. The waves ebb and flow on the shore through the window.

What I will say is my family have welcomed her into their family, yes. She's larger than life, sometimes says things you think you wish she hadn't said, especially in emails. You know she rattles them off and doesn't check them afterwards. My older sister died about six years ago and we usually meet up on the anniversary of her death and my daughter's been to a couple of those but when we're sitting around having lunch afterwards she tends to take over the conversation. One of my nieces in particular just can't handle it; she says we're here for Susan's day, it's not Penny's day. So there's a bit of friction there but they don't see much of each other, so... She doesn't get any of that from me as I'm a very reserved person. I don't know if her outgoing nature is to do with being brought up in Canada; you know, Canadians are like Americans, they talk nineteen to the dozen, so ... She looks like me, oh God yes. She looks like me at that age. She sent me a picture after she made contact by email. No, I didn't have any baby pictures of her. That's right; all those years I didn't know what she looked like. I don't really see any of my personality traits in her, no. So, it's nurture not nature in that respect. [Coughs.] *I will find you a picture of her.*

She didn't tell me much about her childhood, no. One time when we were at her house, she brought out some pictures of her when she was growing up but I have never asked her anything; I've waited for her to volunteer. In fact, most of the contact we've had I've let her lead it rather than hassle her. There were the odd times I'd ring her up and she just wouldn't have time for me so that's why it's best if I wait for her to ring me really. Although it's getting better; it's better than it used to be. Later this month, we've got a big family gathering on my father's side – my dad was one of 15 children – there's something like 400 descendants of my grandparents and about a 150 are all gathering at the end of the month and she's coming to that. But again, she'll blow in and take the room over.

Her adoptive mother died about five years ago, and what was strange was that after her mother died, she rang me every single morning for about two weeks when she went back to work, just to chat really. And I've never been a mother so I don't really know how to be a mother. It's difficult to explain. But, er, yeah, weird. She doesn't call me Mum or Mother. She either calls me by my first name or she calls me Grandma if her daughter's around. I'm sure you've seen Long Lost Family, haven't you? It all looks so idyllic when they meet, doesn't it? And at the end, they put a footnote, oh they've been meeting up and doing this together, but I've heard of so many reunions that have been euphoric to start with but just fizzle out. Lots of things can go wrong. It can become obsessional; you've heard of Genetic Mutual Attraction, haven't you, where a birth parent and child become sexually attracted when they meet as adults? Sometimes, it goes on to a sexual relationship or they get very close and their partner gets pushed out and it's very difficult to cope with.

I've told my story many times before; I talk on behalf of all the women who can't talk. I'm involved with Natural Parents Network, which supports women who have experienced forced or coerced adoption, and I'm also involved in trying to get an apology from the government because we just think that it was wrong, what happened to us. There's lots been written about separating mother and child and how it affects the child, you know, separation anxiety and all that. They talk about separation anxiety for children who are adopted but birth mothers suffer from separation anxiety too. I certainly did. Obviously you think, are they alive out there or are they dead? I knew a lovely lady who battled to get information and finally found out her daughter died aged eight. Then she had another battle to find out where the grave was. That's another thing we'd like that if an adopted child dies, the birth parents should be informed as a matter of routine.

She goes and sees her birth father about once a year. He never married. He's got another son who's about 20 now; he didn't stay with the mother. He got involved in doing naughty things and ended up in prison. He was a very bright young man but put his skills into doing unethical things. [Laughs.] I met my husband when I was 60 at a local singles group. We just clicked straight away; it was lovely. I told him about my daughter on our first date. I hadn't met her at that stage. He's got three children, all in their thirties and forties and they've all got children so we find ourselves going to a lot of children's parties. He was estranged from his youngest son at the time but they are in touch now. Things changed when his son became a father; it changes people, doesn't it? So he sort of understood what it was like being separated from your son or daughter. He was by my side through the reunion process. My daughter met my husband's children once at my seventieth birthday party. Shall I find you that photo now?

Here it is. Yes, she does look like me. There's some more pictures here. That's her and her daughter. See, she does look very dark. I've known her since she was a toddler; a stroppy 15-year-old now, so I'm told, but she always behaves well when she comes here. She's recently bought her partner's half of the house off him so she's completely free of him now. Things are good now. I don't know how you're supposed to feel as I haven't had any more children and I know many other birth mothers who never had any more children; it's like a secondary infertility. She does overstep the mark sometimes though. We've got a Facebook page leading up to this big gathering on my father's side that I was telling you about and for some reason, she had to post something all about her adoptive family, in great detail to sort of explain who she was. 'Although I'm part of your family, I've still got the family I grew up with.' Why does she need to do that? So all the people we're going to be meeting at this reunion will have seen that. Some of them have met her but not many. She's got an adopted sister, who she grew up with. She Skypes her sister and her adoptive dad; she always seems to go to him first for advice, hmm. I met him once. I've been to many visits to court over her ex-partner and I met him once when we came back and he was leaving her house and I said, 'Don't you think we look alike?' and he went, 'I suppose so.' He was very dismissive. I've never sat down and had a conversation with him; I never met her adoptive mother at all. My daughter was 16 when her adoptive parents split up, she was coming up to doing high school or whatever it is they do then, so she didn't want to disrupt that so she stayed with her father.

Have you read many books about adoption? Yes, there are so many. Let me get some of mine to show you. These (Adoption and Loss – The Hidden Grief, Adoption Reunion – Ecstasy or Agony, Adoption and Recovery – Solving the Mystery of Reunion, Adoption and Separation – Then and Now) are by Evelyn Robinson who I was telling you about who talks about disenfranchised grief; you can look her up. She's just been awarded what's similar to being knighted over in Australia, for her work on adoption. A dame rather. They're worth reading. This is Love Child by Sue Elliott – Sue is an adoptee who traced her mum and found out she had a sister and then a few years later, another sister popped up and she's convinced there are more as her mother was a very needy lady who she looked after until she died but there's a lot of history about adoption in there. Pauline Collins's book, Letter to Louise – she's got a daughter and they've had a reunion.

I do a Google Alert on 'adoption' and I think it's every week or every fortnight, a lot of information comes up, articles. This week it was more children are in care but less are being adopted, that was the message. I don't know why; I suppose different kinds of carers are being sought not just adopters, plus there's always a shortage of foster carers and adopters, isn't there?

Yes, I am involved in the Campaign for Adoption Apology. When they were making the television programme, Britain's Adoption Scandal, they soon realised that something was very wrong and took legal advice. They collected a lot of information and delivered it to Amber Rudd, the Home Secretary, and it was looked at by one of her minions. That was November 2016 and it took nearly a year to get a reply and it just said, sorry having looked at all the evidence, it's not worthy of an inquiry. They keep telling us that there are so many intermediary services available for birth parents and that adoption is completely different now and that mothers don't have their children taken unless there's a real call, which is a load of rubbish from what we've heard so …. We were getting on really well and then Mrs May called the election and then someone took over and it had to be the Minister for Children and Families that wrote the reply, so, it was nearly a year since that programme came out. We're going to arrange to meet the lawyers soon; they've done a lot of work pro bono. We'd like an inquiry like they had in Australia; an apology came from the prime minister there four years ago. When the television programme was made, we got an apology from the Catholic Church at the eleventh hour, just as the programme was going out. I went to see the chap. His first words were, 'I don't want to hear about you and your individual children and what happened to you; we're here to just have a chat.' All he could say is how wonderful the nuns were in Ireland that rescued children from cupboards under the stairs. He was, oh God! He wasn't open to listening at all. No. Anyway. We're still fighting on. Seven years ago we started this. Now we're trying to get an all-party group together to form a committee to look into it. But all anyone can think of is Brexit at the moment, I'm afraid.

It's the permanence of it that upsets me, the complete cut-off from the birth family, not just the mother and father but the wider family as well. I know they are supposed to think of them when they go through the process but I know a woman from my gardening club who would have quite willingly taken on her daughter's child but because she was deaf, she was deemed unsuitable. I think more money should be spent on prevention, in trying to keep families together. It costs a lot to take children into care; I know a foster mother who gets paid a lot of money. I'm sure the social workers would love to do prevention work but the workload seems to be so big, doesn't it? There must be a better way. There are a lot of adoption breakdowns, aren't there? There's been a lot in the papers this week about violent children, you know, acting out a lot of stuff. The children's psychiatric services are all being cut off, aren't they? It's very difficult.

People are very angry. I do feel angry. I'm angry at the Catholic Church, the government, the individual people involved. I'm angry at my mother, yes. I didn't talk to her for the last five years of her life. She didn't support me at all. She just did what she wanted. She met my sister's daughter once many years ago. My sister's seeing her daughter this week and I said, please try and get a photo as I'd really like to see what she looks like. She's very private about having photos taken. We lived in a five-bedroom house; there was plenty of room to bring up a child. It was just a silly 'what the neighbours will say' attitude. It's almost converse to what's happening now. The people who didn't have any money back then would probably take their daughter back in and the child would just be absorbed into the family, whereas it was the well-off, the middle classes who didn't keep their children.

*

On leaving, I notice a collection of model scooters at the top of a book case. She tells me her husband has six real Vespa scooters, and actually he's working on one outside in the garage. It's his hobby, she says. Keeps him busy. Then I remark on the elephants. *Ah yes*, she says, *the elephants. I can't remember where I got them all. People give them to me. The elephant is the logo for the Natural Parents Network. We're like elephants, you see? We never forget.*

Sorry not sorry

My mother kept telling me
having looked at all the evidence
I don't want to hear about what happened to you

It would kill my father if he knew
it's not worthy of an inquiry
adoption is completely different now

She just did what she wanted.

Care

When you bring Molly home aged four and a half, all blonde hair and bright blue eyes, picturing play dates and packed lunches, fantasizing about hanging stockings on Christmas Eve, skipping through streets wearing masks and horns asking strangers for candy, dreaming of her wedding, the words you'll write, the way you'll deliver them to the smiling crowd,

you might not be told how alcohol crosses the placenta and affects the brain of a developing foetus; you might not be told about the birth family history of mental health problems or criminality.

When you question her wetting the bed or getting into trouble at school or trashing her room,

you might be told, it's all to be expected, perfectly normal, she'll soon settle down and if it's taking a little longer than we first thought, don't worry, she'll grow out of it eventually.

When you turn around ten years later to see her standing behind you with your Kitchen Devil aimed at the space where your back just was, when she tortures the cat by burning its fur with the lighter she picked up in the alleyway she went down with the man called Pip who she met in the basement of the disused pub where girls like her end up,

you will be told it's nothing to do with her genetic inheritance or the fact she was found soiled and emaciated in her cot aged two, before moving between five foster homes like pass the parcel.

It's all your fault because you are a crap parent who should have done better.

The wrong mother (part I)

Why does she have your child?

I gave him to her.

Why does she have your child?

She's raising him for me.

Why does she have your child?

They say she couldn't have any of her own.

Why does she have your child?

She's a parasite feeding off his flesh.

Why does she have your child?

She stuffed him in a polka dot holdall in the middle of the night and ran off with him.

Why does she have your child?

Because I can't have him.

The wrong mother (part II)

I think about you often,
Some days more than others,
Imagining you, imagining him.

When I first saw your photo,
I hated your nails, the slogan on your tee-shirt,
I couldn't bear your face.

As time has passed,
I've made peace with the idea of you,
Reconstructed you in a thousand images.

Maybe one day, I'll stand before you
And we'll tell each other our stories.

Elephant

Pillar-like legs carry a great
weight as she lifts her trunk,
grasping, gasping, coiling

the long tube of the douche can,
ready to spring, cold and hard,

shooting, her first time again,

the sprinkler rains, cleansing,
forcing out evil, her breath comes
shallow, like the grave she digs

with her tusks, invisible cord
throbbing. Don't look back.

Blue

My eyes are closed but I am
listening to the colour blue,
crashing, crushing, roaring
waves, salty, gushing, waters
breaking, faking, falling into
the sea, the tide, rushing in
and out, the moon, everything
happening too soon, so long ago
that it's now. The sound of blue.

He pulls the blanket over
my body like a shroud.
Pats me on the head,
hovering.

Reference list

Collins, P. (1992) *Letter to Louise: A Loving Memoir to the Daughter I Gave Up for Adoption More Than Twenty-Five Years Ago*, London, Harper Collins.

Elliott, S. (2006) *Love Child*, London, Vermilion.

Everington, S. (2022) '"Sorry Not Sorry", "Care", "The Wrong Mother (Part I)", "The Wrong Mother (Part II)", "Elephant", "Blue"' [Online]. Available at: https://shantaeverington.wordpress.com (Accessed 14 November 2022).

Howe, D. et al (1997) *Half a Million Women: Mothers Who Lose Their Children by Adoption*, London, Penguin.

Natural Parents Network (2022) 'About' [Online]. Available at: https://www.facebook.com/NPNNaturalParentsNetwork/about (Accessed 10 November 2022).

Robinson, E. (2009) *Adoption Reunion – Ecstasy or Agony*, Christies Beach, Clova Publications.

Robinson, E. (2018a) *Adoption and Loss: The Hidden Grief 21st Century Edition*, Christies Beach, Clova Publications.

Robinson, E. (2018b) *Adoption and Recovery – Solving the Mystery of Reunion*, Christies Beach, Clova Publications.

Robinson, E. (2018c) *Adoption and Separation – Then and Now*, Christies Beach, Clova Publications.

11
CONTEXTUAL NOTE

To help the reader make sense of the women's stories, this section seeks to provide a basic overview of the wider context surrounding fertility, egg donation, surrogacy and adoption as it applies in the UK (medical and legal procedures vary from country to country). With the *New Scientist* reporting on 'the first baby to be born using a new technique that incorporates DNA from three people' (Hamzelou, 2016) and an article in *The Guardian* predicting a future of babies growing in artificial wombs outside a woman's body (Prasad, 2017), it must be understood that the reproductive landscape is being constantly stretched and challenged.

Fertility treatments

Many women who struggle to get pregnant naturally choose to undergo fertility testing to try to ascertain the root cause of the problem. Where there is a diagnosable problem with the man or woman, a specific treatment may be recommended. Medicines to stimulate ovulation (the monthly release of an egg) are often the first port of call for women who are not ovulating regularly. Fallopian tube surgery may be needed if a woman's fallopian tubes (the tubes which carry an egg from the ovary to the womb) become blocked or damaged. Laparoscopic surgery may be used in cases of endometriosis (when the womb lining grows outside of the womb), cysts (fluid-filled sacs) or fibroids (small growths in the womb). There are other types of surgical procedures for both women and men, depending on the problem. Often, the cause of infertility remains unknown.

Doctors may recommend assisted conception, namely Intrauterine Insemination (IUI) or In Vitro Fertilisation (IVF). It's easy to get confused between the two. In cases of IUI, sperm is collected from the man, washed and then examined to select the fastest-moving specimens. The sperm is inserted into the womb using a fine plastic tube that enters the cervix (neck of the womb). This must be done at a specific time in a woman's menstrual cycle to coincide with ovulation. IVF is a complex procedure requiring a woman to take fertility medication to stimulate the production of eggs, which are then collected from her ovaries. The sperm and eggs are mixed outside the body and allowed to develop as embryos (hence the term 'test tube baby') before being put back into the womb. There is also a method called Intracytoplasmic Sperm Injection (ICSI), where the sperm is injected into the egg. Many people undergoing fertility treatments choose to have counselling to cope with the emotional turmoil.

Egg and sperm donation

If there is an identifiable problem with either a woman's eggs or a man's sperm that cannot be solved using fertility treatments alone, egg or sperm donation may be considered. This will also be necessary for same-sex couples who wish to conceive: a female couple will need a sperm donor and a male couple will need a surrogate and an egg donor (one woman could fulfil both roles). Donated sperm can either be introduced to the woman's body via artificial insemination, that is using a syringe to insert the sperm into the vagina, or using IUI, as outlined above. Women using donated eggs will usually undergo IVF. If a baby is conceived using donated sperm or eggs, they will be genetically related to the egg or sperm donor. However, the donor is not their legal parent and will not be named on the birth certificate. The UK law changed on 1 April 2005 so that egg and sperm donors can no longer remain anonymous. As a result, from 2023, those conceived via egg or sperm donation are legally entitled to find out the identity of the donor when they turn 18 years old. Laws vary in other countries and some people from the UK choose to travel abroad for anonymous egg and sperm donation. In the UK, it is illegal to pay an egg or sperm donor apart from 'reasonable expenses', although commercial egg donation is available in some countries.

Surrogacy

'Intended parents' may use a surrogate mother if the intended mother is unable to carry a baby in her womb, or the intended father(s) is a single intended parent or gay couple. Surrogates may be 'straight' or 'host'. A straight (or traditional) surrogate will get pregnant using artificial insemination of donor sperm, using her own eggs; she will therefore be the baby's genetic mother. A host (or gestational) surrogate is genetically unrelated to the baby, who will be conceived via IVF using donor eggs or the eggs of the intended mother. In either case, the surrogate mother is the baby's birth mother and is named as the legal mother on a UK birth certificate. The intended parents will need to apply to the courts for a Parental

Order to transfer parental responsibility from the surrogate. Some intended parents travel abroad for surrogacy services – laws will vary from country to country. In the UK, it is illegal to pay a surrogate apart from 'reasonable expenses', although commercial surrogacy is available in some countries.

Adoption

Adoption is a permanent legal process whereby a child who cannot be raised within their birth family is placed within a new family; an Adoption Order transfers parental responsibility from the child's birth parents to their adoptive parents. Although some prospective adopters come to adoption after exhausting fertility treatments, for others adoption is their first choice for building a family. Potential adoptive parents are vetted by adoption agencies, such as local authorities or charitable organisations. The process usually involves attendance at training days, a home-study period and assessment in the home by a social worker, who will also interview family, friends and employers. Potential adopters then need to be approved by an 'approval panel' and matched with a child by a 'matching panel'. Current UK adoptions primarily involve children who have been removed from their birth family by social services; a smaller number of children are voluntarily given up for adoption. Potential adopters are trained to prepare them for the challenges of adoptive parenting and taught how to talk to children about their origins and identity through life story work. Ongoing contact with birth family through the post via an intermediator, known as 'letterbox contact' is generally encouraged.

Fostering

Unlike adoption, fostering is a temporary arrangement whereby a child is placed with foster carers, who are paid to look after the child until the child can either return to their family of origin or a new permanent family can be found. When a child is taken into care, it can take some time before a decision is made about who should look after them longer-term. For example, birth parents may be undergoing treatment for addiction or taking part in parenting training to enable them to meet their child's needs, or other birth family members, such as aunts, uncles or grandparents, may be assessed as suitable carers. This can result in babies and young children being fostered for some time and then being moved, which results in broken attachments during a critical developmental period. However, in schemes known as 'concurrent planning placements', babies and children under two who are likely to need adoption are placed with concurrent carers who are dually approved as foster carers and adopters – these carers initially foster the child but may adopt them later if the courts decide that the child cannot live with their birth family (First4Adoption, 2019).

Reference list

Hamzelou, J. (2016) 'Exclusive: World's First baby Born with New "Three Parent" Technique', *New Scientist* [Online]. Available at: https://www.newscientist.com/article/2107219-exclusive-worlds-first-baby-born-with-new-3-parent-technique/ (Accessed 15 January 2020).

First4Adoption (2019) *Concurrent Planning* [Online]. Available at: http://www.first4adoption.org.uk/who-can-adopt-a-child/fostering-options/concurrent-planning/ (Accessed 15 January 2020).

Prasad, A. (2017) 'How Artificial Wombs Will Change Our Ideas of Gender, Family and Equality', *The Guardian* [Online]. Available at: https://www.theguardian.com/commentisfree/2017/may/01/artificial-womb-gender-family-equality-lamb (Accessed 15 January 2020).

PART III
Conclusion

12
CONTRIBUTING TO NEW UNDERSTANDINGS OF MOTHERHOOD THROUGH EXPANSION AND ANALYSIS OF LIFE WRITING FORMS

The stories in this book tell of the overwhelming desire to become a mother, of joy after heartbreak, of families built by unconventional means, bound by unconditional love and acceptance. Long after the interviews are finished, I'm left thinking about the mothers who didn't get to tell their versions of the truth. I picture Tracey walking away from Alison, fingering her silver necklace; she'll get beaten up again; she'll probably get pregnant again, have another baby removed and taken into care. I see a woman sitting on a narrow threadbare bed in a surrogacy dormitory that she can't leave. I am fascinated by the untold stories of the mothers' mothers, the mother Charlotte hasn't seen for 18 years, the mothering relationships we pass down, consciously or unconsciously emulating or rejecting. Charlotte and Robin felt compelled to help others create families; are their actions altruism, or do they fulfil a deep-rooted need? And just what will the children make of it all when they are older? I remain haunted by the image of Caleb in his blue fleece blanket at the train station; I wonder what happened to him, whether he was eventually adopted by another family or whether he languishes in care, social workers devising new promotional footage for new prospective parents. The ghosts of nearly children are never far away. The babies we couldn't bear, the fertility treatments that failed, the pregnancies that didn't make it, the children who were removed. Other mothers and nearly children hide in the shadows, always there in the background.

★

I would like to conclude by returning to the stated aims of my research, as set out in my application to the OU Human Research Ethics Committee (HREC) at the beginning of my PhD (Everington, 2014). Ultimately, it aims

DOI: 10.4324/9781003290179-15

to contribute to new knowledge by applying and extending existing life writing methodology to the uncharted territory of motherhood via adoption, surrogacy and egg donation. The aim of the project was to create a collection of biographies which extend our understanding of what it means to be a mother, contributing to discourse which challenges the assumptions that to be a mother, a woman must be biologically related to her child/and or have given birth to her child, helping to broaden understanding about the complex nature of mothering. It also explores the unique and hidden relationships that exist between adopters and birth mothers, egg donors and women who become mothers through egg donation, and surrogates and women who become mothers through surrogacy.

Revisiting Chapter 2, I assert that just as Sally Cline speaks of biography as serving as a window on the times, that her writing on Zelda Fitzgerald's life 'became not merely a window into a destructive marriage but also a window into an unjust time in history for women who wished to achieve' (Cline in Cline and Angier, 2010, p. 25), my biographical portraits of mothers illuminate the diverse and changing landscape of motherhood. Curating and creating stories of adoption, surrogacy and egg donation obtained via interviews with mothers caused me to reflect on the wider context of the subjects' lives, leading to a deeper understanding, not just of one particular life, but of the wider social and cultural factors impacting on motherhood via adoption, surrogacy and egg donation. In the 1986 introduction of the updated *Of Woman Born*, Adrienne Rich discusses the fuzzing of 'the personal is political' with a 'New Age blur of the-personal-for-its-own-sake' (Rich, 1986, p. x), causing me to reflect on the wider relevance of the mothers' personal narratives as 'collective empowerment' as opposed to 'individualistic telling', as differentiated by Rich. The juxtaposition of diverse stories and voices, alongside my own responses to the edited interview material in the form of poetry, fiction, personal essay and quotations, allows a richer interpretation and understanding of the labyrinth of motherhood, than that afforded by a single-voiced memoir.

The research's original contribution to knowledge lies in its approach to the untold stories of motherhood via adoption, surrogacy and egg donation, in its expansion and analysis of life writing techniques and in its exploration of ideas of 'authorship'. The editing of the interviews is a creative act, allowing patterns, motifs and themes to emerge, while revering the interviewee's individuality and personal diction. The work broadens a reader's understanding of the multi-layered idea of 'mothering' and in particular, exposes and explores the relationships between adopters and birth mothers, egg donors and women who become mothers through egg donation, and surrogates and women who become mothers through surrogacy. It is a political work, drawing on autoethnographical approaches, showing how personal experience is always socially and culturally rooted and how that rootedness has consequences. The curation of the mother's stories is offered context and texture by the inclusion of quotation collage and further supported by the creation of original material, namely poems, reimagined scenes and lyric essays. By including my own personal experience and responses as a seventh voice, I aim to embrace and foreground the subjectivity and experience of myself as the researcher. The resulting experimental life writing – with its roots in oral history, creatively developed using a collage approach – finds the hybridity of form that is required to embody the complexity of its concerns.

What next?

I believe that the experimental approach to writing lives undertaken here – a literary tapestry, a hybrid form of curated material (edited interview) and created material (poetry, reimagined scenes and lyric essay), accompanied by a critical metanarrative – could be used in future research to explore other aspects of motherhood, and indeed other social topics. I have spoken of Adrienne Rich writing *Of Woman Born: Motherhood as Institution and Experience* to examine motherhood – her own included – in a social context, as embedded in a political institution: in feminist terms. In Chapter 2, I highlighted that researching the experiences of mothers who walk away from their children, opting not to participate in raising them, would be a fascinating area for further life writing study. A related area I am interested in is navigating the menopause, the end of women's childbearing years, and their changing identity, emotions and socially constructed roles.

As a writer-researcher, I am also interested in further exploring practices of co-authorship. For this research, I was subject to the stipulations of the OU HREC, which meant that I was unable to share the edited interviews with the participants for approval. Adams, Holman and Ellis identify four goals for evaluating autoethnographical approaches: (1) contributes to knowledge, (2) values the personal and experiential, (3) demonstrates the power, craft and responsibilities of stories and storytelling and (4) takes a relationally responsible approach to research practice and representation, which includes being as collaborative, committed and reciprocal as possible (Adams et al., 2015). With these principles in mind, a future focus would be to further critique my role as researcher in terms of power dynamics and further develop a collaborative process of co-creation with interviewees.

Readers of this work may be interested in exploring other research blending creative and critical approaches, in the fields of creative writing, experimental life writing, autoethnography as well as research expanding ways of conceptualising motherhood. The references provided at the end of each chapter offer some useful starting points.

Reference list

Adams, T., Holman Jones, S. and Ellis, C. (2015) *Autoethnography*, New York, Oxford University Press.

Cline, S. and Angier, C. (2010) *The Arvon Book of Life Writing*, London, Menthuen Drama.
Everington, S. (2014) 'Open University Human Research Ethics Committee (HREC) Application; HREC reference no.: HREC/2015/1922'.
Rich, A. (1986 [1977]) *Of Woman Born*, New York, W. W. Norton.

INDEX

abortion 19, 153
Adams, T. 171
adoption: assessment 129; as a baby 16; books about 156; breakdowns 158; celebration day 66; and counselling 93, 132; forced 154; matching process 130, 150–151; order 54, 164; politics of 43; post adoption centre 132, 142, 154; preparation and training 130, 148–149; statistics 146–151
The Adoption Barometer 146–151
Adoption of Children Act (1926) 43, 69
Adoption UK 19, 35, 144, 146–151
adoptive family 150, 157; *see also* adoptive father; adoptive mother; adoptive parents
adoptive father 40, 157; *see also* adoptive family; adoptive parents
adoptive mother 40, 135, 155–157; research as an 10; voices 9, 18, 19; writing as an 6, 8, 41; *see also* adoptive family; adoptive parents
adoptive parents 16, 153–157, 164; age and sex/gender 43; meeting with 17, 136–139; writing about 8; *see also* adoptive family; adoptive father; adoptive mother
Alexievich, S. 10–12
Alvesson, M. 46
Angier, C. 11, 41, 170
Annie 20–22, 69–71

anonymity: of donors 54, 57, 75–78, 89, 107, 163; of research participants 34
appropriation and authentication 38–42
articulating the other 41
artistic considerations 10–26
authorship 10, 33, 35, 170, 171
auto/biographical 5, 6, 9
autobiographical writing 17, 19, 30–31, 33, 35, 40
autoethnography 6, 31, 171: analytic 31; evocative 31

Bakhtin, M. 11
Banville, J. 11
Barfoot, J. 33
Barlow, Y. 128
Barthes, R. 20–21
biographical: methods 34; portraits 31, 170; post-biographical 26; subject 34, 37, 42; writing as an act of empathy 10; writing as self-reflection 6–10; writing on motherhood 30–31
birth mother: anxiety 156; interviewing a 8, 10, 35, 37; letterbox contact with 68, 140, 164; meeting with 12, 17, 60–62, 136–139; reunion 8, 135, 156–157; stories 33; tracing one's 130–131; voices 9, 17–20; *see also* birth parents
birth parents: contact with 140; group 17, 36, 131; intermediary services for 157; tracing 89; *see also* birth mother

Breen, D. 128
Brochner, A. 31

Campaign for Adoption Apology 157
Campbell, J. 5, 8
Cassidy, T. 128
character 7, 10, 12, 16, 38, 40–42, 44; absent 15–17, 44
child abuse and neglect 19, 43–44, 93, 148
child-free 33
Cline, S. 10, 170
collage: as an evolution beyond narrative 20–26; as a kaleidoscope 22; literary mosaic 21; literary tapestry 171; quotation 22–23, 25–26, 71, 128
Collins, P. 157
Coram BAAF 148, 150
counselling 35, 89, 143, 145, 154, 163
Couser, G. T. 38–40
Cusk, R. 5, 30

de Groot, J. 45
Deveaux, M. 43
discursive site 20–21
Donor Conception Network 35
Donovan, S. 13, 71
Dorris, M. 40
Douglas, S. 44, 127
drug addiction 39–40, 126, 130, 140–143

Eakin, P. 8, 40
ectogenesis 32
ectopic pregnancy 23, 40, 93–94, 145
egg and sperm donation 163
egg donation 74–89, 92, 162–163, 170; politics of 43; writing about 10, 12, 13
Ellington, L. 31
Elliott, H. 14
Elliott, S. 157
Ellis, C. 6, 31, 35, 37–38, 171; *see also* Adams, T.; Brochner, A.; Ellington, L.; Holman, S.
endometriosis 96
Enright, A. 5, 30
ethics 7: beneficent acts 38; consent 34–35, 37–38, 41, 53–54, 86; Human Research Ethics Committee 33, 169; procedural 33–37; relational 37–41
ethnography 34; *see also* autoethnography
Etter, C. 18–19
Evans, E. 47–48
exploitation 41, 107; Child Sexual Exploitation 19

feminism 29: feminist ideas 8; feminist interviewer 36, feminist revolution 48; feminist scholars 44–45; feminist terms 30, 171; the women's movement 29
fertility testing 75, 162
fertility treatments 32, 54, 90, 117, 145, 162; Intracytoplasmic Sperm Injection (ICSI) 163; Intrauterine Insemination (IUI) 162–163; In Vitro Fertilisation (IVF) 162–163
fiction 12, 21, 33, 170; fictional cloak 11; fictionalised 15, 17–19, 46; historical 42, 45; metafiction 45
First4Adoption 164
foetal alcohol syndrome 40
form: finding a 10–26; premeditated 22
foster care 13, 56, 61, 67, 133, 139, 164; concurrent planning placements 54; statistics 148
foundling token 22

Galloway, J. 12
Gato, J. 32
gender 31–33, 43, 116; cisgender 32; diverse 32; gender-neutral 124; genderqueer 32; identity 32; transgender 32
Goldblatt, D. 42
Goldsworthy, V. 45–46
grand narratives 44–45
Grant, C. 47–48
grief 20, 114, 115, 154; disenfranchised 154, 157

Hadfield, L. 34, 36
Hamzelou, J. 162
Harman, K. 5, 30, 47
Harrison, K. 40
Heilbrun, C. 44–45
Hesketh, S. 18
heteroglossia 11–12, 23
Holman, S. 171
hooks, b. 9
Howe et al 43
hybrid form 6, 11, 20–21, 25–26, 44, 171

infertility 10, 23, 30, 42, 59, 104, 126, 127, 162; secondary 4, 92, 115, 153
intended parents 117, 125, 126, 163–164
interviews 7, 10–18; adoption 149–150, 164; dynamic 36; edited 6, 10, 11, 13, 15, 20, 24–26, 46, 171; ethics of 33–37; interpreting 46; as public performance 7–8; response to 7, 18, 21–24, 44, 170; transcribing 10, 12, 15, 33

Index 175

Jackson, R. 33
Jolly, A. 71, 128

Kay, J. 5, 9, 12, 13, 18
Kehily, M. J. 34, 36
Kincaid, J. 9
Kriegel, L. 22
Lavender, B. 48

life story book 8, 141, 164
life writing 6, 10–11, 15, 29, 37; expansion and analysis of 169–171; experimental 24, 31, 51–161, 171; motherhood and 30–31; narrative 34; representing others in 33; *see also* metanarrative
literary docu-memoir 11
lived experience 10, 30, 45
Lopate, P. 22–23
Lowe, M. 128

Makichen, W. 15, 127
Mansfield, S. 5
Mantel, H. 128
Masters, A. 41
matriography 5
memoir 8, 12, 45; controversial 40; motherhood 5, 30; parental 38, 40; single-voiced 6, 170; *see also* literary docu-memoir
metanarrative 6, 41, 45, 171
metaphor 19–20, 23
methodology 5, 34; life writing 5, 170; sociology 36; *see also* interviews
Michaels, M. 44, 127
mother: and baby group 3–5; definition of 6, 31–32; gender and society 31–33; mothers who leave 33; as social construct 10, 32
motherhood: alternative routes into 5, 31; labyrinth of 6, 170; new understandings of 169–171
mothering 5, 6, 14, 32, 47, 169–170
Myerson, J. 12, 39–41
myths 7, 58, 136; mythology 19; of parenthood 32

narrative 7–9, 44; arc 15, 24; auto/biographical 5; biographical 9; constructing 10–20; dual 39; linear 46; poem 25; prose 10; strategies 33; unified 11; *see also* collage, as an evolution beyond; grand narratives; life writing, narrative; metanarrative

Natural Parents Network 17–19, 35–36, 131, 144, 154, 156, 158
NHS 23, 78, 90–94
non-fiction: creative 20; published 22

Oakley, A. 29, 36–37, 41, 44
oral history 7, 171
Overall, C. 32, 43
ownership: of children 13, 21; of stories 10, 33

parental responsibility 164
parents *see* adoptive parents; birth parents; intended parents
Parker, T. 7, 10–12, 18
Parnell, J. 6, 11
participants: connection with 38; Information Sheet for 34; karmic 71; recruitment of 35; right to withdraw 35
personal essay 7, 11, 16, 22–23, 25–26, 40, 44, 47, 170
personal testimony 23, 44
poetry 6, 7, 9, 11, 18–20, 22–26, 39, 44, 46, 170, 171
politics: of adoption, surrogacy and egg donation 43–44; of form (and the nature of truth) 44–46; the personal as 29–31; and power 29–49
postmodernism 45
post-traumatic stress 20, 114
power 8; dynamic 38, 41, 171; of stories 171; *see also* politics and
Prasad, A. 162
pregnancy: ectopic 23, 40, 94, 145; falsified 14; ghost 70; loss 16, 20, 23, 25; stages of 23, 90–93; termination of 39; test 79, 91, 114, 121, 153
privacy 34, 35, 40, 146

re-imagined scenes 6, 13, 15, 20, 22
research: motivation, significance and approach 5–6; original contribution to knowledge 170; questions 6; *see also* ethics, Human Research Ethics Committee
rhyme 19–20, 24
rhythm 11, 13
Rich, A. 29–30, 44, 127, 170–171
Robinson, E. 154, 157
Root, R. 21
Rossini, M. 48
Ruddick, S. 32

Sampson, F. 44
Schaefer, C. 71

Sebag-Montefiore, C. 31–32
SEED Trust 35
self: self-discovery 22; self-image 16; self-reflection 6–10; versions of self 8–9
Sharpe, S. 34, 36
Shields, D. 21–22
silent partners 5, 70
social worker 43, 56, 60–61, 129–130, 140, 143, 147–150, 158, 164
Stanley, L. 9
stories 45, 169–171; birth mothers 33; fusion of 18–19; painful 5, 30; recording 29; untold 6–8; writing 6–16; *see also* ownership, of stories
surrogacy 4, 31, 74, 89, 96–107, 111–123, 126, 169–170; agency 86; agreement 107; conference 116; gestational 123–124; host 123–124; politics of 43; writing about 10, 14–16, 23–26; *see also* intended parents

Surrogacy UK 35, 74, 128
Swann, D. 18–19

Tasker, F. 32
Thomson, R. 34, 36
truth 11, 20, 44–45, 169

unauthorised: biography 38; material 37

ventriloquism 42
verbatim 7, 12, 16, 18, 24, 46
voices 6, 23, 26; curating and creating 26, 46, 170; fictionalised 18; idiosyncrasies of 7, 12; juxtaposition of 170; women's 30, 46; *see also* adoptive mothers, voices; birth mothers, voices; heteroglossia; single-voiced memoir

Winterson, J. 5, 8, 13, 45, 71
Worth, J. 128

Milton Keynes UK
Ingram Content Group UK Ltd.
UKHW022039070923
428267UK00017B/99